Named in remembrance of

the onetime *Antioch Review* editor

and longtime Bay Area resident,

the Lawrence Grauman, Jr. Fund

supports books that address

a wide range of human rights,

free speech, and social justice issues.

The publisher and the University of California Press Foundation gratefully acknowledge the generous support of the Lawrence Grauman, Jr. Fund.

Obstacle Course

Obstacle Course

THE EVERYDAY STRUGGLE TO GET AN ABORTION IN AMERICA

David S. Cohen and Carole Joffe

UNIVERSITY OF CALIFORNIA PRESS

University of California Press
Oakland, California

© 2020 by David S. Cohen and Carole Joffe

Library of Congress Cataloging-in-Publication Data

Names: Cohen, David S., 1972- author. | Joffe, Carole E., author.
Title: Obstacle course : the everyday struggle to get an abortion in
    America / David S. Cohen and Carole Joffe.
Description: Oakland, California : University of California Press, [2020] |
    Includes bibliographical references and index.
Identifiers: LCCN 2019031072 (print) | LCCN 2019031073 (ebook) |
    ISBN 9780520306646 (cloth) | ISBN 9780520973725 (ebook)
Subjects: LCSH: Abortion—United States. | Abortion services—United
    States.
Classification: LCC HQ767.U6 C65 2020 (print) | LCC HQ767.U6 (ebook) |
    DDC 362.1988/800973—dc23
LC record available at https://lccn.loc.gov/2019031072
LC ebook record available at https://lccn.loc.gov/2019031073

Manufactured in the United States of America

29 28 27 26 25 24 23 22 21 20
10 9 8 7 6 5 4 3 2 1

To the abortion patients who navigate an obstacle course to obtain the health care they need, and to the providers and allies whose work is essential in overcoming these barriers.

Contents

1 Introduction

THE TURBULENT STATE OF ABORTION IN AMERICA

In an ideal world when you need medical care, a somewhat routine series of events takes place: you discover you need help, make a decision about it, find a provider who can care for you, figure out insurance and payment, go to the provider, and then get the care. Because we don't live in an ideal world, familiar hurdles—some often insurmountable—such as health care costs, appointment availability, and family and employer support can interfere, but the goal is for care to be driven by a combination of patient choice and evidence-based medicine.

TALIA

Yet, consider Talia's story of trying to get an abortion. Talia was fifteen years old and had just started getting her period earlier in the year. As happens with many young women, her period was erratic, so she didn't realize she was pregnant until several months had gone by. When she did find out, having just graduated middle school and essentially raising herself thanks to a father who wasn't around and a mother who wasn't dependable, she was certain that she wanted and needed an abortion.

1

But making the decision herself was not an option for Talia. Like young women in about three-quarters of states, as a minor Talia was not entitled to make her own choice. In Talia's state, one parent had to be notified and give consent to the abortion. The consenting parent had to provide government-issued identification so the consent could be notarized. Talia had the support of an adult in her life—her boyfriend's grandmother—but she didn't qualify under state law as a person who could consent. With one parent missing and the other only sporadically involved in her life, Talia's only option was to go before a judge who could, after a hearing, sign off on her abortion.

Going before a judge in any circumstance is not an experience most people would relish, but doing so when you are a minor faced with an unwanted pregnancy can be terrifying. Thankfully, Talia lived in a state that had a well-run organization whose sole purpose was to assist minors navigating this process. Talia contacted the organization, who connected her with an attorney to help her fill out the paperwork and appear before the judge.

However, before Talia could do that, she arranged to have an initial appointment at the local abortion clinic. Where Talia lived, state law required a minor to make a separate trip to the clinic twenty-four hours before the abortion. She made the appointment and showed up at the clinic for her preabortion counseling and ultrasound.

When she got to the clinic, she realized something was wrong and that the building she had entered wasn't an abortion clinic after all. Rather, she was in a fake women's health center, generically known as a crisis pregnancy center, or CPC, but also sometimes called a fake clinic. This center, which was not a medical facility but rather posed as one, was located directly next door to the real abortion clinic and did everything it could to make itself look like the clinic—the same building design and a similar name. Talia was tricked into going there.

Once Talia was inside, the people there, who wore white coats to look like doctors, pretended that they knew Talia had an appointment. But when Talia told them that she wanted to have an abortion, they tried to persuade her otherwise. They told her that they would help her support her baby with money and other forms of assistance. When Talia remained confident in her decision, they brought someone in who told Talia that she herself had had an abortion and that it had ruined her life. Finally, when Talia said she still wanted an abortion, the people at the center brought out the most dangerous lie of them all—they told Talia that they could perform the abortion but that Talia had to wait a few weeks because they didn't have an open appointment. Talia was already nineteen weeks pregnant, and waiting a few weeks would have put her over the state's limit on when a woman can have an abortion. In other words, the center lied to Talia so that she would never be able to exercise her right to choose.

When Talia left the appointment at the CPC, she called the organization that helped minors through the process. The people there quickly identified the fake clinic and told Talia that she was at the wrong place. Talia was shocked. "I thought I was in a real doctor's office. I don't get it." Thanks to the help of the organization, the attorney, and then the real abortion clinic, Talia was able to get the judge's approval without any problems.

But Talia's journey to get an abortion wasn't over. She still needed to come up with the money. She didn't have health insurance that covered the abortion, so she had to come up with $4,000 out of pocket. She and her boyfriend's grandmother pulled together some money, but it wasn't enough. Thankfully, local and national organizations dedicated to helping low-income women pay for abortions stepped in. They made up the difference, and Talia was able to get her abortion just before the state's limit kicked in.

With her abortion behind her, Talia started ninth grade, free to pursue her education without being a parent when she didn't want to be. But for her to get to this point, she had to navigate the complex web of laws that deprive young women of their autonomous decision-making, the deception of fake clinics, the time pressure of a state's gestational limit, and the difficulty that low-income women have in finding money for a procedure many insurance companies don't cover. Talia was successful, but with so many hurdles in place, other women aren't always so fortunate.

BRITTANY

Or take Brittany's story about trying to get in to have an abortion in Colorado. When she was twenty-one, she found out she was pregnant. She had been on Depo-Provera (an injectable contraceptive) at the time, so she was surprised by this development. Brittany knew that, as a college student who was working full time, she "wasn't ready physically, emotionally, or financially to be a parent," so she decided to have an abortion.

When Brittany called the clinic, the woman on the phone asked Brittany if she wanted to have someone walk her from her car into the clinic. Brittany, not realizing why she was asked this question, said no because she already had two companions to accompany her to her appointment. She arrived at the clinic and quickly realized why. Several older men swarmed her car after she parked. When Brittany refused pamphlets that one of the men shoved at her, he screamed, "How can you do this? You're killing your baby to continue on your whore life, you jezebel!"

Then, the men began tossing baby-doll parts at Brittany. These doll parts, covered in red paint, fell to the ground after hitting Brittany and her companions. While throwing the doll parts, one of the men yelled, "This is what you're doing to your baby! Look at the street! It's strewn with the blood of your baby. That's your baby scattered across the street!" The men in front of the clinic then turned to one of Brittany's support people, her aunt, and began yelling at her, calling her "Grandma" and asking her how she could let Brittany go through with the abortion.

Brittany had to withstand this harassment while crossing a wide street to get from the parking lot to the clinic. Once inside, she thought it would be over, but while sitting in the waiting room she could hear the protesters yelling the same types of things at every woman coming into the clinic. And, when the doctor came to work, she heard them yell, "Murderer!" and "Butcher!" Brittany was worried that the protesters would still be there after her appointment, but the doctor assured her that they had left after he arrived. Brittany was so shaken up by what happened that she would have waited until they left if necessary. Overall, she called the experience with the protesters "heinous" and used the "horror" she went through as a source of strength. "If I can make it through that, I can make it through the rest of this day."

WANDALYN

Now consider what it took for Wandalyn to get an abortion. Wandalyn was twenty weeks pregnant when she received terrible news. Her "baby," using her word, was diagnosed with trisomy 18, a life-threatening chromosomal disorder that often results in stillbirths or babies who can't survive to their first birthday because of conditions related to breathing problems or heart deformities. It was a devastating diagnosis for Wandalyn and her fiancé, who had been overjoyed about adding a son to their blended family of five—the two of them plus her two daughters and his son.

After quickly learning everything she could about the condition, Wandalyn reluctantly made the decision to have an abortion, calling it "the most painful decision we have ever made." The closest abortion clinic to Wandalyn had lengthy wait times and told her the procedure would cost $7,000, time and money that Wandalyn did not have. So, with the help of the doctors who diagnosed the fetal anomaly, she found a different clinic that could perform the abortion the same week as the diagnosis, but that clinic was almost two hours away.

Although the abortion would be less expensive at this other clinic, Wandalyn was told that it would still cost over $2,000, money she did not have. Wandalyn, a new immigrant to this country who had successfully run a business in her home country and had resources there, had not been able to find work in the United States. Her family lived off her fiancé's meager income, and Wandalyn had no health insurance. What little money they had went to their three children.

As an undocumented immigrant, Wandalyn was ineligible for public health insurance in the state where she lived, so she was responsible for paying for the abortion herself. When she talked with one of the abortion clinic staffers by phone, she explained that she didn't have enough money. The clinic told her that private charities could help, but Wandalyn would have to come up with some of the money herself. She went to work trying to find the money and was able to stitch together seventy dollars, mostly money that her fiancé had put aside for her prenatal care visits. Despite this amount being far short of what the clinic wanted her to contribute, the staff told her that they would waive the remaining portion of the fee.

With the cost of the procedure no longer a problem, Wandalyn had to tackle the next issue—traveling to the clinic. She and her fiancé didn't own a car, so she couldn't drive herself to the appointment two hours away. Help from friends was impossible too, as Wandalyn had been in the United States for only a short time and had not yet developed a supportive network. The state's public transportation network wouldn't help either, as it was too costly, took too much time, and would only get her as close as several miles from the clinic, not to the clinic itself.

So she once again called the clinic. The clinic itself couldn't help, but the people there connected her to a newly formed volunteer group that helps women travel to abortion clinics and, if needed, hosts them for overnight stays. The two-hour drive for Wandalyn to get to the clinic would mean that each volunteer who helped her would have to drive four hours—two hours to get her and then two hours to the clinic. Wandalyn, who could not afford a hotel, also needed an overnight host and rides to and from the clinic from there because her twenty-week procedure would take two days—the first for dilation of her cervix and the second for the abortion. The volunteer group jumped into action and found five different people to help Wandalyn with each step of the process. The morning drive on day one went off without a hitch, and Wandalyn showed up at the clinic ready for the procedure to start.

Nothing worked easily for Wandalyn, though. When she arrived at the clinic Friday morning, it was closed. Unfortunately, state inspectors had come for a surprise full inspection (such surprise inspections are not an infrequent occurrence for abortion clinics). The clinic protested, but the inspectors prevailed, forcing the clinic to cancel all the patients scheduled for the day. Stuck in the parking lot two hours from home with a volunteer who had just driven for four hours, Wandalyn was one of them. Rescheduling at a clinic in the neighboring state was impossible for Wandalyn because that state would have required her to wait twenty-four hours between her first visit and when she could have had the abortion, which would mean too much time away from her children without any reliable child care backup.

Since she needed a two-day procedure and the clinic was closed Sunday, there was nothing for Wandalyn to do but return home, delaying her procedure even more. Getting home was also tricky, though. Wandalyn was sitting in a stranger's car in a parking lot of a closed clinic. She couldn't stay there forever. The volunteer who had driven her from home that morning didn't have time to drive her home but was able to help Wandalyn a bit more and drove her to another volunteer's house to stay while the group found her a ride home. Luckily, the person who was scheduled to drive Wandalyn home on Saturday was able to quickly adjust her schedule and drive her home Friday afternoon instead.

All that effort, and Wandalyn was back to square one—carrying a wanted pregnancy with a devastating chromosomal abnormality and having trouble getting the abortion she now sought. She felt bad for the drivers who had wasted their time and frustrated that another hurdle was in her way. But she never reconsidered her decision to have an abortion because she knew too much about trisomy 18 and what that meant for her "already-loved baby."

The same clinic was able to reschedule her for Tuesday of the following week, a week after the initial diagnosis and now into the twenty-second week of her pregnancy. She just had to, for a second time, get to and from the clinic and find a place to stay overnight for the two-day procedure. The same volunteer group came through once more. A new driver took Wandalyn to the clinic Tuesday morning, another driver took her to a host Tuesday night and back to the clinic Wednesday morning, and two other drivers tag-teaming took her home Wednesday. The Wednesday leg was the hardest part of the trip for the volunteers because it was such a long drive in the middle of a workday. They solved the problem with one driver taking her halfway, then handing her off to a second driver who lived closer to Wandalyn. The second driver, found through networking nationally with like-minded abortion rights supporters, was able to take Wandalyn all the way home.

Wandalyn's journey from diagnosis to abortion was a constant struggle because of the obstacles thrown her way. All told, she spent more than ten hours in the car, was assisted by almost a dozen volunteers, and utilized charitable funding and clinic discounts that were made available to her. She overcame the absence of available nearby clinics, state insurance barriers, affordability issues, and state inspectors to finally get the medical care she sought—an abortion for her wanted pregnancy.

ABORTION EXCEPTIONALISM AND ITS CONSEQUENCES

Talia's, Brittany's, and Wandalyn's stories are emblematic of the many—though certainly not all—abortion patients who face multiple, compounding roadblocks in their search for care. What makes these stories important is how they highlight the wide variety of obstacles standing in the way of people accessing abortion.* These struggles to get an abortion differ significantly from the accounts of other Americans' efforts to access health care services. Of course, many people face difficulties getting the health care they need. Too many Americans remain uninsured or underinsured, many who live outside population centers have to travel long distances to reach necessary services, and wait times to be seen by providers can be excessive. These and other problems are endemic to *all* forms of medical care in the United States.

But what these three stories highlight are just a few of the many difficulties that women in the United States have in accessing abortion care because of barriers specific to abortion. These barriers represent *abortion exceptionalism:* the idea that abortion is treated uniquely compared to other medical procedures that are comparable to abortion in complexity and safety. These barriers thwart access to care in ways that compound the other problems that are shared by many people who seek other forms of medical care. These barriers are about abortion and abortion alone, and represent the thorough politicization of this branch of reproductive health care.

That abortion is one of the most divisive issues in American politics and culture is well known. One need look no further than the front page of most media outlets in the first half of 2019 (when this book is being finalized) to see this dynamic. Some of the country's most anti-abortion states are racing one another to ban abortion earlier and earlier

---

* Throughout this book, we mostly use the word *woman* to describe who receives an abortion, but we recognize the reality that some people who do not identify as women receive abortions, including transgender men and gender-nonconforming individuals. We use gender-neutral language at times, such as referring to *patients* or *people*, but use *women* and similar language more frequently. We believe striking this balance accomplishes the twin goals of being inclusive but also reflecting the reality of who receives most abortions. By using language in this way, we do not intend to erase the experiences of those who do not fit in the category "woman," people who have the right to receive abortion care as unhindered from abortion barriers discussed in this book as anyone else. s.e. smith, "Women Are Not the Only Ones Who Get Abortions," *Rewire*, March 1, 2019, rewire.news/article/2019/03/01/women-are-not-the-only-ones-who-get-abortions/. For further discussion of the use of both *women* and gender-neutral terms in a book about reproductive health, rights, and justice, see Loretta J. Ross and Rickie Solinger, *Reproductive Justice: An Introduction* (Oakland: University of California Press, 2017), 6–8.

in pregnancy—Missouri at eight weeks; Georgia, Kentucky, Ohio, and Mississippi at six weeks; and Alabama at conception. Given their obvious unconstitutionality under current law (described in more detail below), it will be years, if ever, before these laws take effect. Yet even though these laws will have no short-term practical or legal effect, they have captured the nation's attention, propelling abortion once again to the front of the national political consciousness.

At the same time, some of the country's most abortion-supportive states are engaged in an opposite endeavor—working to make abortion as safe, accessible, and protected as possible. In the first half of 2019, New York, Rhode Island, Vermont, Illinois, Maine, and Nevada have passed laws that would protect abortion if the Supreme Court ever overruled *Roe v. Wade* and that will expand its accessibility in very concrete ways. These changes will have repercussions not only for pregnant people living in those states but also for those who travel for care. While the media attention has focused mostly on the threats that the anti-abortion states pose, the developments in these abortion-supportive states are arguably just as important, if not more.

In this book, our goal is to discuss something that often gets overlooked in the nation's battle over abortion, even by those sympathetic to abortion rights—the everyday *consequence*s, for those who seek abortions and for those who provide them, of the onslaught of the attacks against abortion care since *Roe v. Wade* legalized abortion in 1973. Every step along the way, from the moment someone finds out she is pregnant to the point of getting an abortion, law and politics interfere with the decision and process. In this book, we document the impact of this interference, the lengths to which abortion providers go to nonetheless provide high-quality medical care in this environment, and the tenacity patients must have in order to make the process work for them.

Political attempts to interfere with abortion have been a constant in American political life since *Roe*. The anti-abortion movement has tried almost everything possible to try to stop legal abortion—it has attempted to amend the Constitution, change the composition of the Supreme Court, decrease the number of medical schools teaching abortion, stop women from entering clinics, reduce the number of professionals performing or assisting in the performance of abortions, and promote a culture of shame and stigma for women considering abortion. The movement's methods to accomplish these goals have ranged from the perfectly legal that are well within the bounds of normal democratic politics (for instance, electing politicians who are opposed to abortion and nominating anti-abortion judges) to those that are blatantly illegal (such as assassinating and targeting abortion providers). In the middle of these two extremes sits another strategy of the anti-abortion movement—enacting new legislation that regulates every aspect of abortion. While passing new laws is certainly a normal part of the democratic principle that "to the victor go the spoils," laws that restrict fundamental rights are different.

Legislative efforts to restrict abortion ramped up in 2010, after Republicans made significant electoral gains. Altogether, more than 1,200 restrictions of various kinds have been passed by the states since 1973, but over one-third of them have passed since 2010. On the basis of types of restrictions each state has, the Guttmacher Institute, one of the leading research organizations studying reproductive health, classifies states as supportive, middle-ground, hostile, or extremely hostile with respect to abortion. As of the beginning of 2019, there are now twenty-one states that are very hostile or hostile to abortion. Given the population of these states, that means that 43 percent of women live in a state that is hostile or very hostile to abortion, whereas 22 percent of women live in a state that supports abortion rights.

The story we tell in this book conveys the disturbing consequences of these legislative restrictions and the numerous obstacles women face trying to exercise their rights to a legal health care service, as well as the herculean efforts often needed to overcome them. Given that Donald Trump has, thus far in his presidency, been able to add two Supreme Court Justices who are widely suspected of being hostile to constitutional protection for abortion, the attention of many Americans is understandably currently focused on *Roe v. Wade*'s fate. While that is certainly a major concern, the reality is that many women in the United States *already* live in a world where the quest to obtain abortion care is enormously challenging, especially when combined with complicating factors such as poverty and racism, as well as special circumstances such as being incarcerated or undocumented.

WRITING THIS BOOK

In spite of the extensive literature that exists on almost every aspect of abortion, relatively little has been written documenting the actual *experience* of getting an abortion amid all the obstacles in America today. Both of us are scholars of abortion, one from the legal world, the other from sociology, and we have long known the difficulties that patients face in accessing abortion and that abortion providers face in providing quality medical care despite political interference. But we both decided that a full accounting of these obstacles— from the moment a woman finds out she is pregnant through, if she is successful, getting the abortion she seeks—is essential to understanding the reality of abortion in contemporary America. For these reasons, we wrote this book telling the story of abortion now, a story that captures the disturbing reality of the sometimes insurmountable barriers women face trying to exercise their constitutional right to a basic medical procedure.

This book is based largely on more than seventy interviews we conducted in 2017 and 2018. We interviewed people working in all fifty states plus the District of Columbia and Puerto Rico. We interviewed *abortion providers,* those who work in various jobs in clinics or hospitals that provide abortions (not just clinicians), and abortion access allies and volunteers. As we use these terms throughout the book, *allies* are people who are not in an abortion facility but instead work for an outside organization that helps patients access abortion, and *volunteers* are people who are not paid to provide this support work but do so on their own time. The people we interviewed spanned the various jobs in the world of abortion provision and represented the various settings where abortions take place— local Planned Parenthood affiliates, independently owned clinics, doctors' offices, and hospitals—though, consistent with abortion provision generally, most were from the first two categories. Our interview subjects were also diverse in age and race (though not in sex, as only two were men).[†]

[†] Throughout the book as we refer to the people we interviewed, for the most part we use names from a website that generates fake names and identify where the people work on the basis of the four different regions of the country (Northeast, South, Midwest, West) used by the Guttmacher Institute in its studies of abortion provision. We do this to protect our interview subjects' identity and safety. However, some of the people we interviewed wanted to be identified by their real name, so we do this when it is appropriate but without flagging the difference.

The interviews with providers, allies, and volunteers covered three main topics. First, we discussed the barriers patients face in accessing abortion where they work. Second, we discussed how quality abortion care or access is made available in light of those barriers. Third, we discussed how these barriers affect the people that they see. By talking with providers, allies, and volunteers from every state and major territory in this country, we were able to get a complete picture of the comprehensive nature of the various barriers that exist across the country, how abortion care manages to be provided despite them, and how they affect abortion-seeking women.

To complement the original interviews, we draw heavily on other sources throughout the book. Increasing numbers of women have been publicly telling their abortion stories, and we have used many of those stories to show a personal side to the barriers that we discuss. Additionally, throughout the book we cite relevant empirical research from many different fields that has documented the barriers patients face as well as the benefits (or lack thereof) that these barriers may have.

Each chapter of this book covers a different step in the abortion process, from learning you are pregnant to, if successful, getting a procedure. In order, the chapters cover making the decision to have an abortion, including special restrictions for minors (chapter 2), finding and getting to an abortion provider (chapter 3), paying for the abortion (chapter 4), getting into the abortion clinic (chapter 5), counseling at the clinic (chapter 6), waiting before the procedure (chapter 7), and the procedure itself (chapter 8). Not every abortion follows this linear progression from start to finish, but this ordering is the most sensible way to convey the entirety of the abortion restrictions a woman faces. By covering abortion barriers in this progression, we are not focusing on any one state or territory, or saying that every— or even any—woman in the United States faces each one of these barriers. There are different abortion paths in different parts of the country based on individual clinic practice and particular state and local laws, with some people facing many of the barriers that we explore and others facing none.‡

---

‡ In each chapter, we discuss the different types of restrictions and recount the number of states that have each one. The numbers we use are accurate as of the summer of 2019, but given the ever-changing nature of abortion restrictions (more being passed in restrictive states, some being struck down by courts, a small number being removed in liberal states), the exact numbers may not be accurate at the time you read this.

In the end, the book concludes that the myriad barriers that exist around the country—such as those highlighted in the three patient stories that start this introduction—make it extremely difficult for women, particularly those who are poor and racial minorities, to access abortion services. Nonetheless, for the most part, thanks to their own commitment as well as the dedication and innovation of providers, allies, and volunteers, women in America who seek an abortion still, for now, get legal, safe abortions. As one abortion provider we interviewed told us, "Women will walk over hot rocks to find an abortion provider. If you need one, you need one, and you go where you can."

ABORTION IN AMERICA: A SHORT OVERVIEW

To situate the material in this book, here we offer some basic background about the current landscape of abortion in the United States. Most fundamentally, the story of abortion in this country is impossible to tell without focusing on the demographics of the women who have abortions. A substantial majority of women seeking abortions are low income, with half living below the federal poverty level and another quarter living between 100 percent and 199 percent of the poverty level. Relatedly, more than a quarter of abortion patients have no health insurance at all. Just over a third have Medicaid (though, as discussed in depth in chapter 4, Medicaid pays for abortions in only sixteen of the fifty states, with the result that one in four women receiving Medicaid who would otherwise have an abortion is forced to continue her pregnancy), with the rest having private insurance (including insurance through the Affordable Care Act). About 60 percent of abortion recipients already are parents.

Additionally, while abortion in this country is inescapably linked to poverty, it is also very closely associated with race. Women of color are disproportionately represented among abortion patients. Three in five abortion patients are women of color, with black women representing 28 percent, Hispanic women 25 percent, Asian or Pacific Islander women 6 percent, and women of other races or ethnicities 3 percent. White women make up 39 percent of the women having abortions.

Overall, the demographic breakdown of abortion indicates that the barriers this book discusses largely affect poor women of color. This racially disproportionate burden is consistent with our country's long history of coercive policies around reproduction and parenting targeted at women of color. As a result, along with other issues related to birthing and parenting, abortion access has been a key component of the reproductive justice movement since its inception in the early 1990s.

Reproductive justice is a newer framework for thinking about and critiquing reproductive politics in the United States. The movement relies on the notion that government and society need to guarantee comprehensive reproductive autonomy for everyone, especially women of color and poor women. In particular, reproductive justice focuses on the right to not have a child (which is where abortion fits), the right to have a child, and the right to parent children in a healthy and safe environment. While this book's focus on abortion alone means that it is not a reproductive justice book, we draw heavily from the principles of the movement, especially its teachings that reproductive policy must be evaluated by paying special attention to race and class.

Though the numbers are declining, abortion is very common in this country. Every few years, the Guttmacher Institute produces the most accurate numbers with respect to abortion. Its most recent count indicates that there were 862,320 abortions performed in clinic settings in 2017. This number has been decreasing for some time, as it is down from 1.21 million in 2008. The abortion rate in this country is now lower than has ever been recorded since *Roe*. Put into more relatable numbers, the Guttmacher Institute has calculated that about one in four women will have an abortion by age forty-five. This is down from what had been a commonly stated mantra of "one in three," a previous rallying cry that emphasized how common abortion is, but it still represents a sizable number of women who will terminate a pregnancy in their lifetime.

Ever since Guttmacher released its most recent numbers, people have debated the reasons for the decline, and the phenomenon is still not fully understood. The anti-abortion movement has tried to take credit by claiming that abortion restrictions and anti-abortion sentiment have combined to produce record-low numbers, but that claim is not supported by the evidence. The abortion rate has declined both in states that have enacted major restrictions on abortion and states that have not. States without any major restrictions, such as California, Hawaii, and Oregon, are among the states that have seen the greatest decline, while states with the most restrictions, such as Arkansas, Mississippi, and North Carolina, have actually seen an increase in the abortion rate. Studies show that laws that regulate the minutiae of running an abortion clinic, laws called targeted regulations of abortion providers (commonly referred to as "TRAP laws"), are the one type of restriction that may be connected with a decline. But while restrictions per se may play a limited role in the decline in abortion numbers, the difficulty that many would-be abortion patients have in simply reaching an ever-decreasing number of abortion facilities is a likely part of this puzzle, a matter we explore in depth in this book.

Much more likely to have contributed to the declining abortion numbers is a widespread decrease in unintended pregnancy. As the Guttmacher Institute explains, "In the absence of sudden, dramatic changes in levels of sexual activity or women's ability to become pregnant (and there is no evidence of either), the most likely explanation for these broad-based abortion declines is a decrease in unintended pregnancy." Births increased over the time frame of the drop in abortions, but by nowhere near the same amount. If the unintended pregnancy rate stayed the same, these numbers would have mirrored one another. Although the most recent data still isn't available, the best evidence shows that contraceptive use has increased in the past decade, partly because of the contraceptive benefits that are part of the Affordable Care Act (these benefits are, at the time of this writing, being targeted by the Trump administration). The increased use of effective contraceptives, including long-acting reversible contraceptives, often referred to as LARCs, which are subject to less user error, has led to fewer unintended pregnancies, resulting in a decrease in the abortion rate.

The decrease in the published abortion rate could also reflect an increase in the number of women self-managing their abortions. Medication abortion—abortion up to ten weeks gestation that involves the use of a drug called mifepristone, followed by another drug, misoprostol, twenty-four hours later—has become more and more utilized by women since this method was approved for use in the United States in 2000. According to Guttmacher, 39 percent of all nonhospital abortions in 2017 were by medication abortion, compared with 24 percent in 2011. These numbers are reflected in the totals already discussed because these abortions start at an abortion clinic with the first dose of mifepristone (and then are finished at home with the misoprostol).

What is not captured by the Guttmacher data is women who obtain these drugs outside the abortion clinic setting and use them on their own to terminate their pregnancies. There has been a renewed focus on self-managed abortion in recent years, with an increasing number of abortion clinics reporting hearing from women who have tried to do so. The total number of women who may have done so while the official abortion numbers have declined is unknown and almost unknowable, which possibly makes the reported abortion rate lower than the actual one.

Regardless, despite the apparent decline in numbers, abortion is still an option pursued by almost a million women per year. Those women, while ultimately successful in finding help, are facing an increasingly difficult time doing so. More than 95 percent of abortions take place in freestanding abortion clinics—independent clinics (60 percent) and Planned Parenthood offices (35 percent)—as opposed to private doctors' offices or hospitals. In part because of expensive state restrictions but also because of the decreasing abortion rate and anti-abortion extremism, clinics have been closing at an alarming rate in recent years. Among independent clinics, 145 of 510 (28 percent) closed between 2012 and 2017. Planned Parenthood clinics also closed during that time frame, though the exact numbers are not easily accessible. As a result of these closures, the 2014 figure that nine in ten counties in the United States had no abortion provider is likely even higher now.

As common as abortion is, it is also incredibly safe. The overall complication rate is about 2 percent, but most of those complications are safely and easily dealt with at the time of the abortion at the same medical office. The rate of major complications that require hospital care is 0.23 percent, or 1 in every 436 abortions. To put that into perspective, abortion is safer than childbirth, vasectomy, plastic surgery, colonoscopy, and liposuction. At the most extreme end of the spectrum of complications—death— childbirth is fourteen times more likely to result in death than abortion, colonoscopy is ten times more likely, and liposuction twenty-eight times more. Of course, none of these procedures is specially singled out for regulation the way abortion is. All in all, abortion has a stellar safety record, as a landmark study released in 2018 by the National Academies of Sciences, Engineering, and Medicine concluded.

WHEN ABORTION IS DENIED

Laws that interfere with people seeking abortion cause a wide variety of harms that are discussed throughout this book. At their most extreme, these laws contribute to women being denied access. When that happens, all evidence indicates that they are harmed in numerous consequential ways.

The best research on what happens to women who can't access a wanted abortion comes from one of the most significant recent studies of abortion, the Turnaway Study from the University of California, San Francisco. In that study, which began in 2008 and was completed in 2015, researchers interviewed almost one thousand women who sought abortions from thirty abortion facilities around the country. The study analyzed outcomes for two groups of women: (1) those who received abortions and (2) those who were turned away from the clinic because they were over that particular clinic's gestational limit and subsequently had a baby. Each participant was interviewed multiple times over the course of a five-year period to determine the differences between these two groups. The results of the Turnaway Study are specific to women turned away from clinics because they were too far along in their pregnancy, but the novel way it compared people who received abortions and those who did not allows us to generalize about what the effects can be when a woman does not get an abortion she wants.

The central finding of the Turnaway Study is that women who are denied wanted abortions are worse off in almost every aspect of their lives than those who are able to obtain one. Looking at economics, women denied a wanted abortion have almost four times higher odds of being poor compared to women who get an abortion. They are also less likely to be employed and more likely to be on public assistance. Relatedly, women who receive abortions are more likely to have positive plans for their future related to their education, employment, finances, family, emotional well-being, living situation, relationship, and other aspects of life. In contrast, women denied abortions are more likely to have neutral or negative expectations for their future.

Other measures show similar negative effects of being denied an abortion. Women who are denied an abortion and who give birth are more likely to stay in a relationship with an abusive partner and less likely to be in a quality relationship five years afterwards. Emotionally, it also appears that being denied a wanted abortion is worse for women than obtaining one. Immediately after being denied an abortion, those women have lower self-esteem and life satisfaction and higher rates of anxiety than women who had abortions, though this evens out with time.

Children are also worse off when people are denied abortions. The existing children of women who are denied abortions fare worse than the existing children of women who get an abortion in terms of both development and poverty. When women have an abortion and are thus able to wait to have kids, they are more closely bonded to those children and more able to take care of them financially compared to children that they have as a result of being denied an abortion. Finally, women who receive abortions are more likely to have intended children over the course of the next five years than women who are denied an abortion.

Women who are denied abortions also face one other major health issue—continued pregnancy leading to childbirth—and the Turnaway Study confirms this. It found that women denied abortions experience much more serious physical health complications compared to women who get their abortions. For many women, of course, pregnancy and childbirth don't pose health problems and are welcome and joyous events. However, for others, pregnancy can be difficult or even life-threatening. Preexisting conditions, such as heart disease, cancer, hypertension, and diabetes, can worsen during childbirth. They can also present a woman with the difficult decision between discontinuing necessary treatment for those conditions, such as cancer, and risking harming her pregnancy. Women who were healthy at the beginning of their pregnancy can later develop serious complications, such as gestational diabetes or preeclampsia. Pregnancy and childbirth can also lead to mental health issues, such as postpartum depression.

At its most serious, continuing a pregnancy to term can lead to death. The United States has the highest maternal mortality rate of any developed country. Even more concerning, that rate continues to rise, while all other developed countries are showing a decrease. Among black mothers in particular, there is a national crisis of maternal mortality, as the rate is three to four times higher than the rate for white mothers. Improved abortion access is only a partial answer to this crisis; as reproductive justice activists rightly demand, all people should also be provided with the means to have healthy pregnancies and to parent the children they have.

Even though we know that abortion is common and safe and that forcing women to have a child against their will results in suffering in almost every aspect of their lives, restrictions that make it more and more difficult for women to access abortion are multiplying. As a result, the process of obtaining an abortion is clouded by extreme laws that place incredible burdens on women. What should be a straightforward process—or at least only as complicated as the process of obtaining any other common medical procedure—is, in many places throughout the country, a labyrinthian obstacle course. And with *Roe* on the metaphorical chopping block at the Supreme Court, these abortion obstacles are bound to get worse before they get better.

ARE ABORTION OBSTACLES CONSTITUTIONAL?

It's clear that when women are ultimately unable to obtain sought-after abortion care, they and their families are worse off. But even those who are still able to obtain care, like Talia, Brittany, and Wandalyn, whose stories started this introduction, suffer the consequences. Most people familiar with American law and politics know that abortion is protected by the US Constitution, so it's reasonable to wonder whether the abortion restrictions discussed throughout this book are even allowed in light of the known ways they detrimentally affect abortion patients.

The answer to that query begins in 1973 with the Supreme Court finding, in *Roe v. Wade,* that laws that made abortion illegal were unconstitutional. Despite vociferous opposition, the Court has repeatedly and clearly reaffirmed that principle for almost fifty years

However, at the same time, the Court has been notoriously vague about what other types of anti-abortion laws—those that regulate abortion but do not make it illegal—run afoul of the Constitution. In *Roe* itself, the Court tried to give a clear framework for evaluating abortion-specific laws. The Court announced that laws restricting abortion in the first trimester would be unconstitutional because the decision had to be left to the woman and the judgment of her physician. During the second trimester, the state could regulate abortion but only to advance the woman's health. Only during the third trimester could a state outlaw abortion, but it still had to have an exception for abortions to preserve a woman's life or health.

For almost two decades, the Supreme Court struggled to apply this framework in a consistent manner, striking down some regulations while upholding others. Much of the unpredictability from the Court came from its changing composition, which became increasingly conservative. In the first twenty years after Roe, six new Justices joined the Court, each appointed by a Republican president. As a result, when the Supreme Court decided *Planned Parenthood v. Casey* in 1992, the Court had moved to the right and was less friendly to abortion rights than it had been in 1973.

Although *Casey* did not, as many people at the time feared, overrule *Roe,* the Court did exacerbate the uncertainty around abortion laws by changing the standard for evaluating abortion regulations. Abandoning its previous framework, the Court said that it would strike down an abortion law only if it created an "undue burden" on a woman's right to choose. The Court attempted to define what an undue burden was by stating that a state could not place a "substantial obstacle" in the way of a woman exercising her constitutional right. But, in applying these terms to the Pennsylvania law at issue in the case, the Court showed just how subjective the new standard was. The Court approved the state laws requiring that all women wait twenty-four hours before getting an abortion and go through an expanded and biased informed-consent process that no other medical procedure required. It also allowed the state to force minors to get the consent of a parent in order to have an abortion. On the other hand, the Court struck down a provision that required a married woman to notify her husband before getting an abortion.

What was the difference between the three provisions upheld and the one struck down? The Court explained that a married woman could fear that her husband would abuse her if she told him about wanting an abortion. Thus that would be a substantial obstacle for those women because they would avoid getting an abortion out of fear of spousal abuse. But what about young women who feared getting the consent of their parents or going before a judge (the alternative provided by law)? Or indigent women who lived far away from a clinic and faced the extreme difficulty of traveling and waiting twenty-four hours, with the missed workdays and child care responsibilities that come from multiday travel? To the Court, these were not substantial obstacles. Without a satisfactory explanation of the difference, the standard announced by the Court was left unclear.

In the decades after *Casey*, the Supreme Court approved most, though not all, abortion restrictions that came before it. During this time, a worrisome trend developed that gave politicians much leeway in regulating abortion. The Supreme Court and many lower courts indicated at various times that they would defer to legislatures' judgments about health and safety in determining whether an abortion restriction was warranted. The Court's ultimate statement of this position came in 2007 when, in *Gonzales v. Carhart*, the Court said that legislatures could determine on their own whether an abortion restriction was based in medical fact. Legislatures had this "wide discretion," according to the Court, because "considerations of marginal safety including the balance of risks, are within the legislative competence when the regulation is rational and in pursuit of legitimate ends." Stated differently, when a legislature believed an abortion restriction contributed to women's safety, it could pass the law despite medical evidence to the contrary.

This relaxed standard was the precursor to the burst of anti-abortion legislation in states in the 2010s, but a somewhat surprise 2016 Supreme Court decision seemed to signal that the trend of increasing abortion barriers might have to come to an end. In that summer, the law of abortion appeared to undergo a seismic shift when the Supreme Court decided the case of *Whole Woman's Health v. Hellerstedt*. The case arose out of Texas, where, before 2013, there were over forty abortion clinics serving the second-largest state, both by population and by geographic size.

But in 2013, the Texas legislature passed a very restrictive abortion bill, HB2, that changed the landscape of abortion, not only for the state, but for the entire country. HB2 gave Texas four new restrictions on abortion: that abortion providers had to follow an outdated protocol for medical abortions; that abortions beyond twenty weeks after fertilization were banned; that abortion facilities had to meet the high standard of an ambulatory surgical center; and that abortion doctors had to have admitting privileges with local hospitals.

Only the last two of these four restrictions were challenged in court. If both of these provisions had taken effect, the state would have lost more than three-quarters of its abortion providers, dropping the number for the entire state to under ten, with no providers at all in the huge swath of land south or west of San Antonio. Several abortion clinics sued the state, and the case made it to the Supreme Court.

At the Supreme Court, the issue was whether the state could close down that many abortion clinics simply by claiming that it was promoting women's health and safety. According to the state, abortion clinics that met the requirements of an ambulatory surgical center—large hospital-like operating rooms, wide hallways, sterile environments, extreme safety precautions, and more—would reduce the complication rate for the women who went there. And, also according to the state, abortion doctors who had admitting privileges at local hospitals—contractual agreements ahead of time to treat patients who needed hospital care at a particular institution—would provide better care because of the association with the hospital. Both sides agreed that these requirements would shut down the vast majority of Texas abortion clinics, because upgrading to become an ambulatory surgical center is extremely costly and admitting privileges for abortion clinic doctors were (and still are) rare, especially in a state like Texas where many hospitals are hostile to or don't want to be involved with abortion.

As argued by the state, though, these requirements furthered the goal of patient safety, so they justified any closings. When the Texas attorney general argued the case to the Supreme Court, this strategy was on display. He stated over and over to the Justices that HB2 was passed because the legislature wanted to avoid medical complications, even though he and the legislature had no evidence that abortion complications were anything but rare.

On the other side, the abortion clinics challenging HB2 presented the Court with a wealth of scientific evidence. At trial, many medical and public health experts testified for the clinics that abortion was safe, that neither requirement improved safety or health, and that both requirements together would close more than three-quarters of Texas clinics, resulting in disastrous consequences for women's health in the state. In addition, leading medical organizations and social scientists in the field briefed the Court on the same points, supporting their positions with peer-reviewed scientific studies.

Thus the stage was set before the Supreme Court for a clash between the stated beliefs of the Texas legislature—that abortion facilities needed to be safer and that HB2's requirements would make them so—and the overwhelming evidence from the medical and social science community that abortion was already a very safe medical procedure and that HB2's requirements would harm women by decreasing access to medical care. A divided Supreme Court sided with the evidence. Justice Stephen Breyer's opinion for the five-Justice majority clearly took sides, stating that "research-based" testimony and "expert evidence," not legislatures, should decide questions of medical safety.

The Court went even further and tried to better explain *Casey's* vague "undue burden" language. What that standard meant, the Court said, was that an anti-abortion restriction had to have medical benefits that were sufficient to justify the burdens on abortion access that it created. Looking at the expert testimony in the case, the court concluded that HB2 had no benefit—abortion was already a very safe procedure that rarely required hospitalization—but would impose a huge burden on women's access—most clinics in the state would close. The overall effect of the law, according to the Court's majority, would be "harmful to, not supportive of, women's health."

With its decision in *Whole Woman's Health*, then, the Court answered two important questions about abortion restrictions. First, the test for whether an abortion restriction is an unconstitutional undue burden is a balancing test—whether the burdens the law creates for women are outweighed by the benefits the law furthers. Second, evidence in the form of peer-reviewed research and expert testimony is essential in evaluating this test. The announcement of these two principles, which would guide the evaluation of abortion restrictions going forward, was celebrated by abortion rights supporters. They believed, as in the *Whole Woman's Health* case itself, that scientific evidence was on their side. Armed with this new understanding of what an undue burden is, restrictions on abortion access were going to fall by the wayside as unconstitutional burdens with no accompanying benefit.

And yet, several years after the Court's decision, although some restrictions have fallen under this new standard and some new creative lawsuits based on *Whole Women's Health* have been filed, abortion stories like

Talia's, Brittany's, and Wandalyn's, which began this chapter, remain common. In Texas itself, only a small number of the abortion clinics that closed in the wake of HB2 have been able to reopen after the Supreme Court decision, with logistical problems caused by shutting down proving insurmountable for many. And beyond Texas, thanks to an extensive array of abortion restrictions that remain in place around the country along with stalwart conservative legislatures committed to keeping them on the books and enacting even more, people seeking an abortion in many places throughout America still, even after *Whole Woman's Health*, have to navigate a difficult system of hurdles and barriers.

Furthermore, with Justice Anthony Kennedy—a judicial conservative who supported the basic rule of *Roe v. Wade*—retiring from the Supreme Court in 2018 and being replaced by conservative and likely-anti-*Roe* Justice Brett Kavanaugh, it is hard now to imagine *Whole Woman's Health* being expanded and abortion access in this country improving any further. Rather, with an even more conservative Supreme Court as well as an increasingly conservative federal judiciary as a whole, we are likely to see more and more abortion barriers—such as the Louisiana admitting privileges law the Supreme Court agreed to hear as this book was being proofread—survive constitutional challenge. And if this newly constituted Supreme Court were to overrule *Roe v. Wade,* abortion could be outlawed in some states or could even become illegal everywhere if the Court determined that a fetus is a person entitled to full constitutional protection. To be sure, we aren't there yet, as abortion is still legal everywhere in the United States, but the storm clouds are gathering.

Drawing on the commonsense notion from *Whole Woman's Health* that the burdens of anti-abortion laws must be evaluated using empirical evidence, in this book we take a comprehensive look at the vast assortment of restrictions that affect a woman's experience of trying to terminate a pregnancy in modern America. We do so by breaking down the steps a patient would take on the path from finding out she's pregnant to getting an abortion. For each step, we examine how burdensome the various restrictions are and whether they confer any benefit on women's health specifically and society more broadly.

And yet, in spite of the many obstacles in place, for the most part large numbers of people in this country who seek an abortion are still able to get one. Notwithstanding state interference, they do so thanks to their own incredible determination to control their bodies and lives, the creativity and commitment of abortion providers who are able to provide quality medical care despite the barriers that exist, and the assistance of a mostly unheralded army of abortion allies and volunteers who work tirelessly and in ways almost completely foreign to other areas of medical care.

However, women should not have to move mountains to get basic health care, medical care providers should be able to determine their care based on evidence-based medicine rather than politics, and no one should need a vast network of allies and volunteers to make it all possible. A much better alternative to this system exists, as we explore in the conclusion in chapter 9. This alternative, as seen in the states that treat abortion like any other medical care, would put us on a path to a more just system for people seeking reproductive health care.

2 Making the Decision

COPING WITH ROADBLOCKS, DECEPTION, AND LIES

The mom of four who can't afford another child, the teen who isn't ready to be a parent, the twenty-two-year-old who doesn't want to derail her education and future with a baby, the couple who desperately want a child but who have learned that the fetus was diagnosed with a deadly anomaly. In some sense, they and everyone else who has an abortion do it for the same reason—they don't want to be pregnant anymore and don't want to end their pregnancy by giving birth.

Of course, though, there are many different reasons why someone wouldn't want to be pregnant any longer. Susan Schewel, the former director of an abortion fund in a northeastern state, gave us the list of reasons patients have told her:

> So they can finish high school. So they can go to college. So they can finish college. So they can finish their training program. So they can be a good parent to the kids they have. So that they can get away from guys that are not good for them. So that they can stay with guys that they like who don't want them to have a kid. Because they understand what's involved in parenting, and they don't want to do it. Maybe they want to make art.
>
> But for most of them, it's that they're struggling to get by. They're struggling to put food on the table. They're struggling to afford housing. They're

struggling to have their kids stay in the same school for the full year. They're struggling to stay off the street. They're struggling to stay safe. They don't want to be in a shelter. They are trying to keep their kids away from the county agency.

All of these reasons and more are supported by the most authoritative study looking at abortion decisions. That study, in which researchers asked over 1,200 abortion patients the reason they had an abortion, found that women have abortions for many different reasons, but the most common are a sense of responsibility to others and concern about limited resources.

Specifically, the two reasons that were both offered by almost three-quarters of the women surveyed were (1) that having a baby would interfere with work, education, or caring for children or dependents and (2) that they could not afford to have a baby at this point in their lives. Those who answered that they were not able to afford a baby explained that it was because they were unmarried, students, or unemployed, didn't have enough support from a partner, were on public assistance, or could not afford child care or the basic needs of a baby's life. Other reasons offered by a substantial percentage of the women interviewed were that they had completed their childbearing already, were not ready for a child or another child, or did not feel mature enough to raise a child or another child. About one-eighth of the women in the study said that there were physical health problems affecting the health of the fetus, and about the same fraction said they themselves were experiencing health problems.

When the researchers asked the study participants to identify from among all of their reasons the most important reason they had an abortion, about a quarter said they were not ready for a child or another child at that point in time and another quarter said they could not afford a baby now. Almost one in five women said that the most important reason was that they were done with childbearing or that they were caring for other people already. Less than half a percent said that they were having an abortion mainly because their partner or parents wanted them to have one.

The reasons in this study fly in the face of some of the common myths about abortion: that women have abortions because they are irresponsible and are thinking only of themselves, or the converse, are pressured by others to do something they don't really want. The reality is that women feel a deep sense of responsibility to other people in their lives—whether it's the children that they already have or other dependents who rely on them. Because they think of those people in their lives and realize that having a baby would compromise their ability to care for them, whether emotionally or financially, they have an abortion. For other women, they have an abortion because they are making careful decisions about their future—future career plans, future education plans, or future family plans. They make the responsible choice that having a child now would interfere with the future they see for themselves and others in their lives. And for virtually all women, they make this decision on their own, not on the basis of pressure from others in their lives.

If this were any other medical procedure, women would be able to make this medical decision on the basis of their own reasons, and they alone would be able to decide whether to consult others. For instance, before someone has cataract surgery or a tooth pulled, that person will evaluate her own feelings about the procedure, based on taking stock of her body, life, and finances, while also consulting—if she wants—medical professionals, trusted friends and family, and any reliable information she can find about the condition and procedure. Once she does that, she makes her decision on her own, and no one else has a say in the matter. Other issues may come into play, such as the availability of providers, the cost of the procedure, and insurance coverage, but the decision is the person's own to make.

The same is far from true for making the decision to get an abortion. People who have abortions for any of the reasons mentioned here or any of the other possible reasons there might be to have this procedure routinely encounter roadblocks that people making other medical decisions never experience. They are cared for by doctors who give them misinformation that is protected by law. They go to publicly funded health centers that are prohibited by law from talking with them about their decision. They are told by law that they cannot have an abortion for certain reasons. They encounter fake clinics or anti-abortion websites that give them false information about abortion. Or they are minors who are forced by law to have a parent or guardian be involved with their decision, possibly even overriding it.

These and other barriers make the abortion decision different from all other medical decisions. They tell pregnant women that their reproductive health decisions are not their own and that others can interfere in ways that are unheard of in other areas of medicine. At their essence, they tell women that they are not autonomous human beings whose choices are trusted and decisions respected.

THE MYTH OF UNCERTAINTY

To the abortion providers we talked with, nothing was more important than their patients being certain about their decision. Kathleen Anderson, a patient advocate at a southern clinic, told us the story of a patient she counseled who was hesitant about her decision. This woman came to the clinic very emotional and wouldn't stop crying. She told Kathleen that she was financially stable and could afford to have a baby to add to her family of three but that she just didn't want to have another child. As Kathleen later told us, the woman felt social pressure to have a baby since, in Kathleen's words there was "no real reason they couldn't have another child." Because of this pressure, the patient was having trouble saying simply, "I just don't want to be pregnant. I just don't want any more children."

Kathleen knew that the patient "was just way too emotional to stay" at the clinic and have her procedure that day, so Kathleen suggested she go home to think about it more. Kathleen explained that "any patient who's ambivalent like that, the first thing I say to them is, 'You can leave and come back, but there's no do-over for this. If we do this procedure, I want to know that when you wake up tomorrow morning you are going to be sound with what happened today.'" That kind of support gave the patient the space to make the decision she needed to make for herself.

Two days later, the patient came back to the clinic, certain that she wanted to have an abortion. Kathleen asked her what had happened, and the patient said that when she had gotten home from the clinic she "realized she regretted not having an abortion." So she returned to the clinic and had her abortion. Kathleen said that the patient "was very appreciative" that Kathleen had supported her by encouraging her to make her decision on her own.

Concern about patient certainty is real among abortion providers. As Erica Valverde, a doctor who provides abortions in a western state, explained to us, "If the patient is uncertain, we would rather reschedule the appointment than proceed with a procedure they don't want or will regret." The reason is simple. An abortion is irreversible, so patients need to be sure and need to be clear in expressing that certainty to their provider. Echoing the concerns of others we interviewed, Erica described just how much this haunts her:

> I've had nightmares about performing an abortion on someone who didn't want one. In real life, I once had a patient burst into tears after the abortion, and I thought, oh good heavens, I have just done an abortion on somebody who didn't want one, and I'm panicking now. And I asked her what was wrong, and she said it was the protesters outside who judge her and shame her, and I was relieved but also of course felt bad that I couldn't take that pain away from her. But my first thought was panic about having done an abortion on someone who didn't want one.

As it turns out, Erica and her professional colleagues work in a field where patient uncertainty is very rarely a problem, especially when compared to other fields of medicine. Studies have long shown that most abortion patients are certain of their decision, including one study showing that, at every point over a three-year period after their abortion, 95 percent of patients believed that their decision was the right decision. But it wasn't until 2017 that researchers compared certainty about the abortion decision to certainty about other comparable medical decisions. In that study, researchers talked with abortion patients when they first showed up at the clinic, before they had any interaction with a counselor or health care provider at the clinic. As a result, the study captured patient attitudes unadulterated by anything the clinic might say to them.

What researchers found was that abortion patients were as or even more certain about their decision than patients who underwent other medical procedures. The study found that five out of every six abortion patients had low levels of uncertainty. That one out of every six had some level of uncertainty may seem high to some, but compared to other medical procedures that level is very low. The research shows that other women's health care decisions have a much higher level of patient uncertainty, such as mastectomy after a breast cancer diagnosis, invasive prenatal testing after an infertility diagnosis, and antidepressant use during pregnancy. Uncertainty is also much higher for health care decisions that men might make, such as reconstructive knee surgery and prostate cancer treatment.

This study, as well as the others that came before it that looked just at abortion certainty, disprove one of the common myths about women deciding to have an abortion—that they are conflicted in ways that require special state intervention. However, just because women as a whole are more certain about their decision to have an abortion than other procedures doesn't mean some women aren't conflicted. With those women, abortion providers are cautious. Shelley Sella, an abortion doctor in a western state, told us that this is a small percentage of the patients she sees, but they do exist. "In those patients, we spend even more time with them. Sometimes we send them away. Sometimes they come back. Sometimes they don't come back." To Shelley, what's important is that the decision be right for that particular patient, and if more time is needed, so be it.

For the pregnant women who are uncertain, there are resources, including local and national hotlines. Parker Dockray is the executive director of one of those hotlines, and she explained the help it provides to pregnant people. She said that some people "are really hungry for a place that truly doesn't have a stake. Like even if they have someone to talk to that they feel like is relatively supportive, like a loved one, they always have an opinion." Parker and the people she works with try to provide that unbiased counseling. About a quarter of her callers want to talk through all of their options, from abortion to carrying the pregnancy to term, from adoption to parenting, what Parker calls "true options counseling" (as opposed to other services the hotline offers). For those callers, Parker and her colleagues listen, talk, and ask open questions. "Sometimes our advocates will role-play with people or do exercises with them, the standard counseling tools. Like, on a scale of one to ten, how certain are you about your decision? Or on a scale of one to ten, what is your head saying you should do and what is your heart saying you should do?" Parker said that the goal is to support people in whatever option they ultimately choose, something with which all of the abortion providers we interviewed agreed.

WHEN MEDICAL PROVIDERS INTERFERE

When women find out they're pregnant, like other patients dealing with medical conditions, they often talk with their own medical care provider about their situation. The problem is, as many of the people we talked with explained, the culture around pregnancy is that most providers' immediate reaction is some expression of joy or congratulations. Parker Dockray has heard this story from many of the people she has counseled. What this reaction does is "leave no space for a conversation about what if you're not excited that you're pregnant."

This mistake of excitement is common even among medical care providers who support abortion rights, but not every provider is supportive of the decision to have an abortion or even of the process of considering abortion. Fausta Luchini, someone who helps train medical care providers in the South and Midwest to provide comprehensive counseling around abortion, said that ideally, if a care provider does not support a patient having an abortion, that provider will give a "warm handoff" to another provider who will be supportive. This is more than just giving out someone else's business card; it means actually connecting the patient to this other provider with an introduction and some facilitation.

That doesn't happen all the time, though. Some providers actively sabotage their patients when it comes to deciding to have an abortion. Chloe Hebert manages the National Abortion Federation Hotline Fund, a national abortion referral and assistance hotline. She has heard from patients who have faced all sorts of sabotage, such as primary care physicians who withhold ultrasound results from patients who request them when going to an abortion clinic, or physicians who misinform patients about ultrasound results so that it seems that the patient is too far into her pregnancy to have an abortion. Other medical professionals refuse to refer patients to an abortion provider or won't return phone calls from patients they know have decided to have an abortion. When we interviewed her, Chloe finished this list exasperated, saying, "I will never get over medical professionals who willfully sabotage their patients' access to abortion."

Chloe was far from the only person we talked with who dealt with patients facing this experience. Millie Johnson, a doctor in a western state, worked at a hospital where some of the other doctors on staff were anti-abortion. Those doctors would sometimes show women who were seeking abortion their ultrasound while saying to them, "Why do you want to kill your baby?" They would also refuse to refer the patients to an abortion clinic and would pray over them during their exams.

Doctors who sabotage their patients' abortion decision-making can place those patients at risk of increased suffering or even real danger. Jennifer Pride, an administrator who runs a clinic in the Midwest, had a patient who had a molar pregnancy, a pregnancy complication that occurs when a sperm fertilizes an empty egg and that, left untreated, can lead to cancer. Even though a molar pregnancy never results in a live birth, the patient's doctor, who practiced in a small rural town and opposed abortion, told the patient that the pregnancy would eventually turn into a baby and she didn't need to do anything. The patient wanted an abortion regardless of the diagnosis, so she ultimately found her way to Jennifer's clinic where they performed her abortion. But Jennifer was concerned that if the patient had listened to the doctor and never came to her clinic, she could have suffered needlessly.

Almost unbelievably, in the state where Jennifer works, this doctor is free to misdiagnose the patient and sabotage her decision to have an abortion without any legal consequence. This is so because her state is one of the roughly half of states that prohibits "wrongful birth" lawsuits. This type of lawsuit seeks to hold medical care providers responsible for failing to inform a pregnant woman about possible birth defects or other pregnancy complications, thus preventing her from getting an abortion. Some of these states allow lawsuits when the medical care provider acts intentionally, as opposed to negligently, to sabotage a woman's right to choose, but others prevent all such lawsuits.

For example, both Oklahoma and Idaho prevent all wrongful birth lawsuits. In Oklahoma, the law was enacted in 2010 with the explicit purpose of preventing women from having abortions. The state representative who introduced the law wanted to immunize doctors who, in his words, "failed to convince the mother to abort a child," and the law was passed by the state legislature along with other anti-abortion bills. In Idaho, the law states that no one can sue if the information that was withheld meant that the child "would have been aborted."

Even laws that allow for lawsuits for intentional withholding of information but prohibit them for negligence interfere with a pregnant woman's decision-making process. When Utah passed such a law in the 1980s, legislators supporting the law intended it to prevent abortions by reducing the amount of information that a woman received from her doctor that might lead her to make that choice. As a justice of the Utah Supreme Court noted when reviewing the law, its purpose was to "eliminate informed choice" by discouraging doctors from fully informing patients.

Because of these laws, if an anti-abortion doctor dismisses a woman's concerns about possible birth defects or other problems, she won't receive the information that she needs to make an informed decision. As many who have studied the issue have concluded, this will result in anti-abortion doctors carelessly treating patients when they know that abortion might be an option. This is not a controversial assessment of these laws, as anti-abortion scholars openly agree that bans on wrongful birth lawsuits favor childbirth over abortion. When anti-abortion medical professionals, with the full support of the law, fail to fully inform their pregnant patients, women don't get all the information they need to make decisions about whether to continue their pregnancy.

ABORTION GAG RULES

In some places, medical care professionals who want to counsel their patients about abortion are prohibited from doing so by law. Fausta Luchini explained to us that there is an "ethical obligation" that medical care providers give their patients all of the information they need in order to make an informed decision. However, in some jurisdictions, there are what she calls "gag rules" prohibiting them from doing so. For instance, in Kentucky, nurses who examine patients in hospitals following a rape are prohibited from talking to those patients about abortion. To Fausta, not only does this prohibition violate medical ethics, but it also creates a real barrier for patients.

Kentucky is alone in having this particular prohibition, but some states prohibit medical professionals from counseling about abortion in other situations. Women who seek medical care from Arkansas, Michigan, Nebraska, Ohio, and Wisconsin providers who receive state funds related to family planning or other sexuality-based programs will encounter providers who are prohibited from counseling them about abortion.

A much bigger threat to comprehensive counseling looms on the horizon as the Trump administration's 2019 changes to Title X funding go into effect (as of final editing of this book, courts have allowed the changes to take effect while litigation over them moves forward). Title X is a federal grant program that gives financial assistance to health care providers to provide contraceptive care to low-income women throughout the country. Over four thousand health care providers received Title X funding, and under the previous version of the law, recipients of Title X funding were required to provide comprehensive counseling, including about abortion.

Andrea Hillman is a nurse practitioner who works closely with these Title X recipient clinics in a northeastern state. She explained that, because of the pre-Trump regulation requiring all-options counseling, she was "confident that within family planning clinics patients got thorough options counseling." In fact, Title X's counseling as it previously worked was so effective that Andrea pointed to private providers as the bigger problem. Because Title X regulations don't reach them, Andrea told us that "bias gets to enter into the counseling," with doctors sometimes telling patients that "they don't believe in abortion so therefore they wouldn't even talk about it."

However, under the Trump administration's change, staff at Title X-funded clinics will be allowed to do the same and refuse to counsel about abortion if doing so violates the staff member's or the clinic's beliefs. The new rule also bans referrals to abortion providers unless the patient explicitly asks for them, and even then, the Title X recipient still has the option to refuse. Because of these new regulations and their impact on comprehensive patient care, in the summer of 2019, Planned Parenthood, previously the largest recipient of Title X funds, announced that it was no longer going to take these federal dollars.

A similar assault on comprehensive options counseling for pregnant patients has previously been given the Supreme Court's stamp of approval. In 1988, President Reagan changed Title X regulations to prohibit recipients from talking about abortion. The regulation was never implemented because it was held up in court challenges and ultimately rescinded by the Clinton administration. In the interim, in 1991 the Supreme Court ruled that the restriction was constitutional. According to the Court, the gag rule still allowed medical care professionals to talk about abortion outside of their Title X clinic, so it did not restrict their First Amendment right to free speech. Moreover, women who might be denied this information at a Title X clinic could obtain it elsewhere and obtain abortions from other providers, so their constitutional rights would not be violated. Although the regulations never went into effect, this case remains binding precedent at the Supreme Court and forms the legal basis for the proposed Trump regulations. It is yet to be seen what the ultimate legal fate of the new Title X regulations will be, but with the 1991 precedent still on the books and the Supreme Court arguably even more conservative now, if they get to the Supreme Court, the Trump regulations seem to have a good chance to remain in full effect as long as he (and any subsequent Republicans) stay in office.

ONLY FOR AN APPROVED REASON

Regardless of the reason a woman wants to get pregnant or carry a pregnancy to term, the law allows her to do so. She can get pregnant in order to try for a daughter when she already has a son or decide to have a child in order to produce more children who are of a particular race or who are biracial.

In many places around the country, though, abortion is different. To be sure, providers themselves are divided about the appropriateness of having an abortion for reasons related to sex or race. However, there is little evidence that abortion happens in the United States for these reasons. Nonetheless, several states have taken action to stop this practice. Nine states ban abortions because of the fetus's sex, and two states ban abortions done because of the race of the fetus. Many more states have considered such bans in recent years, with Congress doing the same multiple times over the past decade. The federal Prenatal Nondiscrimination Act, although receiving a healthy dose of national attention, has yet to make it through either house of Congress.

The effect of these bans depends on their wording. In some states, sex or race cannot be *any* of the reasons that a woman has an abortion. Gabrielle Goodrick is a doctor who provides abortions in a western state that has one such ban. Because of the law, she has to sign a notarized statement for every patient saying that she was not aware that the patient was having an abortion for any of the prohibited reasons. If she fails to do so or is aware of a reason that violates the law, she can be sued by a patient's family member or can even go to jail. In the years that this law has been in place, she has seen only two or three patients who have said they want to have an abortion because of sex, and she has had to tell them that she can't help them. Gabrielle is so concerned about the law that she won't allow the patient to "backtrack"—change her mind about the reason for the abortion once Gabrielle has told her that sex can't be the basis. "I try to help people, but at some point I have to protect my office and I can't take that chance."

In other states, sex can be one of many reasons for an abortion but can't be the *only* reason. This leads providers to question patients about their reason for having an abortion beyond what they would ordinarily do. Jen Moore Conrow, a clinic administrator in the Northeast, runs a clinic in one such state. She normally doesn't ask patients, nor does she test for sex of the fetus, but sometimes the patient already knows. If the patient says that sex is the reason for the abortion, Jen has to find out if there is another reason as well. "We had a patient where she's starting to say some things that maybe it's going down this path of sex selection, but ultimately there were multiple other reasons to end the pregnancy. It wasn't the sole reason." If sex selection is the only reason, Jen has to tell the patient, "If that is your only reason, we can't help you. But is there anything else happening with this pregnancy?" To Jen, even though this law is not as burdensome as those in other states, it still is "infuriating." As she explained, "If somebody's not going to be able to love or care for or provide based on the sex of their baby, then that seems like a perfectly valid reason not to continue a pregnancy."

In states where sex-based abortion is banned, providers are sometimes put in difficult situations with patients. Several of the providers we talked with said that, in order to avoid those situations, they intentionally do not determine the sex of a patient during any ultrasound or other prenatal testing. As Floyd Moore, a doctor who provides abortions in multiple southern states, explained, he tells patients that this is not "clinically useful" information for a patient having an abortion. By not scanning for sex, he is able "to be honest with the patient" and tell her that he doesn't know, even if she wants to know. This practice also ensures that he is never in the situation of having to question whether a patient is having an abortion for the purposes of sex selection.

Issues of race and ethnicity are inextricably intertwined with these "reason" bans. Race bans are based on the common anti-abortion talking point that abortion clinics target people of color by intentionally locating in neighborhoods that are majority minority, something that is not true. Sex-selection bans play on stereotypes of Asian patients, with the common belief that Asian women want to abort female fetuses in order to have more sons. Though there is little evidence of this happening in the United States, the result of the stereotype and the laws that prohibit such abortions is distrust of Asian and Asian American women's choices. These laws also further the idea that Asian and Asian American patients are foreigners who have dangerous values inconsistent with American notions of equality.

No court has ruled on the constitutionality of a race- or sex-based abortion ban, but there is an ongoing battle in federal court over another reason-based abortion ban—abortions based on fetal anomalies, such as in utero diagnoses of anencephaly, Down syndrome, or incomplete development of organs, such as the bladder, stomach, and brain. Seven states have passed such bans, while several other states have required particularized counseling before an abortion based on a genetic anomaly. Many other states have considered these bans, with more being introduced each year.

The stated rationale behind these bans is that society should respect people with disabilities. However, a significant number of disability advocates have criticized the laws for using disabled people as props for an anti-abortion agenda. These criticisms seem valid, especially in states that provide very limited support or services for people with disabilities. As with other reason bans, these laws often force abortion providers and counselors to second-guess their patients. Kathaleen Pittman runs a clinic in a southern state that has passed one of these laws, and she explained to us the difficulty she faces with her patients: "How do you tell somebody, 'If you want to have an abortion because you just don't want to be pregnant, that's legal, but if you want an abortion because there's something severely wrong with your pregnancy, well, it can't be done.' I mean, how do you do that? That makes no sense."

So far, the courts have agreed with Kathaleen. Multiple courts have found that these bans on abortions based on fetal anomalies are unconstitutional because they interfere with a woman's decision to have an abortion. And, in May 2019, the Supreme Court refused to hear a case out of Indiana raising the issue, leaving the matter to be resolved another day.

MISINFORMATION AND LIES

People deciding to have an abortion face another major battle—overcoming the abundance of misinformation and lies about the procedure. Chloe Hebert has heard it all, particularly from patients who have done "research" on the internet. They tell her that, contrary to all medical evidence, they know that abortion is dangerous and that they might not be able to have children in the future, but they need to have one anyway. Or that they think that, contrary to the current reality in every state, abortion is illegal, but they are so determined not to have a child that they are willing to break the law.

A small but not insubstantial percentage of women seeking abortion cite problems finding trustworthy information about abortion at the point of decision-making. Anti-abortion lies that have seeped into the national consciousness, deceptive websites, stigma around talking about abortion with family or friends, medical care professionals who have not been trained or kept themselves informed about abortion—all of these and more present challenges to women trying to make an informed choice.

One of the most hotly contested sources of misinformation about abortion that influences women's decisions is fake clinics, or, as the anti-abortion movement calls them, crisis pregnancy centers or pregnancy resource centers. Fake clinics are religiously affiliated and often state-funded centers that provide assistance to pregnant women that is biased against abortion and in favor of continuing a pregnancy to term. While research indicates that the number of women considering abortion who actually go to fake clinics is much smaller than the amount of attention focused on these fake clinics, they are nonetheless a source of misinformation.

For instance, Cherisse, the mom of a fifteen-year-old son, has publicly written about how a fake clinic deceived her. In a boldly titled piece "I Love My Son, but a Crisis Pregnancy Center Tricked Me into Having Him," Cherisse explained that her life is still being affected by the fake clinic's deception. When Cherisse was pregnant, she made up her mind to have an abortion. She saw an ad about abortion care, so she went.

> When I arrived at what looked like a private doctor's office, I was questioned about being on public aid, subjected to guided counseling, shown graphic abortion procedure videos, and, once they realized that their initial tactics had not changed my mind, sent to another of their locations for an ultrasound where I was told that if I had an abortion, I would not be able to have another child. I trusted that I would be given medically appropriate info and guidance, but instead, my trust was exploited.
>
> The [clinic] nurse convinced me that if I had an abortion, I wouldn't be able to have children in the future—a lie—and so I continued the pregnancy though I knew there was a strong possibility that I would have to raise that baby alone. . . . After manipulating me into continuing my pregnancy, they sent me home with a bottle, a onesie, and a rattle. To date, that is the last support of any kind I ever received from them. When I lost my job, not even a year after my son was born, then had to navigate accessing food stamps and help getting child support, they were nowhere to be found.

As the title of the piece indicates, Cherisse loves her son, but she feels that she was manipulated into bringing him into a world that has difficulty supporting him. "My son deserved to be born to a mother who would not be left hanging to raise him alone. He deserved to be born into a social infrastructure willing to provide his mother with the necessary social supports to live." As a woman of color, Cherisse is keenly aware of how her story of the fake clinic attacking her "God-given right to self-determination" is just another chapter in the American legacy of infringing on the reproductive freedom of women of color.

In 2006, Congressman Henry Waxman released a report detailing the misinformation these fake clinics peddle. An overwhelming majority of the centers that Representative Waxman studied provided false information, such as that abortion is linked to breast cancer, has a negative effect on future fertility, and destroys women's mental health. A decade later, the providers we interviewed reported similar forms of misinformation, as they were almost all well aware of the difficulties that fake clinics' lies and misinformation pose to their patients' decision-making process.

The misinformation fake clinics give patients about abortion knows no bounds. Shelly Jones is an advocate in a southern state who has organized a deep investigation into her state's fake clinics. At those clinics, patients are told that "birth control is wrong and can wreak havoc on your body." Regarding abortion, one fake clinic told patients that "if you have an abortion, you'll commit suicide within three years." Hannah Miller, a clinic director also working in a southern state, told us that the fake clinic that her patients have to deal with is located in an RV parked in front of her clinic. In that fake clinic, Hannah's patients are told that "you're killing a baby, and that your baby has a heartbeat after fourteen days." Pam Monroe, an administrator at a series of clinics in the West, said that the local fake clinics tell patients that abortion will "make them depressed, leads to alcoholism, breast cancer, and permanent sterility."

Providers also reported a different kind of misinformation—misread ultrasounds. Many fake clinics offer free ultrasounds, targeting patients who don't have insurance or are underinsured. People we interviewed told us repeatedly that the promise of free ultrasounds draws patients into the clinics, where they are then given false information. As Hannah Miller explained to us, on the basis of her years of listening to the fake clinic's supporters speak publicly, the fake clinics see "the ultrasound machine not as a medical test but as a communication tool from God."

Mary Lofton, a doctor who has worked in clinics in both the Northeast and the West, has seen many patients who went to fake clinics where their ultrasound was misread. The women were told that their ultrasound revealed they were either farther along in their pregnancy than they actually were or, conversely, that they weren't as far along as they actually were. If they were told they were further along than was true, they might think they had no choice any longer because they were too far along to have an abortion given the state's gestational limit or the local clinics' capacity. If they were told they weren't as far along as they really were, they might think they had more time to make a decision, only to wait and find out that they were too far along. Either way, as Mary explained, the misinformation "messes up their plans."

The local fake clinic near Kathaleen Pittman uses an insidious tactic meant to confuse patients. The fake clinic does the usual things, such as "praying over them, mainly making them feel guilty about even thinking about abortion." But beyond that, the fake clinic will sometimes have a woman sign what looks like a legal document saying that she doesn't want an abortion. The document explains that, if the woman signing it ever goes to an abortion clinic, the fake clinic will fax the form to the abortion clinic. The goal of doing so is to try to convince the abortion clinic that the woman doesn't really want an abortion and that there might be legal consequences if the abortion clinic goes forward. As Kathaleen's clinic is the only one in a large geographical area, the fake clinic makes a point of forwarding these documents to the clinic.

A copy of one such form from a different part of the country is available online. The online document states that if the person signing this paper comes to an abortion clinic, the clinic needs to be aware that she is "not in a position to freely give legal consent for such a procedure. Should you perform an abortion on me despite being informed of this fact, you may be subject to criminal prosecution and/or civil liability." When Kathaleen has received these documents, she doesn't follow them. She told us, "That's not something we're going to forever refuse her. She's certainly welcome to change her mind." Kathaleen knows that this fake legal contract is just another tactic that fake clinics use to take away women's decision-making and autonomy by scaring and intimidating them into not having an abortion.

When these fake clinics are successful, it is because they prey on patients by advertising pregnancy support that they only partially deliver. Andrea Hillman explained that the fake clinics sometimes provide baby clothing and baby coaches, important help that many pregnant women can't afford on their own. "So you walk in and you have all this stuff that they're going to give you, and it tends to be the disadvantaged who go there because they're the ones looking for resources." Parker Dockray expressed disappointment, though, that these clinics fail to live up to their promise because services like free diapers and free pregnancy tests are valuable "to fill the gap" for those who can't afford them. The problem is, according to Parker's experience with these fake clinics, they rarely offer enough diapers or enough clothing, often providing just a few items to make it seem that they are helping. Meanwhile, once inside, the woman is given misinformation to try to influence her not to have an abortion.

Over the past decade, multiple states along with some cities have tried to rein in fake clinics with laws and ordinances aimed at their clients. The laws vary in their specifics, but the basic idea behind them is to require these clinics to let women know that they are not real medical clinics and that they can get complete and accurate information about their options elsewhere. In a very real sense, these are consumer protection laws so that women are aware of what fake clinics really are before they rely on the information given.

Unfortunately, in the summer of 2018, the Supreme Court struck down one such law, making it very difficult for others to be enforced or enacted. In the case, a California law required fake clinics to tell patients about comprehensive and free state-provided services and required unlicensed fake clinics to tell patients that they were not licensed to provide medical services. In a 5–4 decision that split along ideological lines, the Court's conservatives found that this law violated the clinics' First Amendment right to free speech.

In many ways, this decision gives fake clinics more constitutional rights than real abortion clinics. As explained further in chapter 6, the Court has allowed states to force real abortion clinics to tell patients things that are medically false or unnecessary for treatment, such as the inaccurate claim that abortion leads to breast cancer. Yet somehow fake clinics can't be required to give patients accurate information. For patients, what this means is that these fake clinics can continue to give out biased and inaccurate information to influence women's decisions, and there's very little states can do to stop them.

SECOND-GUESSING MINORS

In 2017, the story of "Jane Doe" captivated the nation. Jane was a minor who had crossed the border into the United States without an adult, so she was being held in special federal detention for unaccompanied minors. While there, she discovered she was pregnant, so she sought an abortion. The head of the federal agency holding Jane at the time—who, it was later revealed, had been keeping a spreadsheet tracking the menstrual cycles of immigrant teens held in custody—took the unprecedented step of visiting Jane personally at the detention center to attempt to dissuade her from having an abortion. Rather than support and facilitate her medical care decision, as it was supposed to for any other medical care she needed, the agency blocked her from getting her abortion. She had to file emergency court petitions and appeals before she was ultimately able to get her abortion, many weeks following her initial attempt to do so. A class action lawsuit challenging the Trump administration's pattern of blocking unaccompanied minors' access to abortion while in custody is still working its way through the courts.

Jane Doe's experience was brutal because she was in immigration custody, but her particular experience shouldn't obscure the fact that minors in most states throughout the country—regardless of immigration or custody status—are thwarted from making their own decision to have an abortion. Minors face all of the issues already explained in this chapter in making their decision plus something entirely different—required parental involvement in their decision. This is not true for general prenatal care and childbirth. About three-quarters of states specifically allow minors to consent to such care without their parents being involved, while most of the other states have no official policy on the matter.

Abortion, on the other hand, is different, as about the same number of states require that minors involve their parents in the decision in some way. The involvement takes different forms: eighteen states require one parent's consent to the abortion; three states require both parents' consent; ten states require that one parent be notified of the abortion decision; one state requires that both parents be notified; and five states require both notification and consent. In other words, even though almost everywhere in the country minors can make the long-term life-changing decision to have a baby on their own, in most places they cannot make the decision to have an abortion without consulting someone else.

Regardless of what a state requires, research confirms what every provider told us—that most minors willingly involve their parents in their abortion decision in some way. In fact, Jen Castle told us that in the north-eastern states where she has worked as a nurse practitioner, her clinics were "able to demonstrate that we had higher parental involvement with-out a statute requiring it than folks did in states where it was required by law." As Jenifer Groves, a clinic director in the Northeast, told us, "The kids that can, do. That's something I've learned over the past twenty years. Even sometimes when they think they can't tell their parent for that kid reason, like 'I don't want my parents disappointed in me,' they do. That's very different than 'I'm going to get the shit kicked out of me.' Those kids are never going to be able to tell, but the kids that can, do."

Likewise, many providers encourage minors that they care for to involve their parents in the decision and abortion. Naomi Rangel runs multiple clinics in two southern states. She told us that she encourages minors to involve their parents. She often tells patients, "Listen, you have no idea what your parents may have gone through when they were your age. So it's important, though if you don't feel comfortable, fine, then we'll help you navigate the system." Sylvia Raskin and Kathleen Anderson work together at a southern clinic, where they encourage minors to tell an adult, especially for a two-day procedure. Sylvia said, "It's not a requirement, but at this point we try to encourage them to have an adult involved if they are able to, even if not a parent." Kathleen agreed and nudges patients because "they really should have an adult with them to manage it."

But even for those minors who do involve their parents, the require-ment can be difficult to navigate. Cindi Cranston is an administrator at a clinic in a midwestern state that has a parental involvement law. Cindi's experience is consistent with the research in that most of the young people she sees talk with their parents. But for them, the state's requirements can still be onerous. Cindi had recently worked with an undocumented minor who was here in the United States with her aunt but whose parents lived in her home country. Her aunt functioned as her guardian, though she had never been officially designated as such. Under the state's law, this minor could not get the permission of her aunt and instead had to fax the forms to her parents in her home country, have her parents notarize the documents in that country, and then have them return the documents to the patient. As Cindi explained, this patient was determined and could talk with her parents, so she was lucky compared to patients who cannot have that conversation with their parents.

The parental involvement forms required vary by state, with some states making minors produce multiple forms, some of which have to be notarized. Where Millie Johnson works, the minor and her parent have to come to the clinic prepared. "The parent has to provide identification, and the youth has to provide picture ID, which many youth don't have if they don't have a driver's license. And then they have to provide a birth certificate. This is a huge barrier." As a result, Millie has seen many teens whose parents consent, "but they can't find their birth certificate. And then by the time they get it, they're past the state's gestational limit."

For some minors, it's almost impossible to comply, even with supportive parents. Edna Macklin, who runs a clinic in a southern state, told us about a minor who was caught in an unsolvable situation because, as Edna explained, "families are complicated." This minor's mother had turned over custody to her parents when the minor was very young. In Edna's state, the birth certificate gets changed when this happens. Now, many years later, the minor was pregnant, but one of the grandparents had died and the other was in hospice, so the minor was back in the care of her birth mother. However, no one in the family had changed anything with the state. Thus, even though the minor's birth mother consented to the abortion, Edna couldn't accept it because the birth certificate indicated someone else was the minor's guardian.

Jenifer Groves explained another problem with the system for patients who willingly talk with their parents. In Jenifer's state, the parent has to consent to the procedure, plus the law requires that the parent both be present for the mandatory counseling twenty-four hours before the abortion and be at the clinic on the day of the abortion. That means that even if the parent consents, her child might not get an abortion because the parent can't take the time off work. This confounds Jenifer. "What's the rub here? Mom's supportive, mom gave her okay, mom's in. But mom can't be here because she'll lose her job if she misses another day of work. Now the kid can't get an abortion?" The same problem arises if the parent has a substance abuse disorder or is in jail or if the minor is being raised by a relative who doesn't have a court order saying she is the guardian or anything else that can get in the way of the adult consenting and being present for the procedure. In those situations, the minor feels the brunt of the adult's inability to be a part of the process.

Parental involvement requirements are even more burdensome for the minors who don't want to tell their parents or seek their consent but who do involve them because of the law. This can have serious consequences. Studies have shown that minors forced to involve their parents face increased conflict and negative emotions with their parents and experience a decreased sense of autonomy. Shannon Gibbons, who works with a program that helps minors in the South, said that the situation is "frustrating for the minor because oftentimes they feel like they're mature enough to make this decision."

Nonetheless, many minors still choose not to involve their parents. They do this for many reasons, such as not wanting to disappoint or ruin their relationship with their parents, feeling that they have support elsewhere, wanting to maintain their own autonomy, fearing abuse or other difficult family dynamics, or thinking they'll be kicked out of the house.

In a very small number of states, when the minor can't tell her parents, the doctor can waive the parental involvement requirement for the minor if the doctor believes that she is mature and that the abortion is in her best interest. Linda Johnston, a clinic director who works in two different southern states, explained that this waiver process is a flexible option that respects the minor patient's autonomy. It allows her physician to "talk directly to the client about her decision and actually help frame a decision based on that conversation as to whether they feel the minor is mature enough to make this decision on their own. And I would say that's usually the case."

For these minors who still won't involve their parents and who live in a state where the doctor cannot waive the requirement, there is an option. In 1979, when the Supreme Court established that states can constitutionally require minors to involve their parents in their abortion decision, it said that there has to be a system for minors who don't want to. This system, called a "judicial bypass," allows the minor to go before a local judge to approve her abortion decision. According to the Supreme Court, this judge is supposed to assess whether the minor is mature enough to make the decision on her own and, if not, whether the abortion is in her best interests.

A case that Naomi Rangel relayed to us perfectly captured the puzzling nature of these two inquiries. Naomi was working with a sixteen-year-old who was a "very, very bright, straight-A student." When the minor went to court, she told the judge that she was too young to have a baby and that her father was a deacon in their church, so she could not tell him or her mother. Nonetheless, the judge denied the minor's bypass, claiming that she was too young and not mature enough to make the decision. As she recalled to us, Naomi sat there in court flabbergasted, thinking, "But she's old enough to have a baby?" This quip exposes the central absurdity of the judicial bypass process.

Common sense tells us that asking young women to go before a judge to approve their decision to have an abortion is onerous. Research confirms this. Even in places where judges and court personnel know how to handle a judicial bypass request, numerous studies show that asking a young woman to testify in court about her sexual and personal decisions can be a terrifying experience that only serves to humiliate and punish her.

An omnipresent problem with the judicial bypass system is confidentiality. Even though the process is required by law to be confidential, in small towns this is almost impossible to guarantee. Suzie Carter runs a clinic in a midwestern state with many small towns and counties. The law where she works requires the minor to have her bypass procedure in the county where she lives. But in some of these counties, the minor's dad might be the clerk of the court or her mom might be a judge. In those cases, Suzie can help the minor petition for a change of venue to avoid the confidentiality concern, but that just extends the process even longer for the minor.

Another problem that many providers talked about is the timing for the process. Jada Curry works in a clinic in a midwestern city where the "court's hours are school hours." For minors, that means that if they go through the process, "they have to miss school, and if they miss school, the parents will be notified and find out."

Scholars who have studied judicial bypass have shown that most local courts are unfamiliar with the process and have no system in place to help minors. One such nonfunctional system is in Hannah Miller's state. The judges who have seen her patients almost never accept minors' reasons for wanting an abortion, and "most of them are turned away." At her high-volume clinics, she sees only one or two successful judicial bypass cases a year. Naomi Rangel also runs clinics in the same state and has the same problems Hannah does.

Cindi Cranston works as an administrator at a clinic in a big city in a midwestern state. That state changed the law relatively recently so that the minor has to have her judicial bypass hearing in the county where she lives, not the county where the clinic is located. "If they're from a small town in a rural part of the state, it means they have to go to the little courthouse where everyone knows each other. That's the goal. It was meant to keep the big urban city liberals from giving abortions to young people." The system is very difficult for minors to navigate, and there's no organization working to make it easier in the state. As a result, in the last two years before we interviewed Cindi, her clinic saw just three successful bypass patients each year.

There are success stories, though. Where they exist, it is because of the in-depth work that providers and other local organizations have done to create a functional local judicial bypass system. And surprisingly, these success stories exist not only in liberal urban areas but also in some very conservative areas of the country. The common thread in these good jurisdictions is a committed group of advocates that includes providers and allies as well as court personnel and judges who are predisposed to or who have been educated to treat minors respectfully.

Alice Campbell runs a clinic in one of the jurisdictions that unexpectedly has a functioning system. To Alice, this works because of one very sympathetic judge. This judge helped establish the system and approaches each case with the attitude that "it's the state's responsibility to prove that she is not mature enough to make this decision. She shouldn't have to prove anything to the state." Nonetheless, the minors who go before him "are scared. They're frightened." Given what she has seen in other parts of the country, Alice knows that her system is "prime under the circumstances. But I would prefer we didn't have to go that route."

In some states, there are organizations committed to helping minors navigate the system. Shannon Gibbons runs one such organization. Minors call her organization either through a recommendation from the clinic or by finding out about it online. "Usually when they call us they're pretty clear about what they want," Shannon told us. "There's not much ambivalence that they've decided to go forward." Nonetheless, Shannon's group has to work with them to navigate the system. First, to prepare the minor for meeting the judge, the group asks the minor all sorts of questions about her situation, including about her family, her pregnancy, what she knows about abortion, whether she has considered adoption, and more. Then the group sets the minor up with a local attorney to represent her before a local judge. Because the hearing has to be in the minor's home county, the hearings vary greatly depending on the judge. Some judges are quick and reasonable, others take hours and grill minors about everything from their detailed knowledge of abortion procedures to their sex life.

Shannon told us a patient's story that exemplifies the unpredictability of the system, even with the support of Shannon's group. The minor was from an immigrant family and was the first in her family who was set to go to college. She worked in a corporate office as an intern and attended a good private school, where she had a full scholarship. As Shannon explained, "She had everything going for her, but the judge felt like she should involve her parents because her parents were Catholic and opposed abortion, and that she should consult them," so the judge denied the petition. Rather than tell her parents, the minor traveled out of state for her procedure, where she could make the decision alone.

The system is even more difficult for minors who are wards of the state, in a juvenile detention center, or in immigration custody. "We help them because obviously they don't have a family support system," Shannon said. However, "The system makes it so hard that it sometimes pushes teens out of the time where they could get the abortion."

Even in places where the judicial bypass system works, it's far from ideal, and providers uniformly expressed their frustration. Gabrielle Robinson, who runs a clinic in a midwestern state, captured this well. She told us that her local judicial bypass system works well and, at this point, seems "like a normal part of the day." However, she stressed to us that it shouldn't be acceptable. "We get so used to the oppression that we just adapt."

Nancy Hubbard is a lawyer who represents most of the minors in judicial bypass hearings in her northeastern city. She has done so many hearings, she said, that "I think now my name might be on the girls' bathroom door in some high schools." Nancy's system is a well-oiled machine supported by helpful judges who have never denied a minor. Nonetheless, because she has to meet with the minors beforehand and then bring them to court on a different day, the process can stretch into weeks. When she needs to move quickly, she does, but it will always depend on the minor's availability and ability to travel without her parents knowing. With all of her experience helping minors Nancy definitively stated that the system, even when it works relatively well, has no value. "It's just hoops to jump through. If the clinic perceives that the minor is not psychologically ready, they don't do it. So it just seems to me, by the time I get to the teen, it's resolved that an abortion is what's going to happen. I mean, why are we going through this?"

Minors who are able to navigate this system have the admiration of the providers we talked to. Lynn Thompson, an administrator at a midwestern clinic, is always impressed with how minors handle themselves, even when they are scared. "I just imagine at that age I'd probably be shaking. It's really impressive sometimes that fifteen- and sixteen-year-olds present themselves so well." Diana Sharpe, a counselor and administrator at multiple northeastern clinics, said that these minors "are some of my favorite folks to work with." Even though they are at an age where they are still learning to navigate the halls of their high school, they are "some of the most well put-together human beings I have ever come across in my life. They're inspirational. They come to you, they know what it is that they want to do, and there's this fire in their eyes that nothing's going to stop them from doing it."

With so many obstacles for minors, it should not come as a surprise that the effects of the system are severe. Studies show that minors who live in parental involvement states are more likely to delay their care and choose to travel long distances to get an abortion on their own. Mary Badame, who was a counselor in a northeastern state, told us the story of a teen who traveled over five hundred miles each way to get to her clinic. "She had driven with her boyfriend because if her parents found out what she was doing she would be in so much trouble. So she told them she was staying at a friend's house. I just can't imagine that at fifteen."

Beyond delay and travel, research shows that minors in this system face other difficulties. A 2019 study of the Massachusetts system—the oldest in the country and one that is relatively well-functioning—found that the parental consent and judicial bypass system pushes some patients out of the period of being eligible for medication abortions. The study also found that the law's impact falls most heavily on young women of color and those of low socioeconomic status. At its most extreme, for some minors, the result of the system is that they are denied their abortion altogether. Recent estimates indicate that over the past twenty-five years, roughly half a million minors have given birth because of parental involvement laws denying them the ability to make the decision on their own.

The parental involvement system that minors have to navigate along with the other barriers to autonomous decision-making identified in this chapter undercuts one of the basic premises of health care—that the patient decides. George Tiller, the Wichita abortion doctor who was assassinated by an anti-abortion extremist in 2009, famously had the slogan "Trust Women" posted on his clinic wall. The essence of those simple two words is that providers, politicians, and society should trust abortion patients to make their own decisions about what is best for their own lives. As in other areas of medicine, no one else should interfere with those decisions.

Unfortunately, the reality is that for many woman across the country the deck is stacked against them in this regard. Rather than medical professionals and politicians treating the abortion decision like any other medical choice and following the patient's lead, they thwart many women seeking abortion from getting accurate, helpful information upon which they can base their decision. At the same time, anti-abortion providers and organizations deliberately work to flood the market with misinformation and lies, trying to influence women's decisions to choose childbirth over abortion. And perhaps most egregiously, many states tell women that certain reasons are off the table for having an abortion while a majority of states tell minors that, even though they can seek prenatal care and childbirth on their own, they are not competent to make the abortion decision by themselves.

There is an alternative, and that would be, following Dr. Tiller's lead, trusting women to make the decision. Providers working in states without the restrictions and barriers described in this chapter proudly follow this model.

Using minors as an example, Jenifer Groves explained how this happens in one of the states where she works, a state that allows minors to make the abortion decision on their own. There, a minor can be treated like "just another patient," though Jenifer is always on the lookout for abuse. "The younger somebody is and the less emotionally mature somebody is, the more your radar goes up and the more questions you might

ask, because you want to help and make sure that you're not putting somebody back in an abusive situation." But, as Jenifer made clear, the same
would be true for any patient. Good counseling of minors looks the same
as good counseling of any patient—respecting the minor's decision while
also being alert for issues like abuse. Or, in the words of Edna Macklin,
"serving those minors and trying to figure out what their needs are so you
can best help them."

3 Finding and Getting to a Clinic

HARD TO FIND, HARDER TO REACH

Pat Canon, a woman in her late sixties who lives in the South, volunteers at her state's only abortion clinic to help patients who have trouble with transportation. While working the hotline for the clinic, Pat received a call from Keisha, an African American woman of about thirty with two children. By the time she reached out to Pat, Keisha believed she was twenty weeks pregnant, as her history of irregular periods delayed her discovery of the pregnancy. Working with a caseworker at a national organization, Pat was able to arrange funding for Keisha's procedure and agreed to pick her up and drive her to her appointment and then return her home afterwards. Since Keisha was scheduled for a two-day procedure and lived over an hour from the clinic, Pat also arranged a hotel room for her.

That Keisha had to rely on volunteer driving and coordination from a stranger to get to her medical appointment already put her care outside the normal bounds of medicine, but even this anomaly did not go as planned. Pat explained, "After picking her up at home, I signed her into the clinic and made arrangements to pick her up after the first-day procedure and check her into the hotel. I was surprised to get a call from her after only about an hour to come pick her up. She was over their weight limit, her blood pressure was too high, and the ultrasound at the clinic put her at 23 weeks gestation, so she was turned away." While in the waiting room of the clinic, Pat immediately got on the phone with a caseworker from the national organization she had previously talked with about Keisha. The caseworker suggested that Keisha's best option would be a clinic in Washington, D.C., so Pat canceled her hotel room and started the drive back to Keisha's hometown.

On the drive home, Pat reassured Keisha that she would help her figure out how to get to Washington. "Over the next week I worked with the patient and multiple coordinators and caseworkers at the national organization to make the arrangements to get her appointment and funding in place for the Washington clinic. The patient had to come up with additional money for the Washington clinic as well." Funding was almost the least of Keisha's issues, though. Washington was over five hundred miles from Keisha's home. Pat considered various alternatives, such as flying Keisha, but finally settled on driving Keisha herself. "It was the least expensive and best alternative to get her there and back, especially since she had never flown before. Navigating a large airport and taxi rides would be difficult for her. We tried to get a room with a practical support group in Washington, but they were all taken, so we booked a hotel room."

Early on a late December morning, Pat picked Keisha up from her home and drove for ten hours straight. "Neither one of us talked much on the trip. She was feeling ill and slept most of the way. She was concerned about getting home in time to prepare Christmas presents for her children before they woke up Christmas morning. I told her I would get her home in time for Christmas." When Pat and Keisha arrived in Washington, Pat showed her some of the sights, since Keisha had never seen the White House or Supreme Court. They stayed in the hotel and went to the clinic the next morning, where Keisha was again turned away, again because of concerns about her high blood pressure, something this second clinic mistakenly had thought it could handle.

Dejected, Pat and Keisha went to lunch to talk about her options and what she wanted to do. The national organization's caseworker suggested Keisha try a third clinic, this one in New York City. As they finished their lunch, Keisha decided to give it one last try, so the two of them checked out of the hotel and got in the car for the four-hour drive to New York.

Pat and Keisha arrived in New York that evening, about thirty-six hours after they left Keisha's home. Keisha had never been to New York, so Pat drove her through Times Square en route to a hotel room near the clinic. The next morning, after several hours spent sorting out payment for the procedure, Keisha was finally seen. Her high blood pressure was compounded by other medical problems, but the clinic was able to start the abortion that day, with the plan for her to return the next day to finish it.

Once again, things did not go as planned. During the night, Keisha started having contractions and began to miscarry, as sometimes occurs with an abortion at this stage of pregnancy. Pat called the clinic's emergency number and the on-duty nurse advised getting her to a hospital. Pat told us, "I called an ambulance. There were four EMT people and a hotel security guard who came to the room. She was in the bathroom and had difficulty moving. Finally after about a half an hour, they got her in a position that she could be transported to the hospital. I was able to ride in the ambulance with them." The hospital staff quickly cared for Keisha's medical emergency.

After the hospital released Keisha the next morning, Pat picked her up and immediately started the twelve-hour drive back home. "It was a hair-raising ride with storms, torrential downpours, and high-wind advisories. We made it to her home at one minute past midnight on Christmas Eve, so it was technically one minute into Christmas Day. I kept my promise to her." And more importantly, through all the effort of caseworkers, EMTs, abortion providers, and hospital staff to treat Keisha's medical problems, Pat said, "I truly believed we saved a life that week. I still believe it."

Though the trip with Keisha was the longest and most dramatic, Pat periodically drives patients for considerable distances, sometimes—as with Keisha—sharing a hotel room overnight. "I'm pretty easygoing and accepting of differences and have only had one person in all of the transports I have made that I truly didn't like. She was anti-abortion and spent an hour and a half drive telling me how her abortion was an exception. I still drove her because she made her choice for abortion."

When asked what motivated her to take on this often challenging commitment of driving patients, Pat gave us, in her words, a short and a longer answer. The short answer, "I'm sixty-seven years old, I'm white, I'm retired,

I'm steeped in privilege. I can make these transports because I have a car, I don't have a job, I have a credit card, and I have AAA. All enormous privileges that make it possible for me to be able to do transports." In her longer answer, Pat made reference to growing up in the '60s and developing a social justice sensibility, with a strong feminist component. "My battle cry throughout my life was 'It's not fair,' and then trying to set things right. There is nothing fair about the shame and harassment people face when going to get an abortion. It's a necessary part of complete women's health, but more importantly it is only up to one person whether they get an abortion or not: the pregnant person."

While Keisha's story is extreme, the struggles she faced in getting abortion care—finding a medical facility that would perform her abortion and then figuring out how to get there—are familiar ones for abortion patients across the country. Both of these tasks—depending on where the patient lives and her income—can be quite difficult. As various observers of the US abortion landscape have put it, "A woman's access to an abortion should not depend on her zip code."

But, as this chapter explains, this difficulty is the reality for many American women. The reality for them is that abortion facilities are so relatively rare, and, more significantly, so poorly geographically distributed in the country that some experts have coined the phrase "abortion deserts." Where abortion clinics do exist, finding out about them can be difficult, and reaching them can be even more challenging, especially for low-income and rural women. Thankfully, providers, women seeking abortions, and advocates are working together to overcome these obstacles, but these are obstacles that no patient should have to overcome to get care.

DWINDLING CLINIC NUMBERS

As this book was being finalized, California's governor signed into law a massive change that will increase the number of abortion providers in the state. The College Student Right to Access Act requires all student health centers at California's public universities to provide medication abortion services. Taking effect in 2023, this law will greatly expand the number of abortion providers in the state and make it easier for hundreds of college students a month to access abortion.

Unfortunately, California is an outlier, as the nationwide clinic statistics are sobering. Roughly 90 percent of counties in the United States do not have an abortion provider. Along with a small number of primary care physicians and, in some states, advanced-practice clinicians (nurse practitioners, physician assistants, and midwives), less than a quarter of obstetrician-gynecologists in this country provide abortion, and only a tiny number of these do so in their private practices. Hospitals perform only about 4 percent of abortions occurring annually. It is in freestanding clinics, either independent ones or those affiliated with Planned Parenthood, that the vast majority of abortion care takes place. And abortion opponents are doing everything in their power to shut these clinics down and prevent new ones from opening.

All told, according to the most recent data available from the Guttmacher Institute, there are 1,587 known abortion providers in the United States. This figure primarily speaks to the number of freestanding clinics and hospitals that provide abortions and does not capture all individual physicians who may provide a few abortions annually in their private offices. Nor, of course, does this figure encompass the growing number of women who self-manage their abortions, by purchasing (often over the internet) the drugs used in medication abortion. This figure of 1,587 providers represents a steadily declining number; in 1982, at the high point of abortion availability, the number of identified abortion facilities was over 2,800. Compare this number to the over 3,000 crisis pregnancy centers in the country, with states like Mississippi having thirty fake clinics and only one abortion clinic.

Why are there so few abortion-providing facilities and so few clinicians willing to provide this service? Training is part of the story. Despite *Roe v. Wade*, ob-gyn residencies did not make abortion training a routine part of that specialty. We can attribute the failure to do this to the still potent legacy of the "back alley butchers" of the pre-*Roe* era and the general aversion to controversy on the part of most of the medical community in that period.

But also part of the story is congressional action hostile to abortion. In 1973, almost immediately after *Roe* was decided, legislators passed the

Church Amendment, stipulating that hospitals receiving federal funding and individuals working within those hospitals could be exempt from providing abortions if doing so violated their "religious beliefs or moral convictions." Twenty years later, the Accreditation Council for Graduate Medical Education, in concert with the Committee on Residency Education in Obstetrics and Gynecology, the standard-setting body for residency education in that field, passed a mandate that included abortion training, with an opt-out provision for those with religious or ethical objections. But shortly thereafter, Congress, in a move that was unprecedented in its intervention in medical education, essentially nullified this standard. A measure called the Coats Amendment made clear that no residency would lose its federal funds if it did not comply with this mandate.

Training efforts, however, have gradually improved, thanks to various privately funded programs in which ob-gyns, family medicine physicians, and advanced-practice clinicians receive instruction in abortion. Now it is estimated that more than half of all ob-gyn residencies receive routine training in abortion, and others are able to receive this training on an individual basis.

A greater problem currently is that many of those who are trained in abortion care find it difficult to put their training into practice. Sociologist Lori Freedman has investigated this problem and found that doctors who have been trained in abortion but do not provide it in their practice face many impediments, such as being prevented by their employers from providing abortions or feeling that they can't face the pushback from their local community. As Freedman has detailed, this prohibition can extend even to those who wish to provide abortions outside of the private practice setting, for example at a local independent or Planned Parenthood clinic. Freedman's findings once again show the power of abortion stigma, this time playing out in local medical communities.

Finding property for an abortion clinic can also be a challenge. For decades now, providers have faced challenges because of pressure that abortion opponents put on landlords and those selling buildings. But even when providers are seemingly settled in a facility, with a lease that providers thought was secure, clinics can still lose out. For example, Whole Woman's Health in Austin, Texas, learned suddenly in early 2019 that a Christian faith-based nonprofit had purchased its lease in cash and planned to operate its own crisis pregnancy center out of the same building. As the director of the anti-abortion group that purchased the lease told the press, "We now have an opportunity [to] shine light upon a very, very dark place." Whole Woman's Health, meanwhile, ultimately moved to a new facility in Austin, after a search of eight months in which staff looked at more than eighty properties. As a spokeswoman for the group said, "It just makes you realize how powerful stigma is. We had many conversations with landlords and property owners that had a lot of concerns about an abortion provider as a tenant. In some cases it had to do with their own stigma around abortion, in other cases it had to do with the fear of repercussions."

A similar story of a disruption of an existing clinic occurred in a small town in Tennessee in 2019. The day after carafem, a small network of abortion clinics, opened a new facility in the downtown commercial area, city officials called for a special city council meeting with one agenda item—to pass a zoning amendment restricting surgical abortions to industrial areas. The meeting took all of four minutes, and the amendment passed unanimously. The new clinic, at the time of the meeting, offered only medication abortion but had planned to expand to aspiration abortions.

Even when a clinic has its own property and has found medical professionals to provide care, special laws targeted at shutting down abortion clinics make it difficult to operate. So-called TRAP (targeted regulations of abortion providers) laws, at issue in the *Whole Women's Health* case discussed in the Introduction, which are on the books in twenty-four states, are another major cause of the declining number of abortion facilities. These are state laws that regulate abortion facilities in minute, overbearing, and very expensive detail. They are called "targeted" because they are not applied to medical services of comparable scope, such as colonoscopies, which, as the Supreme Court recognized in the *Whole Woman's Health v Hellerstedt,* have a mortality rate ten times higher than abortion. Some politicians have been very forthcoming in stating that the purpose of these laws is to shut down clinics. For example, Phil Bryant, the former governor of Mississippi, has several times announced, as he signed restrictive laws, his wish to "end abortion in Mississippi."

Though exact numbers are difficult to come by, one estimate is that over 160 abortion facilities have closed since 2010, when the number of these TRAP laws started to explode. Not all of these have closed because of TRAP laws or other restrictions. Some have closed, for example, because of the difficulty in replacing a retiring physician. Others have closed because the declining overall number of abortions taking place in the United States means the facility in question does not have a sufficient volume of patients to stay afloat.

Unquestionably, however, some portion of these 160 or so closures is due to an inability to meet the demands of TRAP laws, in particular the requirement that clinics meet the standards of an ambulatory surgical center (ASC). Upgrading a clinic to an ASC involves such matters as widening hallways, installing new HVAC (heating, ventilation, and air conditioning) systems, increasing storage space, purchasing new sinks of specified dimensions, and other very specific onerous requirements. Such upgrades can cost over a million dollars, as the Supreme Court noted when it considered the impact of Texas's TRAP law in 2016. In that decision, *Whole Woman's Health v. Hellerstedt,* though the Court ruled that there was no scientific evidence that ASC requirements were necessary for women's health, as politicians had claimed, many clinics had already closed prior to the decision—both because of the ASC law and because of the requirement that clinic physicians have admitting privileges at a local hospital—and only a handful have reopened. And because the *Whole Woman's Health* decision was based on Texas's specific abortion landscape, lower courts have been all over the map in applying the ruling to other states, with some using it to strike down similar laws while others have virtually ignored it, allowing their state's laws to continue to burden abortion providers.

The providers we talked with were all too familiar with how difficult TRAP laws make it for them and their patients. Jada Curry, a nurse practitioner in a midwestern state, told us of the difficulties for clinics in her state to comply with the TRAP requirement that there be a transfer agreement with a local hospital in case a patient needs hospitalization. "That is a huge barrier because some clinics don't have the capability of getting a transfer agreement based on local hospitals being Catholic or just not agreeing with abortion. And any hospital receiving public funding, you know, they won't be able to participate in abortion care." Indeed, where Jada works, there is the catch-22 that clinics must have such an agreement but that any hospital receiving public funding is barred from making such an arrangement. Compounding the absurdity of this requirement is the fact that without such a transfer agreement, when the rare complications requiring hospitalization occur, a clinic can always simply send the patient to an emergency room, which is required by law to care for the patient.

When TRAP laws shut down clinics, patients are left in the dark as to why they can't get the care they need. Andrea Ferrigno relayed how mystified her patients were when clinics suddenly closed in her southern state because of a TRAP law. "Patients would come into our clinic and say, 'Why can't you see me?' I remember a patient telling me, 'Here's my money. Here. Take it.' She kept giving me her cash. She was so mad. And we had to explain what happened, but they don't care why. They care that they need an abortion." Andrea expressed great frustration for her patients and was concerned about what this would mean for them long term. "That experience of that humiliation, having to beg for an abortion that you safely could've gotten a week before, that doesn't go away if you reopen the clinic or if the law is quashed. That stuff stays with people. Those are the kinds of things that are not easily overcome."

Despite this hostile environment, a handful of new clinics have opened since 2010. But this has not been a simple process. Not surprisingly, when providers attempt to open new facilities, they often run up against a bewildering set of local and state regulations and a hostile set of inspectors. Jennifer Pride recounted to us the long and challenging road to opening a clinic in her very red southern state. This was the first abortion clinic to open in Jennifer's state since the 1970s, and "a lot of restrictions have passed since then and a lot of changes have been made to the legal code. And we found that the various employees of the state wanted to be difficult at all stages of that process, but also that the department of health just really didn't know what their own policies were to a large extent."

It took Jennifer and her colleagues two years to open the clinic after submitting their initial applications with the state. Along with the typical problems of a new medical office—hiring staff, buying equipment, finding a building—Jennifer faced additional problems that were specific to being an abortion facility. "We were unable to get our final license because they originally had said that we didn't need to have a sink in one of the clinic rooms, and so we hadn't put one in. But then they came back and told us, 'Oh, no, you have to have a sink in that room,' and so that delayed our opening by around a month. We had expected all those hurdles, but they were very frustrating to deal with." Whether the state's changing directive about the sink was due to genuine confusion or deliberate sabotage, the result was the same—an unnecessary delay.

TRAP laws can present difficulties for clinics in finding abortion providers as well. Melody Cook, a clinic director in a southern state, told of her struggle to find more physicians when her state imposed a law requiring abortion doctors to have admitting privileges at local hospitals. "We reached out to every ob-gyn in the metropolitan area and mailed them a letter to see if anyone else wanted to either come into practice with us, share the practice, or just be a backup. We got not one single response to our letters." Robin Flynn, a nurse who works with Melody, added, "I've even spoken to physicians that I have worked with, that I knew personally, they just don't want any part of it. They don't want to ruin their reputation."

Clinic administrators have dealt with the problem of local doctors' hesitation to work in abortion by flying in providers from out of town. Edna Macklin, a clinic director in the South, told us that she had "been blessed over the years with numerous just wonderful human beings that are doing these procedures." When asked if they were local, she responded, "They all come from out of state. They always have. Nobody comes from local. I have one physician here who serves both as my medical director and my backup physician. He started as a backup physician because the state passed a law that said you had to have somebody that would see your patients after hours. And so maybe twice a year somebody needs to see the physician after hours. Literally two times a year. But I have to pay this person a retainer to stay there and be available."

The lack of medical providers is directly related to the lack of clinics. Though in a few metropolitan areas, particularly on the East and West Coasts, there is actually an oversupply of trained abortion providers, as discussed earlier, in many parts of the country factors such as lack of support from the local medical community and concern over protesters keep potential abortion doctors away. Donna Sullivan, another clinic director in the South, told us of having only one physician who worked at her clinic. As she nervously put it, "I am one doctor away from closing down."

In a similar vein, Maggie Wellington, a volunteer who coordinates patient support in a northeastern state, told us about a time when she and her organization were surprised to suddenly see an influx of patients from a city a few hours away, known to have its own abortion clinic. As it turned out, the one doctor at that clinic had broken her hand, which forced the clinic to suspend abortion care until she recovered.

And if it's hard to find clinics that provide first-trimester abortions because of a shortage of providers, it's even harder to find clinicians trained and willing to provide later ones. Nine percent of women who obtain an abortion do so after the first trimester (at fourteen weeks or later), and slightly more than 1 percent of abortions are performed at twenty-one weeks or later. But only about one-third of all abortion-providing facilities offer abortions at twenty weeks gestation and about 16 percent at twenty-four weeks.

The experience of an anonymous abortion storyteller we'll call Frida is a familiar one for patients seeking a later second-trimester abortion, even in a state that has many abortion providers. Because of an initial false-negative pregnancy test, she was sixteen weeks along when she found out she was pregnant. She knew that she was not in a position to have a child, so Frida chose to have an abortion. However, even though she lived in a state where abortion providers were not rare, that she was sixteen weeks pregnant "significantly hindered the services accessible to me." Frida's local abortion clinic didn't go this far into pregnancy, which left her "feeling incredibly panicked and significantly less in control of the situation." There were a small number of clinics in her state that could perform an abortion at this stage, but they were overcrowded, and she would have to wait weeks for an appointment. With family support, Frida was able to fly to another state several hundred miles away, where an abortion clinic there could see her immediately. Though Frida recognized her privilege in being able to get help for the cost, time off work, and travel, she nonetheless firmly believed that she "shouldn't have had to go to a different state to access the services that I needed."

Going even further into pregnancy, there are only five clinics in the US as of this writing that openly offer abortion in the third trimester, with many of their patients presenting with fetal anomalies, threats to their own health, or other serious problems. Shelley Sella is a doctor at one of these clinics in the West. The patients she sees who fit in this category are "such a teeny portion of all abortions but it's a particularly desperate group of women." She explained that there "are just so many different reasons why a woman may not know that she's pregnant or may not be able to access an abortion until later in the pregnancy." She rattled off several—domestic violence, delayed diagnosis, an issue that got worse as the pregnancy progressed, lack of access to care early in her pregnancy, and more. Because of these circumstances, "there will always be a need for third-trimester abortions," and women will always do what they can to find her clinic and travel sometimes all the way across the country to get this care.

Part of the reason for fewer clinics offering abortions after the first trimester are state laws. Seventeen states ban abortion at twenty weeks after fertilization or twenty-two weeks after the woman's last menstrual period, and some even earlier—in spite of the fact that *Roe v. Wade* established a constitutional right to abortion until twenty-four weeks.

State laws aside, often what limits clinics' ability to offer services depends on the preferences and training of a particular doctor and is subject to abrupt changes in staffing. Kathaleen Pittman, a clinic director in the South, told us about such a change in her clinic: "The physician that went to twenty-four weeks left and went to another clinic. And our other doctor at the time—who became our medical director at that point—was comfortable through sixteen weeks, and so we've remained there." She explained that, because of this personnel change, she has to now refer those patients needing abortions beyond sixteen weeks to a clinic in another state.

EVEN SPARSER HOSPITAL-BASED ABORTION PROVIDERS

Patients with pregnancies gone horribly wrong or with such serious health issues of their own that their abortions need to be done in a hospital face even bigger challenges. Only about 4 percent of all abortions take place in hospitals. Why is this so? The answer lies in developments—or more accurately, lack of them—in the period immediately after the legalization of abortion in 1973. The same aversion to controversy, mentioned earlier in this chapter, that led ob-gyn residencies to fail to incorporate routine abortion training after *Roe v. Wade* also led to relatively few hospitals establishing abortion clinics on site. Once the Hyde Amendment—a 1976 federal law that prohibited the use of federal funding for abortions except under very limited circumstances—was passed, hospitals had even less incentive to take on abortion provision. And the growth of the anti-abortion movement in the years since *Roe* steadily made hospital abortion care more difficult; eleven states, for example, have laws prohibiting public hospitals from providing abortions, except when the woman's life is in danger. And even where such laws do not exist, the informal culture in many hospitals, where some staff are opposed to abortion, and where administrators fear protesters, is such that abortions rarely, if ever, take place.

At the same time, part of the reason that American hospitals, as a whole, have not developed abortion services is the very success of the free-standing clinic model. This model was developed in the early 1970s in New York State and Washington, D.C., both of which legalized abortion before *Roe*. It quickly became apparent that abortion care could be done as safely on an outpatient basis as in hospitals, with the added advantages of being considerably less expensive, and that clinics could hire only staff who were supportive of abortion. It therefore makes sense that, in the years since *Roe*, a steadily growing number of abortions take place in free-standing facilities. What is unacceptable, however, is that with few exceptions hospitals have not lived up to their responsibilities to provide care for those women who are dependent on them.

Jen Moore Conrow is an administrator at a clinic within a major hospital in the Northeast, but before this job she worked at a nonhospital abortion clinic in the same region. In a heartbreaking conversation, she told us about patients needing hospital care in the time before her current hospital-based clinic opened:

> In my experience, when I worked at a freestanding clinic, what I would tell those patients is that they would have to continue their pregnancy. If we had a patient who had an ultrasound and had a history of three C-sections and it looked like the placenta was either low-lying or there were concerns for *placenta accreta*, which is where the placenta grows into the wall of the uterus, or even if it was just like a classical C-section, which is where it's a vertical scar, that our physician was like, "You know, she's a second-trimester

patient. There's a greater chance of opening the C-section scars. She needs a hospital abortion," and I would wind up having to tell this patient, "I don't have any place to send you."

The one hospital to which she conceivably could send such patients was several hours away. Unfortunately, that hospital saw patients only through the beginning of the second trimester, which was often too early to determine if there was a problem requiring hospital care. For patients, it was often very difficult to get the specialty care they needed. "And these are low-income women who don't have a great way to travel. At the time, there was no hospital near here that was publicly or very easily doing abortion care. We knew of one or two physicians who would very quietly do abortions in a hospital-based setting, but they weren't always available. It would depend on their private patient load. So we could call their coordinators or their schedulers, but we often couldn't get patients in."

The situation in Jen's region has improved recently because of the hospital-based clinic in which she works. But the situation she describes is still common in many other regions of the United States. Perhaps most concerning is Jen's statement that no local hospital "publicly or easily" did abortion care and that doctors there had done abortions "quietly." Strikingly, the situation Jen describes is in many ways reminiscent of the pre-*Roe* era, when only some fortunate women could—sometimes—access authorized abortions in a hospital, typically when they were the private patients of the doctors involved.

States, as mentioned above, also sometimes limit what state-run or -affiliated hospitals can do, either directly with a government policy or indirectly because of fear of public backlash. Douglas Laube, a doctor in a midwestern state, worked for a public hospital that used to be the only facility in the state that could perform complicated abortions. Because of a change in the state government over the past decade, the hospital no longer does them. As a result, the ninety to one hundred patients per year who need the specialty care the hospital used to offer now have to go to major cities in other states.

The recent trend of mergers between Catholic hospitals and secular ones is another reason that hospital-based abortion care has become so difficult to find. These mergers typically mean that when a secular hospital affiliates with a Catholic one, the former must agree to abide by the Ethical and Religious Directives that govern Catholic health care facilities—thereby prohibiting abortions, as well as other reproductive health services such as sterilizations and contraception. As a result of these mergers, one in six hospital beds in this country is in a Catholic facility.

The challenge of Catholic hospitals dominating a geographical area was brought home in our interview with Rose Brooks, a doctor who provides abortions in a large rural western state that has only a handful of providers, none of whom routinely perform later abortions. Rose explained how difficult it is for women in the military, whose health care program does not pay for routine abortions, to get care. Where Rose works, many of the ob-gyn clinics lease their space from Catholic hospitals. As a result, "They can't do elective abortion procedures within their clinic space, even though they might be trained and supportive of the cause." When a pregnant servicewoman is diagnosed with a lethal fetal anomaly and needs care beyond the gestational limit of the local abortion clinic, Rose and her colleagues have to scramble to find her a provider. "We have developed a relationship with an ob-gyn clinic that has space that's not on the Catholic hospital campus, and they will help us by giving the patient an injection to cause fetal demise." Then the service member can return to her military base presenting with a stillbirth and have her care covered by her insurance. Rose bemoaned the runaround that military women have to go through in order to get care that she and her colleagues could easily provide where they work, but with the lack of second-trimester providers where she practices, along with the dominance of Catholic hospitals, this is the best that she and her colleagues can do for these women. The specific problems women face in accessing hospital-based abortion care are further discussed in chapter 8.

THE STRUGGLE TO FIND AN ABORTION CLINIC

Given the shortage of abortion facilities in many parts of the country—the "abortion deserts"—how do patients find out where to go? One obvious answer, common for nearly all other medical procedures, is to ask one's medical care provider for a referral. Sometimes this works just as it should: the doctor will refer the woman to the nearest clinic or to a colleague who does abortions in his or her office. Sometimes, however, abortion politics intrude. Often medical care providers do not know enough to refer a patient to an abortion clinic, or they let their own personal beliefs get in the way. Moreover, the stigma surrounding abortion is such that some women report they are reluctant to ask their personal physicians for a referral.

Megan Siple, a doctor in a northeastern state, captured these challenges for patients. She told us that "primary care provider knowledge about abortion services and referrals is pretty poor, as in many places. But I think patients know that. Women know that most primary care doctors can't help them if they need an abortion, so they bypass that system and go to the freestanding clinic." She also drove home the point that patients often are ashamed to talk with their doctors. "They're afraid of getting a reaction from them, so they're not going to disclose."

Referrals to abortion services are also compromised by federal regulations. As discussed in the previous chapter, Title X, the federal program that provides grants for family planning services, prohibits its grantees from also providing abortion services; those that do must strictly separate abortion services from other services offered, and under the Trump administration's new Title X regulation, that separation must be both financial and physical. The new rule also imposes a so-called "domestic gag rule" that prevents Title X programs from even referring women to abortion facilities. Similarly, the Weldon Amendment, passed each year by Congress, allows individuals in entities that receive public funding to refuse to refer or counsel on abortion.

Though precise numbers are impossible to obtain, providers have told us that many of the women who come to them initially found them through the internet, which can be an excellent resource. Many different national abortion rights organizations and individual clinics have internet resources that help women find legitimate abortion providers. These resources are essential for some women to find the care they need. Shelley Sella, a doctor in the West at one of the few facilities that does third-trimester terminations, said, "There are quite a few people who find us on the internet. There are fetal anomaly patients, patients who are ending their pregnancy because there's something very wrong with their babies. Their doctors either don't know about us or are anti-abortion and won't give them a referral. And when they're not given the referral, then they go online and they find us. We have a web presence and we're open about what we do."

But the issues of internet misinformation and lack of vetting by online search entities can be problematic because of the deceptive practices of fake clinics. As discussed in the last chapter, fake abortion clinics are religiously affiliated and anti-abortion entities whose mission it is to pressure women into not having an abortion. Women sometimes go to fake clinics looking for help in making the abortion decision, where they are often given misinformation in an attempt to persuade them to choose to continue their pregnancy.

Another tactic of fake clinics is to deceive women into thinking they are going to a real abortion clinic. In the "old days" of Yellow Pages advertising in phone books, the Pages were highly criticized for not differentiating between authentic abortion clinics and anti-abortion crisis pregnancy centers. In some locales, the Yellow Pages were successfully sued to correct this confusion.

Today when women seek help on the internet, they are similarly presented with a barrage of incorrect and intentionally misleading information attempting to direct them to one of the over three thousand fake clinics in the country. One of the southern clinic directors that we talked with, Elena Hunter, told us, "So now with Google, that's the complaint. We're seeing crisis pregnancy centers popping up as though they were an abortion provider. So putting pressure on Google from as many sources as possible could hopefully get them to be more judicious when they vet some of these clinics or organizations and maybe not allow them to advertise under 'abortion.'" Elena said that this problem is "really a challenge, but we have to do something." In June 2018, it's possible that the "something" Elena wished for did occur. As Google was having its annual shareholders meeting at its headquarters in California, activists arranged for a plane to fly overhead with a banner reading, "Searching for Abortion Care? Google Lies." This action coincided with a letter sent to Google's CEO, signed by the leaders of twenty abortion rights groups, asking him to take steps to correct the misleading ads placed by crisis pregnancy centers. In spring 2019, much to the satisfaction of the provider community, Google Ads announced a new policy that stipulated that advertisers who want to run ads using keywords related to getting an abortion will first need to be certified as an entity that either provides abortions or does not provide abortions.

Once someone clicks on one of the fake clinics' links, it can be hard to distinguish them from a real abortion clinic. Elena explained that they have "slick websites" with language like "Are you pregnant? We can help you. Come talk to us," in order to, in Elena's words, "trap women." The websites won't say that they offer abortion, but they do everything they can to look like an abortion clinic's website so that women will be confused.

Fake clinics use similar tactics with their brick-and-mortar buildings. Almost every provider we talked to mentioned that there is a fake clinic near their real clinic, sometimes immediately next door. The most nefarious of these fake clinics name their business in a way that will be easily confused with the abortion clinic. For instance, an abortion clinic named Denver Women's Health might have a fake clinic next door named Denver Women's Help. Many of the people we interviewed expressed frustration at their limited legal options in response to this deceptive naming.

It's not only the name that deceives women. The worst of these fake clinics purchase or rent buildings adjacent to the abortion clinic and then put signs up directing pregnant women to the fake clinic rather than to the real one. Vanessa Barrett, a clinic director in the Northeast, had been dealing with this situation in the months leading up to our interview. The fake clinic renamed itself to be almost identical to Vanessa's clinic and then purchased the building across the walkway. Patients have to walk from the street down the walkway; if they turn right at the end, they get to the door of Vanessa's clinic and if they turn left, they go into the deceptively named fake clinic. The anti-abortion protesters outside Vanessa's clinic also try to steer patients toward the fake clinic. "It's confusing," said Vanessa.

In response to this new development, Vanessa's staff spends time explaining the situation when patients make an appointment. "We try really hard to hammer that home on the phone, but of course we know we're bombarding them with a ton of information to begin with. It's a lot for our patients." Thankfully, so far, Vanessa said that not many of her patients have made the mistake of going to the fake clinic. However, periodically patients do mistakenly go to fake clinics, as shown with the case of Talia in the Introduction.

In other parts of the country, providers have similar stories of fake clinics being located to deceive abortion patients. Where Fausta Luchini escorts in the South, the abortion clinic has no parking lot; however, the fake clinic, located next door to the abortion clinic, does. When an abortion patient drives up to the clinic, the anti-abortion protesters motion for her to drive into the fake clinic's parking lot and "then they try to help them walk into their building and they act like they're at the clinic." Charlene Tipton, a clinic director in the South, told us that the fake clinic next to her clinic has a big sign that says, "Considering abortion? Free pregnancy test" on it, luring her patients into that building instead of hers. Naomi Rangel's clinic in the South is located a short distance off a main highway. A fake clinic that has a name very similar to Naomi's clinic purchased a building on the same street but one block closer to the highway, so that every patient coming to the real clinic sees the fake clinic's building first.

For now, it appears that abortion clinics have little legal recourse because the Supreme Court's 2018 decision upholding fake clinics' free speech rights has put a brake on efforts to rein in their abuses. What this means is that fake clinics are free to continue to try to deceive women into thinking they are going to a real abortion clinic.

GETTING THERE IS EVEN HARDER

Once a woman finds a real clinic amid their declining numbers and the barrage of misinformation and misdirection, she has to actually get to the clinic. Other than the ability to pay for the abortion (discussed in the next chapter), this step is, according to our interviews, the biggest barrier to obtaining an abortion. If a woman does not have her own car and the clinic is not reachable by public transportation (as is the case for many women living in rural areas), she must find someone reliable to drive her to her appointment. And even if she owns a car, often there is a requirement for an accompanying driver. This is because clinics typically use some form of sedation in second-trimester procedures, and increasingly for first-trimester procedures as well. Therefore, providers are insistent that for a woman's safety she cannot drive herself home after a procedure that involves sedation.

Figuring out transportation is a major stumbling block for many, but it is only one of several things to work out. Since about 60 percent of abortion patients are parents, for these women a long day (or sometimes more) spent at an abortion clinic means putting child care plans in place. They must also arrange to take time off work. In some cases, because, for instance, a clinic is far from their home, their procedure is spread over two or more days, or the clinic has a waiting period after their first visit, they must budget for an overnight stay in the city where the clinic is located. In each of these situations, they have to negotiate with—or more precisely, ask for favors from—people in their network who may or may not be supportive of their decision to have an abortion.

Of course, abortion patients are not the only Americans who have to travel for health care, as rural residents in some areas also have to travel for various other services. What is arguably unique about abortion is that in this case arrangements often have to be kept secret from some in the woman's network and can involve stress and shame in dealing with others from whom she is asking help. Just imagine the difference between asking friends and family, "Can you drive me to my dentist appointment?" and "Can you drive me to my abortion appointment?" For some people there would be no difference, but for many people the difference means that it is much more difficult to get to the abortion appointment.

Moreover, the over-regulation of abortion providers that leads to the decreased clinic numbers discussed earlier in this chapter means that abortion-specific state policy directly contributes to the transportation and practical difficulties. Finally, because of restrictions on public funds paying for abortion care (discussed in chapter 4), low-income patients who would normally have transportation for a medical appointment paid for by the state cannot get that assistance for abortion care. Taken together, though transportation and practical difficulties exist for everyone seeking medical care, they are uniquely worse for abortion patients.

What is known about traveling and abortion patients? According to the Guttmacher Institute, "Half of all women of reproductive age lived within 11 miles of the nearest abortion clinic in 2014. However, a substantial minority of women, particularly those in rural areas, lived significantly farther away. One in five women across the country would need to travel at least 43 miles to reach the nearest abortion clinic." Further, the "abortion desert" study revealed twenty-seven cities in the country, spread out across fifteen states in the South and Midwest, that are more than one hundred miles from a clinic. But these broad pictures, useful as they are, obscure the many difficulties some women have, difficulties that in some circumstances can jeopardize obtaining the abortion in time. That there are, as of the summer of 2019, seven states with only one abortion clinic, with some performing abortions only through the first trimester, means that some women are doing a lot of traveling, mostly by car but also by bus, train, or plane. When there is limited access because of travel distance, research has shown that the number of women able to access an abortion drops precipitously.

The poverty of many abortion patients means their cars are often unreliable and gas money is hard to come by. We heard repeated stories of women who were late to their appointments or who were not able to show up at all because of car trouble. Shelley Sella recalled a patient who was coming from another state. "I will never forget this. She was driving to see us with her boyfriend and the car broke down. She called us and said she was going to be late, and then called some friends who were able to meet her and provide another car. When she got to our clinic, she said to us, 'I felt like, oh my God, I'm going to have a child because my car broke down!'" As Shelley wryly added, "That is not a reason why someone should have a child."

Sometimes women will get a ride to the clinic, but the driver will leave before the procedure is completed. Recalling patients whose drivers essentially abandoned women at the clinic, Mary Lofton, a doctor now practicing in a western state, said, "The things that you see with people's driver situations. It's just heartbreaking to see how little social support some people have." Mary Badame, who works at an abortion fund in the Northeast, remarked on how the collapse of this system often leads to patients being later in gestation than when they originally called the clinic. "You have to be dependent on the other people in your life, like your sister to watch your kids, or somebody to give you money for bus fare or to give you a ride. And if any one of those pieces fall, then your plans are shot, and you have to make an appointment in a few weeks." For many patients, these delays of even a week or two can push a woman beyond the point at which the clinic performs abortions. Researchers have estimated that some four thousand women a year are turned away from abortion clinics because they present too late for that clinic to treat them. Not all of these "turnaways" are because of travel difficulties, but a significant number are.

Winter driving in particular can pose problems. Janet Cook, a physician's assistant in a large western state, spoke of "our five months of winter" and the havoc it imposed on patients trying to reach the clinic. Lynn Thompson, a provider in a midwestern state, told of conditions after a snowfall that made it difficult, if not impossible, for patients, who often faced a six-hour drive: "It could be windy, and the snow that fell the day before is blowing across the flat grassy lands of the state, and it's whiteout conditions."

In some cases, extreme weather can cause a shutdown of clinics, further complicating care. However, often inclement weather also makes providers and patients more determined than ever. Jen Castle, a nurse practitioner in a northeastern clinic, told us that "on the worst blizzardy days" she is routinely surprised that all the patients still show up for their appointments. Part of it is that "people are used to traveling in really awful weather here," but the other part of it is that in her experience abortion patients are very motivated.

Suzie Carter saw the same thing during the so-called "polar vortex" of January 2019, which brought record-setting subfreezing temperatures to much of the Midwest. As Suzie told us, "Twenty-seven out of thirty-one scheduled patients arrived despite the thirty-five-below-zero temperature. Several staff had to take Uber or Lyft to get to work as their cars wouldn't start." The doctor on duty that day lived several hours away in another state, but, as Suzie said, even though the doctor's mom called her and urged her not to drive, "The doctor didn't even blink an eye about driving." Suzie herself reported that she became a "maintenance engineer" the day before the deep freeze—"checking and rechecking vent covers, closing some, opening others to maximize heat on the medical floor, pulling out auxiliary heaters. I am not looking forward to the heating bill for this month!" She also made the interesting observation that bad weather, ironically, may makes it easier for patients to leave town for their abortion. "My guess is that with the extreme cold and many businesses closing, they had a bonus day off and didn't have to make an excuse for missing work or school."

Those women who arrive for their abortions by bus or train often face unpleasant situations, especially when rigid schedules mean that they arrive hours before the clinic opens. Suzie told us that she occasionally sees patients who take the train to the medium-sized city in which the clinic is located. As she explained, the problem is that "the train gets in at 2:00 a.m. because it gets to some other bigger city at a more reasonable hour. But that means she either has to have the funds to check into a hotel or sit in the train station, which, you know, obviously is not ideal and/or not necessarily safe."

One of the most grueling travel stories we heard was told to us by Emily Webb, a provider in a large midwestern state. "The patient was home for the summer, in a very remote area with no nearby clinics, and found out she was pregnant. Her boyfriend was still in New York, and she was back with her mom and her stepdad. Parents were very religious. So she rode fifteen plus hours from the northern part of the state on a bus down to our clinic the night before her abortion. When she came to us the next morning, she was covered in mosquito bites because she had spent the night in the bus station. Outside the bus station, actually."

The patient turned out to be further along in pregnancy than she imagined, which meant she had to have a more expensive two-day procedure, so the clinic scrambled to arrange extra funding from a national fund. But now overnight lodging became an issue. "She didn't have anywhere to go. She only had on her the money that she scrounged up to get here on the bus." Emily said, "We reached out to people we knew and who had offered this before, so one of our friends in the local ACLU let her spend the night at her house for two nights and took care of her. We all just took such pity on her. She was a sweet girl who went through a traumatic experience, and we did everything we could to help her. We're very glad that we were able to."

The irregular hours that patients arrive in the city where the clinic is located, whether because of public transportation schedules, car troubles that lead to late arrivals, or bad weather, lead to a need for a place to spend the night. In our interviews with providers, we heard countless stories of patients and their companions, and sometimes even their children, sleeping in their cars in the clinic parking lot. Others, especially those who have driven long distances, need a place to stay if they are in states with waiting periods, which require a return visit the next day or soon thereafter. Some patients, as in the case related above by Emily Webb, find out abruptly that the one-day procedure they had anticipated will actually occur over two days.

Clinics do their utmost to help patients with travel arrangements. Besides connecting patients with volunteer-run organizations that can provide funds for travel, some clinics themselves provide such funding. We heard from several providers that their clinics arrange Uber or Lyft drivers for patients who have no other option. Judith Casella, a northeastern provider whose clinic periodically does this for patients, acknowledged that her staff did not always tell the driver that they were bringing a woman to an abortion facility, fearing anti-abortion pushback. But Judith also told us about a patient who needed a hospital abortion and for whom she had arranged a Lyft driver to bring to her appointment and then home. "So this Lyft driver called me and said, 'You know, your patient is in the recovery room and I told her I would wait for her.' So I said, 'Well, that's nice,' but you know, then she had complications, and she ended up being there for hours, until like eight at night. But he waited for her, because he told her he would."

Sometimes clinic staff themselves will drive stranded patients. Billie Taylor, also in the Northeast, acknowledged that this practice is not without risk, given liability issues. "Every single time a staff member offers to drive someone home, I'm like, 'You understand that this is what you are agreeing to?' Fortunately, all my staff currently have insurance, but there was a time when I had one staff member who did not have car insurance, and I would not let her drive." Billie admitted that though she tries to dissuade staff, she herself periodically drives patients home. "You do what you've got to do."

Patients with children—again, about 60 percent of all abortion recipients—have further logistical challenges when they have to travel out of town for abortion care or even spend a very long day at a clinic where they live. They either have to arrange to leave their children with someone or take them with them to the clinic. Lynn Thompson spoke of the challenges women with children can face. "It's hard when they need child care, because especially if they are trying to do it all in one day, they need to leave really early in the morning and they know they're not going to get back until late in the evening. To arrange child care is difficult, especially because there are times where the patient doesn't want to inform friends or family what they're doing."

Nearly all clinics do not allow children on the premises. This rule is frequently broken in practice, though, simply because some patients show up with children. If another adult accompanies the patient to the appointment, that person will typically try to keep the child(ren) occupied, ideally outside the clinic. Billie Taylor spoke to us with great gratitude of the children's bookstore near the clinic that helped in this regard.

But sometimes there is not another adult to watch the children. Billie spoke with both sympathy and frustration about those situations. "Well, a lot of the women that we see have children and end up coming to the appointment with them because they haven't been able to secure child care, and child care here is notorious—there's not enough of it and it's outrageously expensive." When this happened, Billie said, "We deal with it as best we can. The child goes with them to whatever parts of the appointment they can do. With medication abortion it's not usually an issue as much because those are the shorter appointments. But for surgical abortion, it's a huge issue." When a woman with children present is in the procedure room for her abortion, staff take on child care duty. "It's a big issue, and we don't like to have children here any more than we have to because we don't know how other women are going to react to having kids here when they are having their abortions."

A few clinics have been able to set up dedicated play areas for children, as long as there is an adult, other than the abortion patient, who can watch them. Pat Earle, who works at a southern clinic, excitedly told us of the separate house right next to the clinic that was recently repurposed for this use. This house is also unique in that it is set up for overnight stays for up to eight patients and children traveling long distances. "We just ask them to call us like twenty-four hours in advance, and it comes in real handy." For kids who travel with their parent to the abortion clinic, the house is ready. "The clinic next door is small, and kids don't do well in clinics, and in the summertime we see a lot of patients that have to bring their small children. We have everything over there that kids could need, you know, TV, DVDs, toys. We have playpens, we have the little rockers for the kids, everything that we can try to think of that will keep a kid busy and content over there while their mom or whoever they are with is over here at the clinic getting their needs taken care of."

Another group that faces unique barriers with transportation is undocumented immigrants. As the National Latina Institute for Reproductive Health has explained, some states, such as Texas, have internal checkpoints for undocumented immigrants, which have created special difficulties for them to travel to abortion clinics beyond those checkpoints. One of the providers we interviewed in Texas told us how difficult this was for her patients after one of her clinics closed in southern Texas because of the state's new TRAP law. "So patients would still come to us, and we were trying to figure out how to get them to where they could have an abortion. So the closest clinic was far away, so we would talk about, okay, what kind of transportation can we get you? Do you have immigration papers to go over? Because there's an internal immigration checkpoint in Texas." Patients who did not have these papers could not make this trip.

Undocumented immigrants' problems accessing an abortion clinic do not stop there. Some states require providers to check government identification before the patient can be seen. As Kendra Farrell told us, "A lot of them are just, you know, a little reluctant or hesitant from that point of the process. Because I think they're afraid that we may be allies with ICE or something." But even those who are comfortable presenting their identification may be stuck if the identification form they have, such as a passport, has expired. Because of the state law, Kendra said, "We can't just have an expired passport, you know, we just can't. The thing with that is a lot of them don't have the means or the access to be able to get it renewed. So then here we are, another woman that's possibly going to have to continue a pregnancy that she can't or doesn't really want to continue."

All these logistical problems—the costs and difficulties of travel, the need to arrange child care, the need for overnight accommodations—are exacerbated when clinics find that they have to refer women to other facilities, often out of state, because the woman's pregnancy is too far advanced to have her abortion there. These limitations can be a function of state law, or simply a result of which clinicians, with what kind of training, are on staff at that clinic. Sometimes a woman may be within the gestational limits of a particular clinic, but she presents with previously undisclosed health problems that require the abortion take place in a hospital. In these cases, staff scramble to try to help reschedule the patient at a suitable facility, which typically means not only contacting the new facility but helping the woman with new travel arrangements and what is usually an increased need for funding. More than once in this study, we have heard clinic staff refer to themselves when these situations presented as "travel agents."

ALLIES AND VOLUNTEERS TO THE RESCUE

Though clinics themselves do as much as possible to minimize these barriers, allies and volunteers play an essential role in helping patients to a degree not seen elsewhere in the health care system. Clinic escorting, helping patients make their way into the clinic entrance when anti-abortion forces are surrounding them, is the best-known volunteer activity, which we discuss in chapter 5. But allies and volunteers also provide crucial help with transportation, lodging, and other forms of practical support. The National Abortion Federation Hotline Fund, the National Network of Abortion Funds (which is affiliated with over seventy-five local funds), and the Brigid Alliance are among the best known of the national organizations that provide women not only with funding but with logistical help. But, as abortion care has become more difficult to access, numerous smaller, local groups have sprung up to help women get to clinics.

Maggie Wellington, the coordinator of one such organization in a large northeastern city where many women travel from out of town to access later abortions, described her group's functions as serving both out-of-towners and locals. "The cost of hotels here is pretty prohibitive to a lot of people. For some people, it's out of the question even getting a 'cheap' hotel. They just couldn't do it. So the idea is that by having volunteers host them overnight, we save them the cost of a hotel room." For many, the size of Maggie's city is daunting. Volunteers help these travelers as well. "For some patients, if they have not been here before, it can be pretty intimidating. So it's nice for them to have someone who knows their way around." The group also helps take local patients home from the clinic. "Any time you're getting a medical procedure done and you're getting general anesthesia [something more common in later abortions], you need to have someone to take you home, and some patients don't have anybody who can do that" Maggie said. "They don't have anyone that they feel they can tell. So our volunteers will meet patients at the clinic and bring them back to their homes."

Pat Earle, whose innovative housing and child care arrangements were discussed earlier, coordinates closely with a loyal group of volunteers to get women to the clinic. Describing a somewhat clandestine network of abortion relay drivers, she said, "When people don't have the transportation to get here, we have basically set it up with the volunteers, 'Okay, you're going to drive her from point A to point B, and then so and so's going to meet you at point B, and they're going to drive her from point B to point C.' I've got people in place along the interstate that can say, 'Okay, I can drive her this far. Somebody else can pick her up to here.'"

Some volunteers work as part of an organized group that is run by a small number of dedicated staff. Shelley Sella, who works in one of the clinics offering later abortions, which implies some portion of patients who are distraught over wanted pregnancies gone horribly wrong, spoke of the importance of the help of the local religious community. "The Religious Coalition for Reproductive Choice has a very active chapter here, and their team of volunteers can either put women up in their homes or they pay for a hotel. Their volunteers will drive women back and forth to the clinic. So we have some really good local support."

Folami Eze is the director of a practical support group in the South that trains volunteers in many different states. The need is acute in the region where she works because abortion providers are few and far between. The people she and her volunteers serve need help with transportation, gas money, food, and lodging. As Folami explained, "These things sometimes end up being just as big of a barrier as paying for the abortion."

Folami told us the story of a patient who needed help getting to a clinic in one of the states she serves, a state hundreds of miles away from where Folami is based. "We had a caller who was in a domestic violence situation and living in a shelter. So we had to coordinate with a volunteer with an organization near the clinic in that state who had a friend who formerly worked at an abortion clinic who was able to drive to pick this woman up, take her to her appointment, and then take her back to the shelter afterwards." Folami links her work to the reproductive justice movement because not only are she and the other leaders of the network women of color, but also they try to interact with the patients beyond just their abortion—about their jobs, their children, and their other struggles. To Folami, this "network that we're trying to build seems like sometimes it's a little radical."

The contributions that allied support organizations and volunteer networks make to abortion care in many places are enormous, as Pat Canon's story at the start of this chapter makes clear. But her story, like every story of help from a separate group of allies or volunteers, raises the question of whether this reliance on the sometimes paid but usually unpaid labor of altruistic community members is the best model for delivery of a health care procedure. Certainly not all those with the health complexities of a patient like Keisha can count on a Good Samaritan like Pat to drive them on a grueling four-day odyssey covering over a thousand miles in search of an appropriate facility. And though Pat was able to handle the challenges that Keisha's situation presented, it isn't hard to imagine medical or other emergencies that might arise that should be handled by professionals.

WHERE TRAVEL IS EASIER

Throughout this chapter we have focused on the considerable difficulties that many women have in getting to an abortion clinic, but there are places in this country where abortion care is more rationally organized so that patients have an easier time getting to clinics. These are states where there are enough clinics that getting to one is not an arduous proposition. To ease women's travel burdens even further, some states, including some large rural states where travel is difficult and clinics are far apart, cover transportation as part of Medicaid. As Fariba Rahnema, a doctor in a western state that has Medicaid coverage for abortion, explained to us, because Medicaid covers all travel for patients in her state, it covers travel for abortion patients as well. That means abortion patients' taxis, airfare, and overnight hotel arrangements are covered. Arranging this can take time, but overall, Fariba said, "It's wonderful."

In short, as Fariba's situation illustrates, in these states abortion patients are treated like any other patients seeking health care services. This doesn't solve all problems with finding and getting to an abortion care facility, but it puts abortion patients on the same footing as all other patients, something that is key to a saner delivery system for and the normalization of abortion care.

4 Coming Up With the Money

After introductory pleasantries, we asked everyone we interviewed some version of the general open-ended question, "What do you think are the biggest barriers that patients in your state face in getting an abortion?" For providers in the majority of states in this country as well as D.C. and Puerto Rico, the answer was almost always the same—money.

What these providers' patients face today harkens back to 1977, when Rosie Jimenez tried to get an abortion. A single mother living in McAllen, Texas, Jimenez was putting herself through college to become a special education teacher. To support herself and her daughter while paying for school, she worked part-time jobs, including cleaning houses on weekends. She knew this was a tough time in her life, but she was determined to sacrifice now so that she would have a better life in the future.

In September, Jimenez found out that she was pregnant. She had previously had two abortions, both of which had been paid for by Medicaid. However, by September 1977, a new federal law had taken effect. This law, commonly referred to as the Hyde Amendment, barred federal funding for abortions. Jimenez once again wanted an abortion so that she could stay on track with her schooling, but this time she would have to pay for it with her own money.

In McAllen at the time, the typical price that an obstetrician-gynecologist charged for an abortion was $230. Jimenez couldn't afford this steep price, as she needed her money for school and to care for her daughter. So, instead of going to a doctor, Jimenez found a local midwife, who was not licensed to perform abortions and who charged half of the going rate. In other words, because of her financial situation, Jimenez was forced to go to an illegal abortion provider.

Jimenez had her abortion on September 25. A day later, her cousin and friends rushed her to the emergency room because of a rapidly spreading infection. The infection started in her uterus because of feces- or dirt-contaminated instruments that the midwife had used to perform Jimenez's abortion. The hospital could not stop the infection, which eventually spread through Jimenez's entire body, including her heart. After seven days of intensive care, Jimenez died of organ failure on October 3. She was twenty-seven years old and left behind a four-year-old daughter.

Reflecting on her mother's death almost forty years later, Jimenez's daughter, Monique, explained why she is still pro-choice, despite what happened to her mom. She said, "Well, because my mom was choosing a better life. It would've been such a big struggle to have another child. She was trying to do better for us."

While there have been no known deaths due to an illegal abortion since Jimenez's that have been directly linked to a lack of abortion funding, low-income women seeking abortions continue to face the same "big struggle" she faced—the choice between spending what little money they have on the necessities of life or spending that money on health care. This was precisely the choice that Medicaid and other health insurance programs for low-income and poor people were designed to eliminate. However, because in most of the United States abortion is carved out of these programs as well as many private insurance programs, women routinely are forced to make this exact choice, putting their health, family, and finances at risk.

WHY $500 IS ALMOST IMPOSSIBLE

Compared to many other medical procedures, abortion is not that expensive. According to the most recent data, the average price of a surgical abortion at ten weeks was $508 in 2014, while a medication abortion was $535. The price goes up dramatically at later gestational ages, with the nationwide average for a twenty-week surgical abortion being $1,195. Ancillary services, such as birth control, an interpreter, and transportation, can bring the price even higher.

Specialized or later abortion care can cost even more. As Jen Moore Conrow, the director of a hospital-based practice, explained, "Hospital-based care is bananas expensive." At her practice, a first-trimester abortion is over $1,000, and for patients who are further along in their pregnancy, require sedation, or have more complicated medical issues the price is over $3,000. Abortions later in the second trimester and into the third trimester increase almost exponentially, with the latest abortions approaching $10,000 or more. The travel costs associated with getting to the small number of clinics in the country that do such procedures increase the overall price even more.

While the nonhospital and non-third-trimester averages are not eye-popping compared to the price of other medical procedures, they are incredibly challenging for most abortion patients. Half of abortion patients in the United States live below the federal poverty level, and another quarter live between 100 percent and 199 percent of the poverty level.

With patients at this level of poverty, the relatively low price of an abortion becomes a major problem. Susan Schewel, the director of a local abortion fund in the Northeast, broke this down for us. She explained that in her state a woman on welfare with one child receives just $317 per month in cash assistance. "Even if they get every benefit out there available to them" to help with things such as housing, food, health care, and child care, that small amount of money has to cover two people's other monthly expenses, including diapers, transportation, cell phone, and any costs not covered by the benefits. "All of these things can wipe out that money really quickly," Susan said. Now add on the "emergency expense" of an abortion, which where Susan works costs between $400 and $450 for a noncomplicated first-trimester procedure, and it's easy to see the hurdle for women living in poverty.

This is even more challenging in the modern political climate. Andrea Irwin is an administrator at a clinic in a northeastern state. She contextualized her patients' struggle to pay by talking about the attacks on poor people that are happening both locally and nationally. "It's just challenging for anyone to get by that is low income," she said. She then rattled off a list of cuts in her state and from the federal government—Medicaid, food stamps, welfare, housing assistance, general community support, and "just all of those programs that help people deal with the challenges of daily life." When people living in poverty have to deal with the challenges that come from these cuts, paying for an abortion becomes even more difficult.

The kind of poverty that abortion providers see reaches deep into patients' lives. Susan Hickman is very familiar with the challenges abortion patients face because of poverty. She remarked specifically about the difficulty patients face from the lack of affordable housing. As a result, "We talk with a lot of women who don't really have their own housing, but they are living with family or friends or even strangers." Relatedly, this kind of deep poverty also affects patients' ability to travel to and from the clinic. Melody Cook explained that in her southern state, poverty "limits mobility and limits transportation." Patients living in this kind of poverty "don't own a car, and nobody they know owns a car, certainly not a reliable enough car to get them three hours across the state and back" to get to her clinic.

For various reasons, this level of poverty in the United States is connected to race, sex, and the intersection of both. A 2017 report from the Samuel DuBois Cook Center on Social Equity at Duke University and the Insight Center for Community Development compared the net wealth of black and white men and women on the basis of different characteristics—single or married, college degree or not, and with or without children. What the study found was shocking in some way but not at all surprising in others. Most relevant to those who get abortions, for ages twenty to thirty-nine, on average black women have a much lower net worth than white women, whether married or not, college educated or not. In particular, single black women who do not have a college degree have, on average, a net worth of $0 in this age bracket because, on average, their debt cancels out their total assets (compared to $2,000 for single white women from twenty to twenty-nine, and $0 for single white women from thirty to thirty-nine). With a college degree, single black women are on average $11,000 in debt for ages twenty to twenty-nine (compared to $3,400) and have, on average, a $0 net worth for ages thirty to thirty-nine (compared to $7,500). Overall, the report explains that the "immense disparity in wealth between white and black households has reached its highest level since 1989; for every dollar of wealth owned by the typical white family, the median black family owns only five cents."

This disparity affects almost all people of color. According to the Pew Research Center, in 2014, just over a quarter of black people in the United States (26 percent) and just under a quarter of Hispanic people (23 percent) live in poverty, compared to only 10 percent of white people. Asians also have a higher poverty rate than white people, though not as stark at 12 percent. In 2013, the average net wealth of Hispanic households in the United States was $14,000, one-tenth the net wealth of white households.

Perhaps most relevant to the need to pay for an abortion are measures that look at people's ability to spend in an emergency. The Federal Reserve reports on the economic well-being of American households every year. Its 2018 report indicated that four in ten adults would not be able to afford a $400 unexpected expense. Relatedly, Prosperity Now has measured something it calls "liquid asset poverty." This measure looks at a family's cash savings to determine if the family has enough money on hand to live through an unexpected disruption in income. Although not specifically pegged to abortion, this measure is useful for thinking about whether someone has enough money in savings to access immediately to pay for an abortion. For a family of four to live at the poverty line for three months, this figure is $6,150. More than one-quarter of white families live in liquid asset poverty, which is a high number. But, it's worse for all families of color. As a whole, 51 percent of families of color live in liquid asset poverty: 61 percent of Hispanic families, 57 percent of black families, and 31 percent of Asian families.

Generations of discrimination in the past and ongoing discrimination now contribute to this disparity. The wage gap between men and women is 82 percent, meaning women as a whole earn 82 percent of what men earn. Broken down by race, though, that number shows the continuing impact of racism. Black women earn 68 percent of what white men earn, and Hispanic women earn 62 percent. But the disparity in wealth is not just about current earnings. As the net worth report explains, wealth is also a factor of how money is passed down from generation to generation within a family, such as help with paying for college or a down payment for a house. Because of "past and present barriers that have kept black families from building wealth," the 2017 report on accumulated wealth inequality concludes that "black and white women are positioned differently from one another largely because white women benefit more from wealth being passed down from their families."

WHEN INSURANCE DOESN'T HELP

Patients struggling in the face of this level of poverty find it extremely difficult to pay for an abortion. If this were almost any other medical procedure, Medicaid would cover the cost for these individuals. Medicaid, a joint federal/state program that began in 1965, has for decades alleviated the struggle that people living in poverty face in paying medical bills. Before Medicaid, poor people had to make the daunting choice of using what little money they had to pay for life's necessities, such as housing, food, clothing, shelter, and child care, or to pay for health care. One of Medicaid's most important goals was to eliminate this choice so that indigent Americans could do both.

In particular, Medicaid provides this assurance for low-income pregnant women's health care. Until 2010, Medicaid covered certain groups of people who had incomes up to 100 percent of the federal poverty level (which in 2019 for a household of one is $12,490). With the enactment of the Affordable Care Act that year, states were given the option of expanding Medicaid to all people who had incomes up to 138 percent of the poverty line. Thirty-seven states have expanded Medicaid, many beyond the 138 percent threshold, which means that in the remaining states no one above 100 percent of the poverty line is covered by Medicaid.

But pregnancy is different under Medicaid. The complicated Medicaid eligibility requirements for everyone else do not apply to pregnant women. Rather, Congress requires states to cover all pregnant women up to 138 percent of the poverty line, regardless of whether a state has expanded Medicaid. States are permitted to go beyond this requirement and cover more pregnant women, which every state except for Idaho has done. In fact, half of the states have set their eligibility limit for pregnant women at 200 percent or more of the poverty line. As a result of Medicaid's expanded treatment of pregnancy, it is the largest health insurer in the country that covers pregnancy, paying for nearly half of births in the United States.

Under Medicaid, indigent women pay nothing for their health care related to their pregnancy. The program prohibits states from requiring women to make a copayment, so there are no out-of-pocket expenses for Medicaid's expansive pregnancy-related care. The program covers prenatal care, labor and delivery, and sixty days of care following delivery. While exact program coverage varies by state—for instance, some states cover home births, while others do not—states generally cover a broad range of care for pregnant women to ensure their health.

Except for abortion. In 1976, Congress first passed what is now referred to as the Hyde Amendment. Named after the rabidly anti-abortion Republican representative Henry Hyde, this annual appropriations bill prohibits federal Medicaid dollars from being spent on abortion. Representative Hyde was not secretive about the reasons behind this law. He made it crystal clear during the floor debate of the bill that he was proposing this ban as a way to partially overturn *Roe v. Wade* and end abortion:

> Constitutional amendments which prohibit abortions stay languishing in subcommittee, much less committee, and so the only vehicle where the Members [of Congress] may work their will, unfortunately, is an appropriation bill. I regret that. I certainly would like to prevent, if I could legally, anybody having an abortion, a rich woman, a middle-class woman, or a poor woman. Unfortunately, the only vehicle available is the [Medicaid] bill. A life is a life. The life of a little ghetto kid is just as important as the life of a rich person. And so we proceed in this bill.

As a result of the Hyde Amendment, which has passed Congress every year since 1976, and similar bills covering other federal agencies, federal money cannot be spent on abortions in any program, not just Medicaid. The Hyde Amendment and a bevy of similar riders cover Medicare, the Indian Health Services, the Children's Health Insurance Program, the military's TRICARE health insurance program, federal prisons, the Peace Corps, and the Federal Employees Health Benefits Program.

Furthermore, Congress included a version of the Hyde Amendment as part of a compromise necessary to pass the Affordable Care Act in 2010.

This provision requires that insurers on the Obamacare Marketplace that cover abortion must separate out the abortion coverage so that federal dollars are not paying for it. The compromise also allows states to ban these Marketplace plans from covering abortion entirely, which twenty-five states have done.

In two cases in 1977 and 1980, one involving a similar state law out of Connecticut and the other involving the Hyde Amendment itself, the Supreme Court concluded that the Medicaid ban was entirely constitutional. The Court gave two main reasons. First, it said that even though abortion is a constitutional right, there is no constitutional requirement that the government fund people's access to that constitutional right. All that *Roe v. Wade* means is that the government cannot obstruct a woman from obtaining an abortion. The Hyde Amendment, according to the Court, is not the obstruction standing in the way of the woman getting her abortion; her poverty is. In the Court's words, "Although government may not place obstacles in the path of a woman's exercise of her freedom of choice, it need not remove those not of its own creation. Indigency falls in the latter category. The financial constraints that restrict an indigent woman's ability to enjoy the full range of constitutionally protected freedom of choice are the product not of governmental restrictions on access to abortions, but rather of her indigency." In other words, any burden a poor woman faces getting an abortion is her fault, not the government's, and it is up to her, not the government, to fix that.

Second, the Court ruled that the Hyde Amendment is not discriminatory. Rather than analyze whether the law discriminates against women (all men's reproductive care, such as vasectomies then and including Viagra now, is covered) or against people of color (because people of color are disproportionately burdened by the law), the Court asked whether it discriminates against the poor. In essence, the Court acknowledged that yes, it does. But, the Constitution does not prohibit wealth-based discrimination, so the law is constitutional.

The Court decisions were narrowly split, with five Justices voting to uphold the Hyde Amendment and four voting to strike it down. The dissents were blistering and called the majority Justices out for ignoring the on-the-ground realities of poor people's lives. In particular, Justice William Brennan wrote that "what is critical is the realization that as a practical matter, many poverty-stricken women will choose to carry their pregnancy to term simply because the Government provides funds for the associated medical services, even though these same women would have chosen to have an abortion if the Government had also paid for that option."

Justice Thurgood Marshall, the Court's only African American Justice at the time, took it a step further by noting what would happen to women who could not afford an abortion but still sought one out. "If abortion is medically necessary and a funded abortion is unavailable, they must resort to back-alley butchers, attempt to induce an abortion themselves by crude and dangerous methods, or suffer the serious medical consequences of attempting to carry the fetus to term. Because legal abortion is not a realistic option for such women, the predictable result of the Hyde Amendment will be a significant increase in the number of poor women who will die or suffer significant health damage because of an inability to procure necessary medical services."

Justice Marshall also connected the dots that were laid out earlier in this chapter about the Hyde Amendment, poverty, and race. He noted, "The class burdened by the Hyde Amendment consists of indigent women, a substantial portion of whom are members of minority races. As I [have written before], nonwhite women obtain abortions at nearly double the rate of whites." He concluded with powerful words, stating that the Hyde Amendment "is designed to deprive poor and minority women of the constitutional right to choose abortion." In a related case, he also wrote that the Hyde Amendment "brutally coerce[s] poor women to bear children whom society will scorn every day of their lives."

The Hyde Amendment and its related provisions are nearly but not entirely absolute in banning abortion. Although the exact language has varied at times, the provision has most frequently allowed for three exceptions. Federal dollars can be used to cover an abortion when the woman's life is threatened by the pregnancy and when the pregnancy is the result of rape or incest. All states but South Dakota follow these exceptions in theory (South Dakota unlawfully permits reimbursement only for abortions that threaten the life of the woman), but in practice, abortion providers often find it difficult to get Medicaid to actually reimburse for these limited circumstances. In fact, one study found that only 36 percent of abortions that should have been covered under these exceptions were actually covered, and a 2019 report from the General Accounting Office confirmed that over a dozen states regularly fail to comply with these exceptions.

In the states that do comply with the rape and incest exceptions, how they are applied varies. In some states, only the doctor has to sign a form to have the exceptions apply. Other states require the patient to go to the police to report the crime, and only then will Medicaid cover the abortion. Erica Valverde works in one of the states that requires a police report and is always concerned that patients will have to "relive their trauma" by filing a police report. She, like many of the providers we interviewed, finds the requirement "terribly patriarchal and condescending while missing the point of doing the right thing for the patient."

Iowa takes the rape exception to an extreme that is almost hard to believe. Rather than allow a doctor to sign a form or require a patient to file a police report, the state requires the governor to sign off on every abortion paid for under one of the Medicaid exceptions. This requirement is so invasive that Gabrielle Robinson, who runs a clinic there, explained that her clinic now waives the abortion fee altogether for a patient who has been referred from a sexual assault counselor. She encourages the patient to seek additional funding from other sources, but "someone who has been sexually assaulted has had enough hoops to jump through, so we eventually will waive the fee for these folks" rather than make them take their case to the governor.

The other exception in federal law—when the pregnancy is a threat to the life of the patient—is also a narrow exception. It does not cover when a pregnancy is a threat to the patient's health or well-being but not to her life, and except in a very small number of states it does not cover a pregnancy that will certainly result in the death of the fetus or baby. Jen Moore Conrow explained how difficult it is to meet this exception. She works at a northeastern hospital-based clinic that cares for patients with medical complications and other conditions that make abortion care in a stand-alone clinic impossible. She called the life threat exception a "double-edged sword" for her clinic. Because she and her colleagues at the clinic as well as her colleagues in the high-risk pregnancy department of the hospital are so skilled at treating women with complex medical histories, it's becoming increasingly difficult to say that the pregnancy will threaten the life of the patient. This is undeniably a good thing for patients and public health. But because medical care has progressed and so few women's lives are threatened by pregnancy, "somebody who wants an abortion now can't get it" because the exception no longer applies. Thus the double-edged sword.

The life threat exception is a high bar, but Jen told us about one medical condition that definitely meets it—when the patient is suicidal. She relayed a story to us of one such patient. A social worker from her hospital's psych unit was treating a pregnant patient on Medicaid who wanted an abortion. The social worker told Jen that the patient was suicidal because "she would kill herself before she would have a kid." Jen responded, ironically but truthfully, "You're in luck. If she's suicidal because she's pregnant, she can use her Medicaid."

There is one other way in which the Hyde Amendment is not absolute—it does not prohibit states from covering abortions using their own money. Because Medicaid is a joint federal/state program, some of the money that is used to fund it comes from the federal government, and the rest comes from individual state governments. In seventeen states, this state Medicaid money can be used to fund abortions. Seven of these states have done so because their legislatures have voluntarily passed laws covering abortion as part of their state programs. In the other ten, state courts have ruled that denying coverage for abortion violates a pregnant woman's rights under the state constitution. None of these states, though, provides coverage for people on purely federal insurance programs, such as for federal employees, military personnel, Native Americans and others. States cannot make up for these insurance bans.

Even though seventeen states permit Medicaid to reimburse abortions in theory, not all of them actually do so. Gabrielle Goodrick is a doctor who performs abortions at her own medical practice in a western state that, in theory, covers abortions under Medicaid. However, she explained when we talked with her that in her state reimbursement is "a fiction." In her experience, "Medicaid has never paid for an abortion outside a small number in hospitals, whether it's medically indicated, fetal or maternal indication." In the southern state where Shelly Jones works, Medicaid also covers abortions in theory, but in reality there are a number of hurdles. First, the state covers abortions only under a limited number of conditions that some providers interpret strictly. Second, if a woman enrolls in the state's Medicaid program *after* learning she is pregnant, she is not eligible for an abortion under Medicaid, only pregnancy care. Third, less than half of the abortion providers in the state accept Medicaid because, as is true in many places across the country, the program reimburses at a low rate and takes a long time to do so.

Thankfully, though, other states that cover abortion under Medicaid do many things right. One doctor we interviewed who practices in one of those states described what makes the system work so well. The state allows for same-day presumptive eligibility for pregnant women, which means that women who show up at the clinic without Medicaid coverage can sign up at the clinic and be covered immediately, without the normal waiting period. Immigrants can enroll as well, and even undocumented immigrants are covered because documentation status is not a necessary piece of information for the process. According to this doctor, her state likely "made a deliberate decision to do this because if you don't provide pregnancy care for undocumented people, you have a public health crisis." The doctor further explained that the rate at which providers are reimbursed under Medicaid, which had been historically low, was just increased thanks to intense lobbying following a new statewide tax. However, the rate is still quite low compared to other gynecologic procedures. Moreover, outside of the Medicaid context, private insurance reimbursement is often too low, but the doctor told us that "we want to make sure that women get what they need, so we're willing to accept what we get."

Finally, to round out the picture of insurance bans on abortion, some states have their own bans that go beyond Medicaid. Eleven states ban private health insurance plans from covering abortion. In nine of those states, people can purchase an additional rider that covers abortion, but they would have to take the unlikely step of planning ahead for an abortion. Twenty-two states ban health insurance policies for public employees from covering abortion. These prohibitions go beyond the federal Hyde Amendment and capture a much broader number of people who might need an abortion at some point in their lives.

RELYING ON STRANGERS TO MAKE UP THE DIFFERENCE

Insurance bans often mean that abortion patients are left to the generosity of strangers. Dawn Clay works with an abortion support network in the South. She told us the story of a full-time nursing student who was struggling to care for her multiple younger siblings as well as her drug-addicted mother. The woman had to discontinue her birth control because of cost and soon thereafter got pregnant. Because her period had been irregular, she didn't know she was pregnant until she was over twenty weeks along, which was further than the local abortion clinic's limit for when it would perform an abortion.

When she got that news, she was devastated. The clinic referred her to a clinic in another region of the country that could perform an abortion at that stage of pregnancy, but the price would be almost $10,000. The woman didn't have the funds, and the national abortion fund that she was working with could contribute only part of the money. This left the woman $3,000 short. The local clinic referred the woman to Dawn because her group works closely with the clinic on various matters. Dawn "told her not to worry. I then started a fund-raising campaign online and I got the money for her from online donations." It took Dawn only a few days to raise the money, and when she told the patient, she was crying. As Dawn recognized, "it's kind of a compelling story."

In some sense, the story told here is a familiar one. After all, Americans having difficulty covering health care costs has been the key motivator of health care reform efforts for decades. Even with the increases in coverage seen with Obamacare (some of which are currently under threat by Trump administration changes), people still struggle with medical bills because of out-of-control medical costs, high insurance deductibles, services that aren't covered, or out-of-network hospitals and providers. Others can't afford increasingly out-of-reach insurance premiums, even with the Obamacare marketplace and tax subsidies. These are, unfortunately, common tales in modern America.

But what's different about abortion is that for many people who are well enough off to have private insurance, the cost of an abortion is not so high that it is impossible to cover. Certainly for those who face the increased cost of an abortion after the first trimester or whose abortion is more involved because of medical complications, the price can be difficult, even with insurance coverage. However, for routine first-trimester care, which is the vast majority of abortions in this country, cost is not terribly burdensome for those who are middle class and who may have private insurance, whether they use it or not. However, three-quarters of people who get abortions live in poverty, which means that private insurance often doesn't enter the picture.

Instead, these low income patients are uninsured or covered by Medicaid. For virtually all other medical needs this portion of the population might have, Medicaid would cover the cost without any copay or deductible. This is what patients are used to with Medicaid. Thus several providers explained to us that patients are often surprised when they are told that Medicaid won't cover their abortion. Kendra Farrell counsels patients in a southern state with the Hyde Amendment and said that some patients "are in disbelief" when she tells them their abortion isn't covered; they will even call their insurance company themselves to confirm.

With the Hyde Amendment in effect in so many states across the country, women have to get over their shock and look elsewhere to get help paying for their abortions. Currently, there are two main resources—abortion funds and clinic discounts.

In essence, abortion funds are organizations that distribute money to assist women with paying for an abortion. As Susan Schewel explained it simply, "We raise money from individuals who care and disburse it to low-income people who have chosen an abortion." Some funds do more than this, like provide the practical support discussed in chapter 3, but most are limited to the straightforward task of funding abortions. The National Network of Abortion Funds' website lists about eighty different funds around the country. A small number of these funds are national in scope, while others are statewide, local, or even based in one particular clinic. Abortion funds disproportionately serve African American and young abortion patients.

Although it may seem counterintuitive, abortion funds are not limited to states without Medicaid funding. Many of the states with Medicaid funding have abortion funds that help fill the gaps for patients who are not covered by Medicaid but still find themselves struggling to pay. These can be indigent patients who are ineligible for Medicaid in the state, patients traveling from another state without Medicaid coverage, or patients who have an income level above the Medicaid cutoff but have difficulty with the price associated with a more expensive abortion, such as one with medical complications or later in pregnancy.

Mary Badame, who works with an abortion fund in a northeastern state, told us about one such patient. This patient lived in a state with Medicaid coverage but was insured through a high-deductible private insurance plan. When she found out during her twenty-third week of pregnancy that there was a fetal anomaly that was inconsistent with life, she confronted a huge expense. She lived in a part of the state where abortion providers performed abortions only up to nineteen weeks. The providers in her state that could care for her were hundreds of miles away and charged higher prices because they were located in a major metropolitan area with a higher cost of living. As a result, this patient was forced to drive across the state and pay several thousand dollars for the abortion. "She actually would have been able to afford a much larger portion of her abortion care," Mary said, "but because she had to then pay for travel and child care to access the care that she needed, we ended up covering the majority of the cost of her procedure."

The amount of money these funds have available varies dramatically across the country. Some are able to help thousands of women, while others can help just a handful. Almost all depend on the vagaries of private fund-raising and grants, though in the summer of 2019 New York City become the first city to contribute public dollars to a private abortion fund. If successful and then replicated elsewhere, this effort could vastly increase the help these funds could provide to patients.

Of course, no abortion fund has unlimited money, so most have systems in place to determine who they are going to help and at what level. Even if funds can help patients, they rarely fund the entire price of the abortion, often giving a set percentage or amount per abortion. Susan Schewel said that her fund "pushes women as much as we can to come up with as much money as they can without risking the life or health of themselves or their family. We don't want people selling their food stamps. We don't want people selling drugs." By funding only a portion of the abortion and not all of it, funds are able to help more people. It's also a way for the fund to make sure that the women are not, as Pat Canon, who works with a fund in a southern state, explained, "being coerced just because they have the money funded to them. It stops the argument that we paid them to have an abortion."

Even this limited assistance is often help enough, as Chloe Hebert, the director of the National Abortion Federation Hotline Fund, told us. "The barrier is cost, and being able to reduce that for people allows them to pay attention to the other aspects associated with getting an abortion, such as how they will get there, do they have to stay overnight, can someone go with them? People get incredibly overwhelmed by the price a lot of the time." When a fund can alleviate that, even just a little, women are more likely to be able to put all the pieces in place to get their abortion.

Another important way that funds differ is in who interacts with them— the clinic on behalf of the patient or the patient directly. Either way, the process creates challenges. When the clinic is responsible for contacting the fund to work out payment, the clinic has to devote considerable resources, even one or multiple staff positions, to this task. When the patient is responsible, it puts an added burden on someone who is already struggling with the combination of poverty and an unexpected medical expense. Elena Hunter, a clinic director in a southern state, explained how difficult that can be for patients sometimes. Her clinic doesn't have the capacity to help patients in this way, so the patients have to call the funds themselves. The funds that her clinic works with, though, deal with such a high number of patients that it's often difficult for patients to get through: "We get a lot of calls back from patients saying, 'I couldn't get through because their phone was busy.' So we tell them, 'You can call any time between 6:00 a.m. and 10:00 p.m. Try at the end of the day or the very beginning of the day. You might have the best luck getting it.' So we're coaching them on how to do it. We tell them, 'It's like calling a radio station. Just hit the redial, hit the redial, hit the redial, you know. It's worth it. Just be patient.'" Gabrielle Goodrick described the struggle trying to find funds for her patients because there are a large number of funds to contact, but each has limited resources. "We have a national fund that we work with. We try to get funding from them. We had a statewide abortion fund, but that got closed down two years ago. So we opened up a new one and are running it through a local nonprofit, but that has very limited funds."

When those limited funds still leave a patient without enough money, Gabrielle does what many other clinics do—her clinic pitches in. "We'll offer a clinic discount and try to get them seen." Unfortunately, almost every person we interviewed told us that the abortion funds they and their patients have access to are not able to satisfy every patient need, so they are left doing the same. To many we talked with, this is a matter of mission. As Nellie Baker, a doctor and clinic director in a midwestern state, explained on behalf of almost everyone, "We really don't like turning people away." Jenifer Groves, who runs multiple clinics in the Northeast, echoed that sentiment, saying that almost no matter what, "We make it happen. I don't know how else to say it. If somebody comes in with twenty-five bucks, we're going to figure it out. We're going to write it off, we're going to find as much funding as we can. We're going to do the procedure."

The challenge for clinics and patients is figuring out how to access as much support as possible from outside sources without the clinic discounting so much that it affects business operations. Jenifer explained that at her clinics, "you've got to work the phone, and we have financial advocates on staff that do that. You're working all these different things at the same time, trying to cobble together the amount of money people need to get an abortion. They're working it. But despite all their work, sometimes people come in the door short, and that's where our clinic discounts come into play. We do what we can."

In Billie Taylor's state, the Medicaid restriction is in force. The result is a complicated dance with the patients and her staff. "We do get funding from a national abortion fund, but not a lot. After that, we start making calls if the patient doesn't have the capacity to do so herself." She and her staff will call local churches, specialized national funds, funds from other states where the patient may be coming from. "As a social worker, I believe in accountability, and so we try to get the patients to bring something or call someone, but a lot of patients are struggling and might not have the capacity." The brunt of the work then falls on her staff. They're busy with seeing patients, though, so they have to do what they can to find downtime to make the calls to help patients with whatever amount they can find. The clinic has also started its own fund with money that local supporters want to donate, but according to Billie, "it's not a lot." As a result, the clinic "ends up eating the rest of the cost."

Funds and clinic discounts are an essential part of the abortion landscape in the face of the Medicaid bans and other funding challenges patients face. Chloe Hebert summed up how important they are by talking about what would happen without this assistance. "I think you'd see a lot of dominoes fall. I don't think that a lot of clinics would be able to see the amount of patients they currently do, which would hurt access long term. Some patients would be able to make it happen for themselves regardless, but I think the majority of our patients would not be able to get the health care they want."

SACRIFICE, DELAY, AND WORSE

For indigent patients, this landscape means that while they would otherwise have government insurance to cover their health needs, for an abortion they have to rely on a combination of abortion funds, clinic discounts, and scraping together their last dollars. To Cindi Cranston, it's like "playing a game of abortion Tetris, where you're trying to lock in all of these little pieces into their exact place in order to actually get an abortion."

Rebecca Moore, who runs several clinics in western states, framed the challenge similarly, asking us to think about the initial call to the clinic from the perspective of the patient. She told us that at her clinics, because of abortion funds and clinic discounts in the states where she works that do not have Medicaid funding or because of state funding in the state that does cover abortion, "at the end of the day folks are going to get the help they need. But I just can't imagine that it doesn't feel better to know that when you call our clinic with state funding, we say, 'Are you on Medicaid? Okay, good, it's covered,' compared to in our other states, 'Do you know if you can pay for this?' They're two different conversations, and the second one is probably not very pleasant. On top of everything else you're trying to figure out getting here, time off, child care."

Andrea Ferrigno has the perfect perch from which to evaluate how the insurance ban affects patients. Andrea is an administrator at a group of clinics that operate in states with and without Medicaid coverage for abortion. From that vantage point, the comparison is stark. In states with insurance bans, patients and clinic administrators have to act as co-project managers just to make the funding work:

It becomes like this sort of partnership with most of our patients here, where the patient calls to make an appointment, and we go through the costs and then offer financial support if they need it, and we have to make a plan. I remember doing this myself with many patients, where we say, "Okay, I'm going to need you to call these two funds that only talk to the patient, and then I'm going to call these other funds that only talk to me, and then we're going to make another appointment for us to get on the phone to see who got what." Then the next day, we will get on the phone and say, "Okay, how much did you get? Okay, I got this much." And put it together and say, "Okay, how much more do we need?"

It isn't hard to imagine that, for many patients going through the stress of an unwanted pregnancy while also dealing with the daily challenges of living in poverty, managing this kind of project is extremely difficult and, for some, borderline impossible.

Making the situation even worse, though, is that every day spent tracking down funds or coming up with money leads to delay. Delay, in turn, means that the price of the abortion goes up, as do the risk of a complication and the risk of being pushed beyond the gestational age limit for the clinic or state. "When we were fund-raising with patients that were in their later second trimester, it was maddening," Andrea told us. She and her colleagues would work frantically with the patient to raise the money in the quickest manner possible, but delays "happen all the time." Andrea's clinic would sometimes freeze the cost of the abortion on the date of the patient's first contact with the clinic, rather than the date two or three or more weeks later when the patients finally received care, but doing so hurt the clinic's business "because it costs us more no matter what, but we know that if we charge the patient what it really costs, they're never going to get the abortion they need." For both the clinic personnel working on these cases and the patient, "it's incredibly difficult logistically and also emotionally exhausting and draining. We would love to give abortions away free for everybody that needs one, but we also have to be reasonable and keep our doors open."

The flipside of patients who contact the clinic first and then take time to get together the money are patients who don't contact the clinic until too late because they are trying to cobble together the price of the procedure. Gabrielle Goodrick lamented that these patients wind up delaying to the point that the abortion price has increased even higher. She told us that "there are cases where women are waiting months and months to get their abortions. I mean, I've had patients come in and they have just gone to the website to look at price. They don't bother calling us. And then they come in and they're fifteen weeks, and they say, 'Yeah, I've been trying to come up with the money.' And I tell them, 'Well, I wish you'd called us, because we could have helped gotten you in here at least a month or two sooner.' Because they're waiting paycheck to paycheck to get enough money to get in."

In other words, in states without Medicaid coverage, it's a race against the clock for women who can't afford the procedure. But that is, according to Chloe Hebert, "a tricky place for a fund and clinic to be sometimes." Chloe tries to provide quick assistance for patients so that they don't wind up facing an even higher fee for the procedure. To Chloe, there's a sense of urgency that she tries to impress upon the patients, but in doing so she has to be careful not to rush the patient's decision. "It's challenging to hold these two thoughts together when working with patients: this is your personal decision and you should have the space to consider it for as long you yourself need *and* you can't take too long because each week that goes by, the fee increases and access decreases."

In contrast to the complexities in states with the Hyde Amendment in place, in the states where abortion is covered by Medicaid the entire experience is different for patients. In the state where Andrea works that has coverage, patients with Medicaid don't have to delay or jump through any of the hoops that they do in the other state where she works. Even patients who qualify for Medicaid but don't currently have it can come in and get coverage on the same day. There's no delay, no fuss, and no time whatsoever spent on the difficult task of finding hundreds or even thousands of dollars for the patient's procedure. All in all, Andrea said, there's just "a lot more flexibility and a lot more time and access for the patient." Qualitative studies of women using Medicaid to cover abortions in states that do so confirm Andrea's experience. In those states, the experience is "straightforward and 'pretty easy'" for women.

Jenifer Groves has the same vantage point as Andrea, as Jenifer is the director of two clinics in different states, one with Medicaid coverage and the other without. Jenifer has experienced all of the same issues as Andrea but also elaborated on what the difference means for patients' moods. We interviewed Jenifer in the state that has a Medicaid ban in place.

> One of the things I'm noticing is that the mood in the waiting room for women in the other state as opposed to here is so different. It's like if you talk to some of the people that work here, they say things like, "The populations are so different." But I'm like, "They're not, they're not." The bulk of the patients I see in the other state are from a city where poverty's also huge. All of those psychosocial issues are huge. We see the same population. What's the difference? The difference is that the patients walking into the clinic there aren't worried about how they're going to pay for this procedure, and that, in and of itself, pulls a layer of garbage off of people. There's a levity in the waiting room there that doesn't exist here. People come in here heated, they come in here hot, and I get it. You're not talking about a higher income of the patients that we're seeing over there. It's just money's not something they're worrying about for the abortion. Here, you've got to fight, you've got to beg to get an abortion. You don't have to do that over there. And the difference is mind-blowing.

It's not just in the patient mood that Jenifer notices a difference. The patient experience is different, particularly when it comes to counseling. In the state where Medicaid doesn't cover abortion, some counselors feel that they need to start the conversation talking about money and, in particular, rape. Rape is one of the exceptions to the insurance ban, so if the patient is pregnant as the result of rape, Medicaid will cover the abortion. As Jenifer described it, "The abortion here starts with the rape experience. You're framing the visit around rape. It does not start with what the woman wants it to start with."

This is not a minor paperwork issue. Rather, it changes the patient's entire experience. In the state where Medicaid covers abortion, the patient's counseling session is about what she needs and wants with her medical care. Whether the pregnancy is the result of rape may come up in the conversation, but it may not—it's up to the patient. Talking about interpersonal violence generally is part of that care—"Are you feeling safe in your relationship?" or "Have you been punched or hit in the past three months?"—but asking whether this particular pregnancy is the result of rape or incest is not medically necessary for abortion care. Rather than talk about rape, the counselors can discuss with the patient things like food insecurity, child care, pregnancy difficulties, or anything else she wants to talk about, including possibly rape. But "the only reason," Jenifer said, "we would need to ask if this particular pregnancy was a result of rape is for Medicaid coverage." And doing so, as Jenifer has experienced, changes the patient-clinic interaction.

Mary Lofton, who has also worked in states without Medicaid coverage for abortion, has been in the position of certifying to the state that a pregnancy was the result of rape. She said, in comparison with the state where she has worked that does have Medicaid coverage, this sometimes "creates a system of lack of trust" with patients. As the one signing the certification, Mary is careful to make sure that what she is certifying—that the pregnancy was the result of rape—is true. This makes her ask questions that are "not important medically" but are "very uncomfortable." To Mary, these questions are "not about taking care of the patient and making sure she's okay from the rape," which would be within her expertise, but rather are purely about payment and law enforcement, which are not within her medical training.

The stories we were told of patient suffering within this system were heartbreaking. Jan Dancy, a patient advocate in a northeastern clinic, told us about a patient who had been there earlier the day we talked. The patient had driven from about an hour away to get her abortion. She already had a baby and a five-year-old son. Her sister came with her for the appointment because the patient couldn't drive herself home and needed someone to watch her kids. The patient showed up with twenty dollars to pay for the abortion but told Jan that paying that money would mean that she and her sister might not have enough money to pay for gas to get home and to feed the kids for the rest of the week. Jan couldn't take her money, telling us, "I wouldn't be a part of taking anybody's last dollar. I don't want you to feel like you're making decisions around your family that cost your family as well to such a severe extreme."

Charlene Tipton told a similar story about a patient she had also seen earlier in the day that we talked with her. The patient was sobbing when Charlene saw her with the clinic's receptionist. The patient was on Medicaid, which would not cover the cost of her $575 procedure. However, she had managed to scrape together that money and brought it to the clinic with her that day. In the process of talking with her, Charlene learned that the patient had saved the money by not paying rent, ignoring her utility bills, and telling her kids that they couldn't have Halloween costumes this year. Charlene was able to dig into her clinic's funds to help the patient so that her family wouldn't suffer.

As these two stories indicate, the list of ways that people told us patients came up with the money for their abortion was almost endless. Patients use money that they would otherwise spend on rent, car payments, utilities, child care, and Christmas presents. They sell items on Craigslist, such as televisions, stereos, and other personal goods. Susan Schewel, the director of an abortion fund in the Northeast, said that women her fund worked with would even sell sex to raise money for their abortion, which didn't surprise her given the level of desperation and need. What did surprise her was the one time a patient told her that her family had sold their dog. Capturing the lengths women go in the face of the Medicaid ban, Chloe Hebert said, "A lot of people try and save. They'll forego certain bills. They will borrow. They'll get help from the person involved, although that's pretty rare. Ask family and friends. A lot of personal individual loans usually. Sometimes they'll even do bank loans if they can or credit cards if they have them."

Women do this because, in Hannah Miller's words, they are "desperate." Or, as Erica Valverde explained, "Time is of the essence because you don't become less pregnant with each passing day." But, as patients take these drastic measures, the stress they face leading up to their abortion increases.

Some patients are put in the position of raising their own funds even though help is available to them. Van May, an administrator at a large southern clinic, explained the difficulty undocumented immigrants have accessing funds at her clinic. Although the abortion funds Van's clinic works with will indeed help these patients, the clinic has to screen the patients to see if they qualify for assistance. Van said that "a lot of our undocumented patients would rather pay the full cost of an abortion than get screened." The patients are afraid that the screening process will result in immigration officials being alerted, so they often wind up piecing together the money from whatever source they can. "We know this is an issue," Van said, "but you can't force somebody to be screened for assistance."

Patients also sometimes wind up altering their medical care because of the Medicaid ban. Fariba Rahnema, a doctor in a western state, told us the story of a patient who had insurance through the military, which meant that even though Fariba worked in a state where Medicaid covers abortion, this patient's abortion was not covered because of the military abortion ban, which, unlike regular Medicaid, states cannot change. "The patient thought she had all the money together and, when she came to the clinic, just didn't have enough." As a result, even though she wasn't comfortable doing so, Fariba talked with her about different pain management options based on price. "Now I'm talking about treating her differently than other patients and doing things that are going to be more painful just so we can get her to afford this. And that is the struggle for patients sometimes." The patient ultimately chose to go with oral pain medications rather than any anesthesia. Fariba told us that she had told the patient that this was "definitely not something I wanted to do," but the patient had chosen this option because it was all she could afford.

Mary Lofton also experienced a difference in care because of the Medicaid ban. She now works in a state with Medicaid coverage, and almost all of her patients, both first- and second-trimester procedures, are sedated. However, where she used to work, a state where Medicaid does not cover abortion, patients routinely opted out of sedation because it cost an extra forty dollars and they couldn't afford it. As a result, she and her staff learned to administer what she called "verbacain"—verbal novocaine—because patients who are not sedated can benefit from soothing talk during the procedure.

Thankfully, this doesn't happen everywhere, as some clinics are able to find emergency funding to prevent patients from making this difficult choice. Kathleen Anderson told us the story of a patient at her clinic:

> I had a patient today who was anemic, way anemic, so she couldn't do the abortion pill. So she was going to do the procedure, but she didn't have enough money for sedation, so she was going to do the procedure awake. And she was afraid to tell me that. So I said to her, "Are you doing this awake because of financial reasons?" And she looked at me and she said, "Yeah." I said, "That's not okay. I don't want you to do this awake just for the difference of forty dollars." So we got her emergency medical assistance for the money because that's our philosophy. Doing the procedure awake can be uncomfortable, and not everybody's a great candidate for that. And we never want anybody to have to do that for financial reasons. That's not who we are.

Almost every provider we talked with had the same philosophy—that they didn't want patients to have to alter care because of financial issues. However, not every clinic has access to the kinds of emergency funds Kathleen did, nor are all clinics in a financial position to absorb the cost themselves.

What everyone working to help patients fears the most is that a patient ultimately won't be able to have an abortion solely because of funding issues. According to researchers who have studied the issue, the best estimates are that one in four women who would have had a Medicaid-funded abortion if it covered the procedure give birth instead.

Brittany is one such woman. She found out she was pregnant when she was already in her second trimester and knew immediately that, given her life situation, she couldn't have another child at that point in time. Brittany was poor, sharing an apartment with her sister and three children, and not in a relationship at the time. "I remember thinking that I would just use my insurance, my Medicaid, to pay for the procedure. That wasn't the case, obviously. I couldn't use it, and I couldn't come up with the money. I couldn't even borrow the money." As a result, Brittany carried her pregnancy to term. "I was stressed, I was in a lot of pain, and I would just cry. I was depressed. It was just not a good space for me, mentally or physically." Brittany is clear that she loves her daughter dearly, "but if I'd had the money I would have had an abortion. I did not choose to have a child at that time. And that takes a toll on you—mentally, emotionally, physically, financially. Everything."

For Kendra Farrell, this is unfortunately a common experience for her patients. After voicing "frustration and disappointment" about Medicaid not covering their procedure, some patients "don't return because they can't find the means or they're trying to get the funding but they get frustrated having to try to call, and they just kind of give up." Kendra sometimes has patients who come back for an abortion after having been turned away for an earlier pregnancy because they couldn't come up with the money. As a result, "they continued the pregnancy, delivered to term, got pregnant again, and came back and told her, 'Well, the last time I was here I couldn't afford to come back and I had a baby.'"

Perhaps the most radical and wide-ranging effect of the Hyde Amendment and similar abortion insurance bans is the further segregation of abortion from normal health care. Andrea Irwin, one of the providers we talked with who works in a state where Medicaid does not cover abortion, compared abortion coverage to other medical care, like prenatal care, birth control, or miscarriage management. These other health needs are covered for her patients, which "sends that message that this is part of the normal reproductive health care package and everyone can access it, regardless of income." In comparison, abortion is not covered, which "feels particularly stigmatizing to not cover this one thing out of the whole array of different services we do provide."

In contrast, Nellie Baker explained how much different abortion care can be in a state without insurance bans, public or private. In the facility where she trained, abortion care was integrated into other aspects of health care, partly because, as Nellie described, there were no insurance barriers to coverage for patients, which meant that patients didn't have to stress about money and her facility didn't have to work overtime to find them supplemental funds. Instead, abortion was "routine health care," with abortion patients treated the same as anyone else. With insurance covering abortion like any other procedure, abortion "just wasn't a big deal and was just part of our job."

5 Getting In

CHAOS AT THE CLINIC DOOR

For most people, the biggest issue they might face getting into their doctor's office on the day of an appointment is finding parking or a reliable bus route that will get them to the office on time. Or, for people in a wheelchair or who otherwise have trouble walking, there could be issues related to sidewalk ramps, stairs, or other physical accessibility concerns. And anyone who has had an appointment in a hospital-based doctor's office knows the difficulty with finding your way through the poorly laid-out halls of a large medical institution.

However, at no point when you try to enter your doctor's office will you have to deal with strangers berating you for getting a colonoscopy, trying to convince you not to have cataract surgery, or saying you are committing a crime and going to hell because you have chosen to have a physical checkup. But that's exactly what abortion patients go through on a regular basis. And state and local authorities usually just stand by and let it happen with the blessing of the Supreme Court.

For instance, consider the situation at one of Hannah Miller's clinics, where getting an abortion means wading through a sea of protesters. Hannah is the co-owner and lead administrator for four southern clinics in two different states. She told us that she has regular protesters at all four of her clinics, but at one in particular the situation has gotten almost completely out of hand, with the number of protesters growing "very dramatically" over the year leading up to our interview. This clinic, which has been in operation for over two decades, sees a high volume of patients six days a week. It has a history of being targeted by some of the most extreme members of the anti-abortion movement, including a national leader who has a criminal record for targeting providers.

Understanding the clinic's layout is essential to understanding Hannah's situation. It is located in a large metropolitan area, occupying its own office building at the back of a quiet tree-lined loop just over half a mile from a main thoroughfare. There are other office buildings on this loop, but they are sporadically spaced. As a result, the loop is not heavily trafficked by cars.

On a typical weekday, the clinic gets between twenty and thirty protesters with two large anti-abortion RVs parked outside the clinic along with the protesters. The protesters use the clinic's unique layout to best position themselves to have access to patients. As Hannah explained, "Patients have to drive a loop. Protesters set themselves up on each side of the loop so they can stop people before they make it to our driveway. Then they park themselves and position themselves in front of our driveway opening and on our sidewalks in front of the clinic as well."

This is difficult enough for patients to navigate on weekdays, but it's even worse on Saturdays, when there are between one hundred and two hundred protesters. And several times over the course of the year that we interviewed Hannah, there were special events with thousands of protesters. For those special events, the protesters obtained a parade permit, which allowed them to shut down half the road, reducing it to just one lane. Hannah said that on these event days sometimes the police are helpful in directing traffic but that most of the time "it's a total free-for-all. You just kind of drive and do the best you can." Clinic volunteers station themselves outside to direct patients away from the protesters and the RVs and into the clinic's driveway. The clinic does its best to warn patients beforehand what to expect, though that is challenging, as Hannah explained:

It's just a very Catch-22 situation because you can freak patients out beforehand, and then it turns out there's a light day and you may not have as many protesters as you expected, and you've terrified a patient for no reason. Or, you don't tell them at all and then they freak out. Rightfully so. Typically, we tell patients that there are possible traffic issues and if so, to watch for signage directing them toward the clinic, and that there are escorts—all of our escorts have bright pink vests—and to look for someone in a pink vest that could help them navigate into the clinic. If someone calls and asks, "Am I going to see a protester?" we will tell them that typically there are protesters outside, but there are also these people to help you get into the building safely.

But I try not to use the word *protester* on the phone because of the fact that it just inspires such fear and stigma and shame in women, in patients in general, who are just looking for safe, legal care. They shouldn't have to be protested where they go. It insinuates that whatever they're doing is wrong. Personally, I have an ethical issue with that. I try to use the terminology that there are traffic obstructions. That's usually the word that I use— obstructions.

Hannah described how on some of the days with the largest number of protesters a "prayer march" takes place. One of the organized groups lines both sides of the street with hundreds of anti-abortion protesters. They start at the main thoroughfare and then march down the loop to the clinic, where they congregate directly across from the clinic's entrance. There's no sidewalk there, so this large group is blocking a portion of the road in front of the clinic. Once there, they'll have a "church service" in front of the clinic. But this isn't a typical church service, because mixed in with the prayer are protesters yelling at patients coming into the clinic. They also have a loudspeaker over which they play the recording of a woman talking about how she regretted her abortion. The recording, which tries to shame and stigmatize the women entering the clinic, is the same every time the group is there. The group leaves just before noon when patients stop checking in.

Other protesters regularly bring loudspeakers and megaphones to the clinic entrance as well. The people on the mic mix in a combination of preaching and yelling at patients entering the clinic. Occasionally, they'll invite children who are a part of the protest to do a singalong on the mic. They've even had church choir groups singing over the loudspeaker in front of the clinic. In response, the clinic's escorts and supporters sometimes use their own sound amplification devices to try to "drown out" the protesters, playing audio books about abortion as well as rap music.

Throughout it all, the patients just want to get to their medical appointment, but the protesters are targeting them. They put kids in the middle of the street, creating what Hannah calls a "nerve-wracking traffic situation" where the protesters are "daring people to drive into them." The protesters also walk in front of cars, trying to wave them down. The cars either swerve to get around them or stop so they don't run over the kids or the other protesters. When the cars stop or when a patient is walking on foot to the clinic, the protesters talk directly to the patients and their companions. They tell the patients they are paying someone to murder their baby, they are going to regret the abortion, they could soon be celebrating Mother's Day, and other "shaming" messages. To male companions, the protesters yell how worthless and cowardly they are and that they "don't deserve to have the title of man." Hannah summed up all that patients and companions have to hear as "very hostile and very sexist."

Hannah told us one story of an interaction that happened in the weeks before we interviewed her:

> I try very hard not to interact with protesters. It's something that helps me in my personal well-being and stress levels. But two or three weekends ago, I got right up in a protester's face because he was following patients along the sidewalk and targeting them and screaming at them and calling them these vulgar names. One of the patients that he had stopped he had made so hysterical she was paralyzed and couldn't move. Our escorts had blocked her with umbrellas and we were trying to make sure we could get her into the building without being targeted, and he just stood there in the mouth of the driveway with his wife, screaming at this girl, trying to tell her to leave. I very rarely lose my cool, but that time I did.

At Hannah's three other clinics, the situation is much less charged, though still problematic. At one of the sites, there are about fifteen angry protesters on Fridays and Saturdays who are outside "pushing for adoption and shaming patients," but the clinic is in a residential area that is policed more strictly. At another site in a different state, there had never been protesters until recently, when a fake clinic moved to the property behind Hannah's clinic. Now the situation is "more hostile than it's ever been," with five to ten protesters a day who are "very angry and very hostile, screaming at patients." At the last clinic, there is a "regular crew" of protesters, but they are less disruptive. "It's typically so hot in that city, and it's on a really busy road, that they sit outside for a few hours and then leave and go to Chick-fil-A for breakfast." To Hannah, whose patients face much worse situations at each of her other three clinics, "I'll take those protesters any day of the week."

The specific details of Hannah's story may be unique, but the overall thrust is not. Encountering protesters who intimidate, shame, harass, and harangue people who are doing nothing more than entering a medical clinic is normal around the country for patients trying to get an abortion. In no other area of medicine are patients subjected to this kind of harassment just for walking into a doctor's office. Some localities have tried to limit the impact of these protesters, but the Supreme Court has made that difficult to do. As a result, the burden is on clinics and their volunteers to try to protect patients from this harassment. But even the most effective response still leaves women seeking abortion services feeling at best attacked and at worst physically stressed in ways that hinder good medical care.

LIKE NOTHING ELSE IN MEDICAL CARE

Not every patient who enters an abortion clinic faces a situation like what is happening outside Hannah's clinic, but many do. The Feminist Majority Foundation surveys abortion facilities every two years about violence and protest. Its most recent 2018 report of 218 clinics indicates that about 88 percent of clinics experience some sort of anti-abortion protest activity at their sites.

The Turnaway Study, which interviewed almost one thousand abortion patients at thirty abortion facilities in the country, also looked at onsite protest activity. Of the clinics that were a part of the study, 15 percent reported that the site had no regular protesters that were visible to patients, and none of the hospital-based abortion facilities, which perform less than 5 percent of abortions in the US, reported visible protesters. Margaret Bolin, an administrator at a hospital-based clinic in the Northeast, told us something similar. Her clinic has a very small number of protesters only a handful of times per year. The protest isn't very effective, though. Margaret explained, "One of the nice things about being tucked inside of a hospital is nobody knows where we are. You can't tell because so many people go in and out, so it's very difficult to target us in here or know who our physicians or our patients might be."

Among clinic patients in the Turnaway Study, just over half said they did not see or hear protesters when they entered. For these women, in this regard, the act of entering the clinic was no different from the act of entering any other medical office.

But facilities that report no protesters are in the substantial minority, and almost half of women entering the clinics involved in the Turnaway Study reported seeing or hearing protesters. The Feminist Majority Foundation survey indicates that 23 percent of clinics have daily protests and almost 40 percent have weekly protests. The Turnaway Study had an even higher number among its clinics, with 70 percent saying that the protesters were almost always there. That over half of the Turnaway patients reported, after the fact, not seeing or hearing protesters is no doubt due to several factors, including what memories are retained from the day of their abortion and also the effectiveness of clinic escorts (discussed in more depth later in this chapter) in shielding the patients.

The Turnaway Study also asked about the aggressiveness of protesters. Of the 85 percent of facilities that reported protesters, slightly more than a third said that the protesters were aggressive, and just under half said that they were sometimes aggressive. Protesters are the most aggressive and most frequent in the Midwest and South and at high-volume clinics. Of the women in the same study, slightly under half reported encountering protesters, indicating that some women do not report encountering protesters even when they are there. A significant majority of women in the Midwest, Northeast, and South reported experiencing protesters (with almost three-quarters in the Midwest), while only 10 percent of women reported protesters in the West. While the Turnaway Study data reveal that more contact with protesters led to more upset patients, this contact did not change women's feelings about their abortion.

What happens when patients try to enter the roughly nine out of ten abortion clinics in this country that have protesters? While no one we talked with indicated that they had the same number of protesters as the largest protests in front of Hannah's clinics, many reported numbers that were nonetheless striking. For instance, Mary Lofton, a doctor who has provided abortions in a somewhat conservative northeastern state but now works in a very liberal western state, said that the protests were "much worse" in the western state, especially after anti-abortion extremists released deceptively edited videos about Planned Parenthood in the summer of 2015. Where she now works, there are many more protesters, with one to two hundred showing up on occasion.

Other clinics deal with just a small cadre of protesters. At Cindi Cranston's midwestern city-based clinic, where she works as an administrator, there are just a "few" protesters, but they are in front on a daily basis. "They know when we see patients and when we don't. There's a small group that's always there, and then they're joined by different groups from time to time."

Even clinics that have small numbers of regular protesters, like Cindi's, have to deal with an increased number during "Forty Days for Life." Forty Days, something almost everyone mentioned during our interviews, began as an everyday protest at abortion clinics around the country from Lent to Good Friday. Now it is a twice-a-year event, with the second forty-day stretch taking place in the fall. During this time, almost every clinic sees an increase in the number of protesters. Linda Johnston, a director for two clinics in the South, told us that during Forty Days one of her clinics that usually sees only a handful of protesters, with thirty to fifty at times, has seen up to two hundred.

Amid the tens to hundreds of people in front of abortion clinics confronting patients as they try to enter the building, there are different types of protesters. Elizabeth Wolff, an administrator at a southern clinic, described three different types who stand in front of her clinic. First, there are the "prayers." These protesters walk and pray in front of the clinic but generally mind their own business. Second, there are the people who consider themselves "sidewalk counselors." They approach patients and offer unsolicited help, though sometimes they can be quite aggressive in how they talk to patients. Third, there are the "haters." These protesters yell and do everything they can to intimidate patients. They show graphic photos, shout bloody descriptions of abortion, and call the patients terrible names. Their common refrain is that the patient is a "murderer" and is going to kill her baby. Donna Sullivan, who runs a different southern clinic, also differentiated between the "prayers," like the old Catholic priest who walks up and down the sidewalk in front of Donna's clinic praying the rosary, and the "screamers," protesters who stand in front of the clinic in a very visible location yelling and screaming at the patients as they enter the building as well as at people walking by on the city sidewalk.

Patients will sometimes see children among the adult protesters. Erica Valverde is a doctor who works for a clinic in a very religious conservative western state. At her clinic, the protesters pray more than harass, holding up signs that say "Pray to end abortion." After quipping, "So far I haven't seen any evidence that prayer actually ends abortion," Erica explained how the protesters frequently use their children: "The unnerving thing is that— as with many folks here—there are a lot of women who don't work because they're home taking care of their children, many times more than three children. I've seen them stand outside. So these are women standing outside with their children, also holding signs, but in forty-degree weather with rain and drizzle holding these signs. And I just think how are you going to judge somebody on parenting when you're standing outside for hours with your children in freezing cold rain? I don't understand the protesters."

Susan Smith, an administrator at a northeastern clinic, shares Erica's concerns about the children in front of her clinic. Susan's clinic is in a state that has very cold snowy winters. She explained that many of her clinic's protesters home-school their kids, so they bring their children to the clinic during the day to protest. She said the children, ranging from babies through teenagers, are in front of her clinic on a regular basis. Given where she lives, "In the fall it's one thing. But in the winter, it's really hard to see that because it's really cold and there are these kids out there for hours and hours at a time."

So much of how the protesters interact with patients depends on the clinic's layout. At one of the clinics where Vivian Walker, a doctor who practices in clinics in multiple midwestern states, works, there's a wide public sidewalk on a main city street right in front of the door. Patients must park at a little distance from the clinic and then walk on this sidewalk to get in. Although the protesters are generally, according to Vivian, not the most aggressive in the country, they are able to have an intimidating presence by lining both sides of the sidewalk so that patients have to walk through a corridor of protesters to get to the door. There's a similar layout at Susan Smith's clinic, so patients have to "walk through sort of a gauntlet of protesters on both sides of them." On what Susan calls a "good day," the patients are merely handed information and told not to go inside. On a "bad day," the protesters walk right up to the patients and yell and scream at them.

Contrast those stories to what takes place outside one of Naomi Rangel's clinics. Naomi owns several southern clinics in two different states, where almost all of the clinics have intense protester issues. However, one clinic is on private property and the protesters "can't come near us," Naomi said. "It's in a beautiful building, about 7,100 square feet. You go through this gorgeous atrium to get into the clinic. There's a number of different offices there, so the protesters never know which one someone is going into. It's also far back off the road." As a result, though there are sometimes four or five protesters, they stand on the sidewalk far from the clinic where the patients and workers can't see them. "We're just real fortunate we don't have any issues there."

Frances Easton is an administrator in charge of two clinics, one in the Midwest and one in the South. The layout of her midwestern clinic forces the one or two dozen protesters to stay on the sidewalk that rings the clinic. "They can't come on our property, so that's typically where they stand. They're just surrounding the clinic and our parking lot. And we have like three driveways if you're trying to access the clinic depending which way you're coming from. They typically will try to block those off, which is illegal, but eventually they'll move in enough time where there's nothing you can really do about it."

For patients who arrive by car, as Frances's description demonstrates, being in an enclosed vehicle doesn't offer complete protection. Shelly Jones, an abortion advocate who works in a southern state, explained that, at one of the clinics in her state, patients park in a lot that is shared by the crisis pregnancy center, which has a building directly across the parking lot. The pregnancy center allows the protesters onto the private parking lot, so they can get right next to the patients' cars and confront them with a "full court press, where they're hovering around them until they make it to the public sidewalk, where the security guards help the patients get into the clinic." At the midwestern clinic where Nellie Baker is the doctor and lead administrator, there are two driveways into a small parking lot. The protesters, who number up to fifteen or twenty at a time, stand at both driveways so they can "harass" the patients as they enter the parking lot. When a patient gets out of her car, the protesters then can get within five to ten feet of the patient without being on the parking lot property. From that distance, they yell and scream at the patients trying to stop them from going inside to get an abortion.

One of the most nefarious tactics we were told about in our interviews related to protesters interacting with patients in cars. Megan Siple is a doctor at a northeastern clinic that has a core group of religious Catholic protesters. According to Megan, the protesters there are "more subdued" than the "fire and brimstone" protesters at other clinics, but they are constantly outside trying to "upset the patients." One of the tactics they use is to march across the sidewalk that is part of the driveway for the clinic's parking lot, which is not at all unusual, as the previous stories indicate. The unusual tactic is that they "wait for the patient to bring their car in, and then they tap on the car window and they hold a clipboard so they look like they're an official person. They want to get the patient's name down." Caught off guard, the patients comply and wind up giving their names to the protesters. Megan called this tactic a "subtle" but "effective" invasion of patient privacy because, whether the protesters use this information to further harass the patient or not, just the act of taking this information can be intimidating.

Invasion of patient privacy is par for the course. At some clinics, this involves taking photos or video of the patients entering the clinic. At one of Naomi Range's clinics, one of the protesters stands on a nine-foot ladder using his phone's camera to take pictures of the women going inside. At other clinics, several of the people we interviewed told us about protesters using GoPro cameras to record video of the patients. At the clinic Edna Macklin runs in a southern state, one of the most vocal protesters uses his GoPro to lure patients into talking to him. Before patients come to the clinic, Edna and her staff try "desperately" to tell them to ignore this protester when they try to enter. They even put up a sign that Edna acknowledges probably is not very nice: "Please Ignore This Idiot." However, Edna told us that "people in the South just want to be friendly," so many of her patients wind up talking with this protester on camera. Inevitably, the video recordings of the conversations are then posted to Facebook for the world to see.

Patients are most at risk of being harassed when entering; by the time patients are done with their appointments, most of the people we interviewed told us that the protesters have generally left. However, Vanessa Barrett, who runs a clinic in the Northeast, explained that the protesters at her clinic have a second wave when the patients are leaving, a "more wild crowd." With the luxury of a supportive crisis pregnancy center across the walkway, the protesters are able to lie in wait:

> The protesters seem to be really giving the patients a hard time postabortion. They've got cameras set up that point directly at our doors, and they try to catch people as they're leaving the building. They'll come running out of their building and try to talk to people as they're leaving. It's been very surprising to us. Now that doesn't mean—and I'm not saying that they're not there before too. They definitely are. But these people seem to be focusing right now more on after. Between fifteen and seventy-five will show up on Saturdays at around ten o'clock in the morning, when almost all of our patients have checked in. And they'll be out there in droves, and they'll be in our clinic escorts' and our volunteers' faces, and they'll really be out there giving the escorts and the patients as they're leaving a really hard time and talking about murder, and they're just really loud and vocal.

Patients that Douglas Laube, a doctor in the Midwest, sees also can encounter protesters after their procedure. But he reminded us that not all patients are intimidated by the protesters and that some show real spunk and resilience in the face of being harassed. One patient he recalled was confronted upon leaving the clinic by a protester saying, "Please don't kill your baby." Douglas told us, "She yelled back, 'Sorry, it's too late!'"

When protesters get the opportunity to interact with patients, what they do and say isn't all that original. In fact, Pat Earle, a clinic worker and support person in a southern state, "swears they have the same script." They shout at patients, "Don't kill your baby," "Why do you want to murder your baby," or "You always remember the child you didn't have." Megan Siple told us a few others, such as "You're a mother," "Protect your baby," and "We have help available." Emily Webb, an administrator who runs multiple clinics in a midwestern state, described similar messages and more—"Mommies, don't kill your babies," "Good Christians don't do this," and "You're crying, you're clearly not sure about your decision." Not only are these messages shouted to patients entering the clinic, but they are also chalked onto the sidewalk in front of her clinic. To male companions, as Shelley Sella, a doctor who has practiced in the West and Midwest, described, protesters scream, "Daddy, Daddy, don't kill me."

Patients also frequently face protesters handing them leaflets. Many of the people we interviewed described these. They can be anything from pamphlets that give false information about abortion, such as its connection to breast cancer or depression, to advertisements for crisis pregnancy centers, to brochures about the sanctity of the fetus.

One of the common refrains among protesters is to talk about patients' identities, particularly their race. At the northeastern clinic where Mary Badame has worked in almost every capacity, protesters have a sign that says "Unborn Black Lives Matter," playing off the anti–police violence slogan of "Black Lives Matter." Nellie Baker also explained how the mostly white protesters frequently talk about the patient's race. "They like to talk a lot about how black women shouldn't be having abortions. They yell at a lot of our black patients about how you're killing your own people and this is genocide and how can you do this? And then if someone is white, a lot of times they kind of get into this whole like, 'This is just like Nazi Germany and you're killing all the Jews' and all these things. So they do a lot of talk about how you're killing your own people and murdering people." Nellie explained further: "It's not just 'Don't have an abortion.' They're actually saying things directed to the patient's race or how they look."

Kendra Farrell, a counselor at a southern clinic, notices the same thing. The protesters are mainly white and frequently yell at black women, "Don't kill your black baby." Occasionally there's a group of Hispanic protesters who spend the day yelling in Spanish at anyone who looks Latina. Kendra lamented that "it's terrible what they do." Emily Webb described something similar with Muslim patients. Her clinic is near a large Muslim community. One of the protesters is a Christian from a majority-Muslim country. Whenever the protesters see a patient who may be Muslim, such as a woman in a hijab, they shout, "Incoming Muslims!" so he can target them in Arabic. As Emily explained, "Whatever they see as a weakness, they'll try to exploit."

Pat Earle's location provides a unique backdrop for the racialized harassment her patients face. The clinic is located in a historic location for the civil rights movement. The protesters "appropriate" that and shout things like "Martin Luther King Jr. or Malcolm X would roll over in his grave." Dawn Clay, who is part of an escort group in the South, told us that patients entering the clinic where she works also hear this kind of racial-ized harassment frequently. She told us that "this can be one of the most emotional days of their life anyway," so that adding on racist attacks can make the situation much worse. Some patients just laugh and roll their eyes, with the attitude of "I hear this all the time." But Dawn told us that "every once in a while somebody will just kind of melt into tears and it's very obvious that it's had an emotional impact."

As in Hannah Miller's story that started this chapter, using sound amplification to frighten patients is a regular occurrence at other clinics as well. One of the clinics where Emily Webb works has seen a recent serious uptick in protest activity. A national figure in the anti-abortion movement has begun to target Emily's clinic by appearing regularly and "making a spectacle." The spectacle includes speakers that allow his voice to reach across the open parking lot and into the clinic, where everyone inside can hear. At Pat Earle's clinic, there's a local law that says that protesters can-not use bullhorns, so instead one of the most vocal protesters uses "little toy megaphones that you would find in little kids' cheerleading play sets." He has also used a really large megaphone that was all white, like the "old cheerleader varsity ones." The protester used that on a regular basis until one day the clinic escorts pointed out that the white megaphone made it look like he was "yelling through a KKK hat." Since then, the protester hasn't brought the megaphone back.

For patients venturing into their medical appointment, this can amount to an almost circus-like atmosphere. Rebecca Moore, the lead administra-tor for several clinics in multiple western states, used that exact word to describe the atmosphere outside one of her centrally located clinics—"a circus" that has gotten worse ever since the 2016 election. Besides the larger numbers of people protesting and the usual gruesome and stigma-tizing signs that patients must confront, the protesters have begun to litter the street with stuffed animals and to hang baby dolls by their necks from the trees that border the clinic. Rebecca called the overall effect of these tactics "ghastly" and "ghoulish." Patients and staff, in order to get into the clinic, now "have to drive through this littered field of little furry animals" and dolls hanging from trees.

In another one of Rebecca's clinics in a different state, every year around Easter, a large group of men gather around the clinic, dressed in biblically themed gowns and robes. They circle the block, singing and carrying tablets for a few hours. Rebecca described the costumes involved as "quite something." Something similar occurs outside the southern clinic that Sylvia Raskin runs. She reports that the twenty-five to one hundred vocal protesters who show up on Saturdays are joined by a priest once a month. He not only joins the protesters who are holding up "frightening and medically inaccurate" signs but also sets up an altar and stages a mass outside the clinic. In front of the northeastern clinic where Judith Casella works, the five or six people who protest on a regular basis use a bevy of religious props to confront patients right up to the front door—crosses, flowers, baby carriages, rosaries, and more.

Religious services in front of clinics are common, as are funerals. On some Sundays outside one of Naomi Rangel's clinics, there are almost two hundred protesters. They march up and down the street and then stage a mock funeral, with a wooden box as the casket for all the dead babies. Naomi described the scene as "very morbid." Billie Taylor, who runs a clinic in a northeastern state, told us about a similar annual funeral march in front of her clinic "with white little caskets and rose petals and about five to six hundred people."

The circus atmosphere can also include subjecting patients to harassment using a variety of media. At one of the clinics where Mary Lofton works, a new extremist anti-abortion group appeared across the street with a tent from which they played anti-abortion videos at loud volume directed at the entrance of the clinic. The people standing beside the video tent were aggressive and caused many disturbances. After legal wrangling about property rights, the group was forced to leave.

And things can be even stranger. At one of the southern clinics where Andrea Ferrigno works as an administrator, there is a family medicine doctor who works in a building next door. This doctor is vehemently anti-abortion and lets the world know it. He has "all kinds of crazy banners" hanging from his office expressing his views about abortion. If any of Andrea's patients are confused and park by accident in the other doctor's parking lot, this doctor will tow them. Andrea and her colleagues have tried to talk with the doctor, but he has refused to stop. Instead, he allows the protesters to park in his lot so they can stand there and shout at the abortion patients. But Andrea's clinic had the last laugh about this doctor's anti-abortion antics. He has a huge sign on his building with a big red arrow pointing at Andrea's clinic saying "Abortion Clinic." Of course, his intent is to shame the clinic, but instead Andrea and her coworkers "find it hilarious, because so many patients find us because of that arrow. It's really funny. 'How did you hear about us?' 'I saw the big arrow.' And we're like, 'Oh, excellent!'"

Making the chaos outside some clinics even worse for patients, many of the people we interviewed described conflict between anti-abortion groups protesting in front. Jennifer Pride, an administrator at a relatively new clinic in a southern state, explained that there is a new national anti-abortion group headquartered in a nearby suburb. That group is one of the most extreme in the country, believing in abolition of abortion at any cost. There is another long-standing group that often protests in front of Jennifer's clinic and is more moderate, believing in an incremental approach to ending abortion. When the two groups are in front of the clinic, they don't get along and increase the tension. The new extreme group has even taken to yelling at a local nun who quietly prays in front of the clinic. As Jennifer told the story, "Basically, because the nun comes and prays the rosary outside, they were yelling at her that praying wouldn't do any good, that she needed to take action, and she was saying, 'Oh, I'm not involved with these people.'"

BEING A PATIENT AMID THE CHAOS

The situation at one of Emily Webb's midwestern clinics perfectly captures how this chaos affects patients. Emily is a second-generation abortion provider who grew up watching her parents deal with terrifying threats and harassment from anti-abortion extremists. Ever since the election of President Donald Trump, the protest activity outside the clinic she manages has grown in intensity. Compounding the problem, some national anti-abortion figures have recently latched onto Emily's clinic and drawn attention to it.

As a result, Emily and her colleagues have installed privacy landscaping, such as trees to block the view from the public walkways, as well as black tarp in their fencing. Although these steps have been effective in blocking the protesters from where they had previously been standing, according to Emily, these actions "have really made them very angry." Now, without being able to spread out around the facility, the protesters are instead gathering in large numbers right around the driveway and the street leading to it, doing everything they can to impede traffic entering the clinic. According to Emily, the protesters stop cars turning onto the side street where the driveway is located and put their hands on cars as they turn into the parking lot. The protesters play videos, yell over a speaker, and record patients entering on a GoPro.

> It's terrorizing. They feel harassed and threatened. We try to keep patients calm and get them in the clinic, but it's a constant battle. Yesterday was Wednesday and we had thirty patients scheduled, but we had only fifteen patients come in. We're like, "Oh God, is this because of the protesters?" We're just hoping that it's not a correlation, but we don't know. I do believe it is psychologically damaging to them. I mean, they're already dealing with so much. We try to keep our clinic so peaceful and beautiful, and we want it to be a place of warmth. To have to drive through this gauntlet that hates you is disgusting.

Emily also shared with us copies of forms that her clinic has recently started asking patients to fill out anonymously about the protesters and their effect on the patients' visits. These forms are harrowing to read. In them, patients detail protesters screaming at them, calling them names, jumping in front of their cars and refusing to move, throwing pamphlets into open car windows, recording faces by video, offering to adopt the patient's child or pay for her pregnancy care, preaching at them, and, in one instance, calling out the patient by name over the speaker system the protesters had erected. A small number of patients indicated they were able to ignore the protesters, but the vast majority explained in detail how upset the protesters made them.

The common themes were immediately apparent in reviewing these forms. Many of the patients expressed deep anger and hatred toward the protesters. One of the patients said that the protesters were so "rude" that she "wanted to slap them," while another patient supporter said that the protesters are "horrid people" and he felt "like punching them in the face." Others said that the protesters made them feel embarrassed and horrible.

One such patient said that she felt "even more embarrassed than I already am" and that the protesters "don't help [because] they make you feel like scum."

Similarly, other patients described feeling nervous and fearful. One patient who said that the driveway was blocked by protesters with cameras said that she was nervous because she didn't want them taking her picture. Another patient, who had to stop her car at the driveway in order to avoid hitting the protesters, was surprised that the lead protester knew her name and that she went to Catholic school. After he then said that she was going to die and that "today could be the day God takes [you] before his presence," she said that she was scared. A third patient said that the presence of the protesters and the police trying to control the protesters made her feel "unsafe." To her, "Everything was unclear [because] there seemed to be so many people shouting. It made me very nervous."

Many patients were also upset that the protesters were invading their privacy and trying to control their choices without knowing their lives. These patients called the protesters "judgmental" and "ignorant." One said that the protesters "have no idea why certain people come here," while another said they were "disrespectful" because "they have no clue what is going on in people's lives to be walking up to people giving their opinions." Several specifically said what the protesters were doing was an "invasion of privacy."

Other providers we interviewed also described how varied patients' reactions are to the chaos and protest in front of the clinic. Jada Curry, a nurse and administrator at a midwestern clinic, explained the different reactions she sees from patients:

> There are some patients who really, it doesn't bother them at all. Then you have patients that it really, really bothers them and they really take it hard. I mean, they even don't want to come back in for a follow-up visit or a sexual health visit, in fear of seeing the protesters again. And then some patients feel like they have to talk to the protesters, or they're already struggling with their decisions and they feel that they should talk to them. And then they come in, and I've seen people that have even been just crying hysterically.

Elizabeth Wolff summed up patients' reactions well: "Some of them get mad, some of them cry, some of them are able to completely stonewall it. It just depends on the patient and where she is that day."

Emily's, Jada's, and Elizabeth's observations are consistent with the results of the small number of studies that have looked at this issue. As noted earlier, the Turnaway Study talked with women about how protest outside the clinic affected them. The women in the study who noticed protesters in any way—seeing, hearing, or being stopped by them—were about evenly split over whether the protesters bothered them. Just over half reported being upset by the protesters, with some saying they were "extremely" upset.

Older and smaller studies of abortion patients showed similar results—that many women, though not all, have negative reactions to the ways that anti-abortion protesters act outside clinics. One of those studies completed in 2000 interviewed almost 450 women and concluded that, although the women varied greatly, "on average, they seemed to find these encounters unpleasant" and were "negatively affected by them in the short term." International studies of anti-abortion protesters show very similar results.

These intense emotional reactions just from trying to get into a medical clinic are bad enough, but they are even worse when coupled with physical reactions. These are not uncommon and can be quite serious. For instance, one of the patient forms Emily Webb shared with us had a page of "add-on notes" from clinic staff. The notes indicate the following (with "pt" being shorthand for "patient" and "apt" for "appointment"): "When checking in for an apt, pt stated that a protester tried to jump onto the hood of her car. Pt stated this while having her labwork done as well. Patient appeared very upset by this." The note also indicates that the patient had high blood pressure when examined, complicating her medical care. Research in other medical settings confirms that patients who experience emotional stress immediately prior to a medical procedure suffer from greater pain and risk of complications.

Reactions to protesters can undermine patients' medical care in other ways as well. Jada Curry told us that her patient counseling sessions can sometimes be more difficult after the patient encounters protesters. "They have been so anxious or they're so upset about the encounter that they just have a harder time hearing all of the teaching and all of the information that they're getting here in the clinic. They just really sort of say, 'Tell me where to sign and I just want to get out of here.' Because they felt so targeted by protesters and just shook up by it all."

The Turnaway Study found that the small proportion of women who had a more difficult time deciding to have an abortion were more upset by protesters than women for whom the decision was easier. Kendra Farrell has noticed the same thing when she counsels women.

> There's just so many different reasons why a woman may be conflicted with making this choice, and just coming here and having to deal with all of this unnecessary paperwork or meeting the protesters outside that are judging them, it just makes the decision even more difficult to make for a lot of them when it shouldn't have to. Nobody should have to be met with a judgment because of a choice that they need to make that's best for them, or the mom who was excited about being pregnant, happy about bringing a new life to the world, and they go to their two-month checkup and find out it's a nonviable pregnancy. They're met outside with protesters and are being judged and they don't even want to be here at all. So you have those women that struggle with that.

In an odd twist, some patients blame the abortion clinic for the protesters. Cindi Cranston explained that her clinic has patients fill out a patient satisfaction survey about what the clinic could do to improve. Every year, the number one or number two answer is to "get rid of the protesters." She said that some patients understand that there's very little the clinic can do but that others "don't know why we can't protect them." They write things like, "Why would you allow this?" or "Why on earth would you not tell these guys to get out of here?" One of the studies of protesters' effects on patients reported a similar response from one of the people interviewed: "[The patient] was confused about whether the clinic itself was supportive of abortion generally and of her decision to have an abortion specifically, and understood the protester presence to be evidence that clinic workers did not care about protecting patients like her."

For a particular group of patients—sexual assault survivors—the attacks and invasion of privacy from the protesters can be especially troublesome. In 2013, the Victim Rights Law Center and thirty-nine other individuals and organizations wrote a brief to the Supreme Court explaining how traumatizing it is for sexual assault survivors to deal with abortion clinic protesters. The brief noted that rape results in over thirty-two thousand pregnancies every year in this country. A sizable portion of those victims seek services at abortion facilities, whether for an abortion or for other counseling that can be provided. This population is particularly vulnerable to the protesters because of the extreme trauma they have suffered. As the brief explained, "Rape victims often feel shame and fear, suffer from post-traumatic stress disorder, panic attacks, flashbacks, and depression, and are at an increased risk of suicide." When protesters harass and intimidate patients in this state, the effects described above can be even worse. Their "need for privacy, physical integrity, and personal security" is compromised by the protesters' behavior, making a terrible situation even worse and even running the risk that some victims won't enter the clinic at all.

The entirety of the emotions can be overwhelming for some patients, whether they are sexual assault survivors or not. Jan Dancy, a patient advocate in a northeastern state, can relate. As a patient advocate, Jan is not going through the same experience as the patient. While the patient is pregnant, "I'm always meeting with someone as a body that is not pregnant." However, Jan and the patient always have the protesters in common because "we actually both went through that," with Jan experiencing it on an almost everyday basis. This forms a common bond, especially as the protest has become more "racialized" and "aggressive" in recent years, according to Jan. Jan is Black, like many of the patients at the clinic. For many of the patients, Jan empathizes with how upset and "flabbergasted" they are. Some just "can't believe that this happens in this country and don't let go. They bring it up during the ultrasound, lab work, nursing evaluation, even as they are going to sleep for the procedure or waking up in recovery. They're still talking about the people outside."

PROTECTION THROUGH BUFFER ZONES

In the face of this kind of activity and its effect on patients, one of the approaches some states and localities have tried is enacting a buffer zone. A buffer zone is a fixed distance from clinic entrances—the doorways if the entrance is on a public sidewalk and the driveways if the entrance is from a private parking lot—or property lines where the protesters are prohibited. So, for instance, a thirty-foot buffer zone would mean that no protester could be within thirty feet of the abortion clinic's entrances. State legislatures or local city councils can enact these, or sometimes courts can impose buffer zones as an injunction at the end of litigation against protesters.

A similar but less common tactic is a no-approach or bubble zone. These requirements, less strict than buffer zones, set an area where protesters can be but where patients cannot be approached. Bubble zones can also protect a certain amount of space around a patient. For example, an eight-foot bubble zone in a one-hundred-foot no-approach area would mean that within one hundred feet of the clinic's entrance no protester can get within eight feet of a patient.

These kinds of zones around clinics have many positive effects for the clinic and its patients. Although there have been no peer-reviewed published studies to date about the impact of buffer zones, surveys of abortion clinics have shown that buffer zones improve law enforcement response, decrease violence and harassment, and increase abortion clinic access. In one survey of National Abortion Federation members, three-quarters of facilities with buffer zones responded that the zones improved access to the clinic for patients and staff.

Deborah Levin's experience with a buffer zone is indicative of the benefits. Deborah has been a volunteer clinic escort in the same northeastern city for almost three decades. In that role, as described in depth in the next section below, Deborah's job is to walk with patients as they approach and help them navigate entering the clinic. She and other volunteer escorts try to distract the patients from the protesters and help them remain calm.

In the mid-2000s, the city where Deborah escorts enacted a small buffer zone. Having escorted for more than a decade before the buffer zone and now more than a decade afterwards, Deborah has an excellent vantage point from which to evaluate its effect. Her conclusion was unequivocal: "This is so much better. It's just a zillion percent better for the patients."

Before the zone was enacted, it was chaos at the front door. One of the clinics where Deborah escorted would see up to one hundred or more anti-abortion protesters on Saturdays. Most of them would be praying, but several would very aggressively harass the patients. Deborah described the situation by starting with the clinic layout:

> It was a doorway immediately inside of which was a staircase up to the clinic on the second floor. Between the door and the stairway was where the guard

sat, and there wasn't very much space at all. The door was not opaque, nor was it soundproof. There was a pane of glass in it. When the patients would come in, the protesters would crowd around the outside of the doorway. They would scream at the patients. So really, there was hardly anything in between them and the patients except for us escorts.

There was always pushing and shoving and maneuvering for position, and sometimes they would bring bullhorns, sometimes they would bring huge signs, those huge gory signs that they would hold up. If one patient was actually getting checked in, it was bad enough. If multiple patients arrived around the same time, we can't let them in all at once to respect the privacy of each patient. So while one group was getting checked in, the other group would have to stand outside in that doorway with nothing but us in between them and the antis, and people got really freaked out, frightened, angry, and understandably so.

We escorts would try to distract them from the ugly things that were being shouted at them before the buffer zone came along. And we would have to put our bodies between people and sometimes that was a little fraught.

At the other clinic where Deborah escorted, the situation was even worse. At that clinic, which was more centrally located in the city, there would be upwards of three to five hundred protesters forming a gauntlet for patients to walk through. "The cops would make people form lines so that the patients could actually walk down the sidewalk, but it didn't work particularly well. It was always this threatening mass of people, a huge number of people blocking the sidewalks, interfering with traffic, and interfering with people trying to go about their regular business downtown."

Everything is different with the buffer zone, which "has worked absolutely brilliantly." The central difference is that there is a now a "space in which patients can enter before they get to the clinic door that is at a physical distance from the antis." According to Deborah, with the protesters now over ten feet from the clinic entrance, "It's just so much less frightening for the patients."

To enforce the buffer zone, the city has painted a line at both clinics that demarcates where the protesters can't cross. The buffer zone doesn't stop the protesters altogether, as they still congregate at that line, continuing to approach the patients before they cross and to yell at them afterwards. But because the buffer zone goes into the street at one location the entire area in front of the doorway is clear of protesters. Also, the escorts stand along the buffer zone line forming a "wall" that keeps the protesters away from the patients. Overall, according to Deborah, "The patients now have the same experience as they approach the clinic, of course, but the antis have to stop at a certain point and that seems to ease the tension quite a bit, especially for people who are waiting outside to be checked in. They know that nobody is going to get right up on them. So yeah, it's really made even a bigger difference than we could've anticipated."

Other providers we talked with had similarly positive things to say about buffer zones. Jen Castle, a nurse practitioner who has worked in multiple northeastern states, told us that the buffer zone in one of the states where she worked "was relieving for everyone because the protesters weren't right in people's faces going in the door. They were pushed back to a place that felt safer for everybody." The city where Susan Smith worked had a buffer zone that produced a notable difference with her patients. According to Susan, without the buffer zone, the patients enter the clinic "agitated" because they are swarmed on the sidewalk. With the buffer zone, the patients complain much less about the protesters, so Susan and her colleagues can start the patient's visit by addressing the care the patient needs rather than talking about the protesters.

Unfortunately, the Supreme Court's most recent case on the matter has made it much more difficult to have a buffer zone. In the 2014 case of *McCullen v. Coakley*, the Court addressed a Massachusetts thirty-five-foot buffer zone around reproductive health care facilities. In a brief to the Court, Planned Parenthood detailed the history of violence, harassment, and obstruction that had taken place outside clinics in Massachusetts before the buffer zone, including a shooter murdering two abortion providers and injuring five others in 1994. After the buffer zone was enacted, according to the brief, protests outside the clinics continued, but the atmosphere outside was "much more orderly" with fewer confrontations.

Despite this evidence, the Supreme Court unanimously struck down the buffer zone as a violation of the protesters' First Amendment rights to free speech. According to the Court, the state of Massachusetts hadn't shown enough of a justification that would warrant restricting speech in this serious of a manner. However, the Court confused the situation by saying nothing about whether an earlier decision in 2000 that approved a Colorado zone was still good law. In the earlier case, the Court approved Colorado's eight-foot bubble zone within a one-hundred-foot buffer zone. The Court concluded that this zone was not overly broad and that it protected Colorado's legitimate interest in protecting abortion patients and clinics. After the Court's 2014 decision, lower courts and state and local jurisdictions now have to determine whether a buffer zone is too broad, like the one struck down in Massachusetts, or whether it is narrow enough to survive, like the presumably still-standing precedent from the Colorado case.

This has been a difficult task, and many jurisdictions have voluntarily decided that they are no longer going to enforce buffer zones rather than risk being sued after *McCullen*. Other jurisdictions have fought to keep their buffer zones, but the overall result is that many fewer places around the country now have them.

Judith Casella, a clinic administrator, talked with us at length about what it means when a buffer zone is taken away. Judith has worked at the same clinic for over two decades. Before the buffer zone, her clinic had suffered from violence and harassment. The protesters were able to approach the patients right up to the entrance and "be right in their face" with signs, yelling, and even pushing.

According to Judith, the buffer zone created a "sanctuary around the clinic." She and her colleagues were able to tell patients on the phone that once they got past the buffer zone "they were going to be safe and they weren't going to be harassed." The buffer zone was large enough that in one direction it pushed the protesters into the middle of a very busy street. As a result, the protesters were discouraged from congregating in such large numbers. Now, with the buffer zone off the books after the Supreme Court decision, the protesters once again have access to the patients as they are entering the clinic, creating a more confrontational experience. They have gone back to violating the patients' space and harassing them for their decision to access medical care. The experience for patients is once again, in Judith's words, "scary and pushy and frightening."

TURNING DOWN THE VOLUME

Another way that legislatures or courts can protect patients entering clinics is through a noise ordinance. Many localities have general noise ordinances, unrelated to abortion clinics or health centers. However, some places have enacted them in direct response to the needs of patients entering abortion clinics. Courts have also imposed noise restrictions following litigation against protesters for harassing patients or clinics.

Noise ordinances and injunctions can take many forms. Sometimes they prohibit noise that goes above a certain decibel reading. Others prohibit amplification devices, such as bullhorns or loudspeakers. Still others just impose a vague requirement of reasonableness or against disturbing the peace. Some apply broadly anywhere in a city, others just within a certain distance of a medical facility.

Sylvia Raskin's clinic was instrumental in her southern city passing a noise ordinance. Sylvia explained that after her clinic was burned to the ground by anti-abortion protesters in the mid-2000s, her city council unanimously passed a buffer zone to protect the clinic. However, the protesters challenged it in federal court and won. Rather than appeal the case, the city and Sylvia worked together to pass a noise ordinance that applied to all health care facilities.

At the time, Sylvia's clinic was being bombarded by noise from the anti-abortion protesters. They were screaming through bullhorns, which clinic patients and staff could hear inside the building. Sylvia said, "It was just terrible." She hoped that highlighting her patients' experiences would help get this proposed ordinance passed:

> What ultimately worked for us was to have five physicians attend the commission meeting to testify about the real impact that the noise was having on our patients' health and safety. Speaking to the commission was an orthopedist, an ophthalmologist, an anesthesiologist, and two ob-gyns who discussed what the risks were. They explained the effect that noise has on increasing anxiety and raising blood pressure. These factors can lead to the patient needing more sedation, which can increase risks. The physicians helped the commissioners understand the importance of having a quiet area surrounding all health care facilities.
>
> This ordinance was challenged by the protesters, and then we went back to the city commission with a physician who was the former president of the state ob-gyn organization. He presented extensive global medical research on the negative impact of loud noise on providing safe patient care. The issue really resonated with the commissioners in understanding what was at stake.

Now, in Sylvia's city, there's a noise ordinance around all medical facilities that prohibits sound amplification within one hundred feet. Sylvia has seen how the ordinance has helped patients. Protesters still yell and harass them, but without the use of megaphones and loudspeakers.

The northeastern state where Susan Smith works has a noise ordinance in place, but it doesn't have defined parameters. Instead, it just prohibits interfering with the delivery of health care through noise. Susan said that this has been difficult to enforce because the protesters quiet down once the police show up, then get louder again when they leave. One particular protester stands right outside the door to the clinic and, with a naturally loud voice that carries very well, yells repeatedly into the clinic, knowing that patients can hear him. Susan described the effect: "It is very audible within our health center. So when we're sitting down with patients trying to educate them on the risks and benefits of the procedure, how to take care of themselves after, it is a real distraction to them. The people doing the counseling let me know that it's really loud or that patients are having a hard time focusing."

After many attempts, Susan's clinic was finally able to persuade the police to cite this very loud protester under the local noise ordinance. In response, he sued the city for violating his First Amendment rights. Just before we interviewed Susan, the city's citation was upheld by an appeals court, which found that the law is neutral and leaves open sufficient alternative methods of communication; thus, it did not violate the protester's freedom of speech. Since the decision, Susan said that the protesters have been "a lot quieter" because the city is finally enforcing the law when the clinic or its patients complain.

Like the law in Susan's state, noise ordinances that have been applied against anti-abortion protesters have fared well in courts. In 1994, the Supreme Court addressed the issue in a Florida case involving a court-imposed injunction that prohibited excessive noise outside a clinic that patients could hear inside the clinic. In doing so, the Court addressed the concerns about patients and noise that Sylvia and Susan expressed to us:

> Noise control is particularly important around hospitals and medical facilities during surgery and recovery periods, and in evaluating another injunction involving a medical facility, we stated: "Hospitals, after all, are not factories or mines or assembly plants. They are hospitals, where human

ailments are treated, where patients and relatives alike often are under emotional strain and worry, where pleasing and comforting patients are princi-
pal facets of the day's activity, and where the patient and his family . . . need
a restful, uncluttered, relaxing, and helpful atmosphere." We hold that the
limited noise restrictions imposed by the state court order burden no more
speech than necessary to ensure the health and well-being of the patients at
the clinic. The First Amendment does not demand that patients at a medical
facility undertake herculean efforts to escape the cacophony of political protests. If overamplified loudspeakers assault the citizenry, government may
turn them down.

Since 1994, the Supreme Court has not limited this precedent, and lower
courts have used it to uphold noise ordinances that aim to help patients,
including those going into abortion clinics.

WHAT ELSE LAW CAN DO

When there's no buffer zone or noise ordinance to help patients trying to
enter a clinic, other laws can help. The most directly applicable is the
Freedom of Access to Clinic Entrances Act, a federal law passed in 1994.
FACE, as the law is known, prohibits intimidation or violence against
abortion providers and patients. Because of difficulty in enforcement, this
aspect of the law has had mixed success.

The part of the law that has been incredibly successful is the prohibition of blockades. Before FACE, a common anti-abortion tactic was to
have massive numbers of protesters not just make the front of a clinic difficult to wade through but to actually block the entrance. Operation
Rescue popularized this tactic in the late 1980s and early 1990s with
blockades that involved people chaining themselves to clinic front doors,
parking cars in front of clinic entrances, refusing to move when ordered to
by local police, and more. Now that FACE is in place, the kinds of protests
described in this chapter remain very common, but clinic blockades are
less frequent events than they were before FACE.

Beyond FACE, clinics often rely on generally applicable criminal law to
protect patients entering the building. General criminal laws, such as
those prohibiting trespassing, harassment, assault, battery, terroristic
threats, and disturbing the peace, can be helpful. Local ordinances, such

as those that regulate public signs, distribution of pamphlets, protest permits, and impeding traffic can also help.

Using these laws has mixed results, largely dependent on how supportive
the police department, prosecutor's office, and local judiciary are. Rebecca
Moore has experienced the difficulties at one of her clinics. The police are
generally supportive. "They'll show up, and they'll keep an eye on things,
and it'll cause the noise to go down." But, Rebecca told us, if the protesters
violate the law, the police often don't bother charging them with a crime. "I
know they think, 'Should I spend my time writing up this guy for this infrac-
tion when I know that if I haul him down there, there's not a serious penalty
to this?'" The district attorney has told Rebecca that doing so wastes the
city's resources, so has done nothing; however, the year we interviewed
Rebecca, the city had a new district attorney. Rebecca is optimistic, especially since the new prosecutor has agreed to visit the clinic to see the protest situation for herself. The new mayor also visited the clinic during a
heavy protest time so he could personally experience what the patients have
to go through. The experience was "really powerful," especially because the
mayor is African American. "When he came in they just blasted him with
horrible, racist epithets, so he really got a taste of how bad they can be."

Providers who have good responses from local authorities have put this
kind of personal engagement into the effort. Rebecca isn't the only one
who has asked police and politicians to come visit the clinic to see the
protesters in action; several others that we interviewed have deployed the
same tactic. Pat Earle stressed how important it is for the clinic to have a
relationship with the police "before anything happens." When a national
extremist group announced plans to target Pat's clinic, Pat met with the
police months beforehand and walked them through what to expect with
this type of a group. By doing so, she was able to have the police department "get on board with me" and realize the seriousness of the situation.
Diana Sharpe, a counselor and administrator who works for multiple
northeastern clinics, lauded a unique unit of one city's local police that
specializes in protest situations. They aren't always perfect, but because
the clinic has had a relationship with them for years they are generally
responsive and know how to handle situations that arise.

Those who have not been successful developing a good relationship
with the authorities suffer. Hannah Miller, whose troubled clinic's story is

detailed at the start of this chapter, is disheartened by the local police. When they appear at the clinic during mass protests, it's "obvious" to Hannah and her colleagues that they don't want to be there, and they do nothing more than the minimum to keep the peace. Melody Cook, a nurse who is the director and co-owner of a southern clinic, said that it's an "ongoing fight" to get the police concerned about the protesters obstructing traffic into and out of her clinic. She said that she and her colleagues "call the police repeatedly" but have never found a way to get the police to do anything other than show up. Melody finds the situation frustrating and even got into an argument with one police officer over the situation. "He was unhappy with us calling for what he perceived to not be a problem, and I had to repeatedly ask him to please talk to the protesters about obstructing traffic." He finally did, but Melody said no arrests were made or citations issued, and the problem persists.

VOLUNTEERS PUTTING THEIR BODIES ON THE LINE

Because of the lack of laws to address these issues and difficult relationships with law enforcement, many clinics with protester problems receive community support from volunteer escorts. Escorts like Deborah Levin, whose story about the buffer zone is featured above, help patients get through the protesters in front of the building and into the clinic. Kathleen Anderson and Sylvia Raskin work at the same southern clinic and described what the escorts do to help patients. Kathleen explained how the escorts stand outside, wearing T-shirts and vests identifying themselves, and "greet the patients with a smile," walking them through the protesters and comforting them by "making them feel like we're on your team and we're going to protect you." Sylvia said that the patients, once inside, often remark "how nice it was to have somebody in the parking lot to buffer the screaming and harassing aggressive people on the other side."

There has been little research about the effect of escorts, and the one study that exists is from over two decades ago. In that study, researchers talked with patients who obtained an abortion at a clinic in Buffalo, New York. The researchers found that volunteer escorts are helpful in ameliorating much, though not all, of the negative effect of anti-abortion protest activity. The patients believed that the escorts were "somewhat effective in insulating women against direct contact with the antiabortion demonstrators." Perhaps more importantly, women also said that the escorts improved how they felt while in the clinic and about the procedure afterwards. The researchers concluded that "the escorts helped to protect women against negative psychological effects attributable to antiabortion demonstrators." The study also found that when there were more antiabortion protesters, patients were more depressed about the protesters after the abortion but that the escorts counteracted the effect of more protesters and even improved patients' moods. The one thing that escorts could not help with was to alleviate the negative reaction associated with abortion protest intensity (as opposed to simple numbers). When demonstrations were more intense, the escorts didn't make a difference.

Everyone we talked with shared the view that clinic escorts helped patients deal with the protesters. Take, for instance, Pat Canon and Fausta Luchini, both volunteer escorts at the same southern clinic. We talked with both of them extensively. The clinic where they escort has been under siege from the politicians in the state as well as anti-abortion protesters. The protesters outside the clinic are the usual mix of what Fausta calls "prayers, chasers, and door tenders." The prayers mostly pray near the clinic, though they occasionally yell at patients as well. The chasers chase patients from the parking spot, along the sidewalk, and then as they are trying to enter the clinic, sometimes yelling along the way while other times trying to whisper in their ears. The door tenders hang around the entrance. According to Fausta, "They're all sugar and sweetness until the patient actually gets to the door, and then they're suddenly much more venomous."

As escorts, Pat and Fausta try as hard as they can to minimize the chaos outside the clinic. To that end, Pat said that they have a "total nonengagement policy for the escorts," meaning they never talk with or respond to the protesters. Doing so, these escorts firmly believe, would provoke the protesters and make a tense situation even worse.

Almost all escorts have this nonengagement policy, even though they themselves often become the target of the protesters' vitriol. This targeting is particularly acute for escorts who stand out to the anti-abortion protesters because of their race, religion, or ability. In Pat's group, the

African American escorts receive the same kind of racist taunts that the patients do. For instance, the protesters yell at them, "You're contributing to the black holocaust" or "You're betraying your race." Another escort is an observant Jew and wears a skullcap when he is at the clinic. The protesters target him constantly. They even bring out a special sign that they store in one of the protesters' trunks until this Jewish escort shows up. The sign's message is not unusual, as it repeats the common equation of abortion to the Holocaust, but the protesters save it for when he's there and put it away otherwise.

Pat's escort group also includes someone in a wheelchair and someone who is deaf. Once the protesters discovered the escort was deaf, they passed her a note that said, "Your parents would have aborted you if they had known that you were deaf." And for the escort in a wheelchair, the protesters tell her that she is "lucky" that she was born because her parents would have "murdered her" for having a disability.

There are no private parking lots near the clinic, so the protesters "have access to [patients] the whole way to the clinic." The escorts try to identify patients getting out of the car and then they walk with them, while talking with them about what's going on. Pat begins the conversation by saying, "They're going to try to talk to you. You do not have to talk with them. The best advice is to watch the sidewalk and I'll guide you in." Most patients accept the offer of help, but not all do. Pat always backs off from the patients who do not want her help, but then the protesters surround the patient instead.

Fausta's approach is slightly different. Instead of talking with the patients about the protesters, Fausta "babbles on" about other things. As she takes the patient from the parking lot, Fausta says, "Now you've got your ID with you, right? Because we don't want to have to walk back through this mess to come back down here. Okay, so we're just going to head up the sidewalk this way and I can talk if you want me to but I don't have to." She continues on like that and "can talk all day if they need me to. It really is just babbling on to give them something to focus on that's different from what they're hearing from the protesters."

The group that Pat and Fausta belong to has about sixty-five escorts, though only about twenty-five to thirty are active on a normal Saturday. A small contingent stay at the front of the building to guard the property line, and the rest try to help patients once they park. "We have no more than two escorts walk a patient and companion at a time," Pat explained, because if there are more it draws too much attention from the protesters, who try to break through the escorts to get to the patient. "Larger groups are like blood in the water, and we've had escorts really assaulted badly" in those situations, Pat told us.

Next door to the clinic where Pat and Fausta escort is a crisis pregnancy center, which has created some odd dynamics with the escorts. One week, the clinic had a national extremist group show up to protest outside. The national group brought large numbers who were very aggressive and vocal, so much so that the local US attorney brought a successful FACE action against the group that resulted in a temporary buffer zone around the clinic. The buffer zone helped, but the escorts were still busy shuttling patients into the clinic through the extremists. That week, one of the protesters was so loud outside the abortion clinic that he scared the staff of the next-door crisis pregnancy center. Astonishingly, given the usually antagonistic relationship between the center and the clinic, a member of the pregnancy center's staff came outside to ask Pat if she would send an escort or police officer around back to help someone from the center get inside.

Along those lines, Pat surprisingly told us that she has sometimes even escorted people who have appointments with the center. Those people, who are not getting abortion services, are also afraid of the protesters so they ask for help. When this happens, Pat is happy to oblige. "It's all about choice. If they want to go there, we'll walk them there." Interestingly, one of the northeastern clinics where Diana Sharpe works has the same situation—a crisis pregnancy center next door—but Diana told the escorts to take the opposite approach when people were asking the escorts to direct them to the pregnancy center's open house. She was unapologetic about this. As she said to them, "Think about where it is that you're sending them. I know it feels counterintuitive to you because you are a lovely human being and want to help people, but you'd be sending them to a place that is giving them false information and untrue medical statements."

Back at Pat's clinic, if a patient is not sure about her decision and wants to talk with the protesters, Pat said that her role is to "back up and wait until the patient decides either to go to the crisis pregnancy center with the protester or go to the clinic." She is proud of how she handles these situations, letting the patient make up her mind. As Pat explained, "If somebody is not sure if this is the decision for them, we're going to back up and let them take the time because we don't want anybody to be forced or coerced into an abortion who doesn't want one." But if the patient tells the protesters, "Leave me alone, no, leave me alone," Pat and her fellow escorts keep going, no matter what the protesters do or say.

In alignment with the research on this issue, both Pat and Fausta feel that escorting is very effective in helping patients. It does not alleviate all of the trouble of walking through loud and harassing protesters just to get medical care, but it makes a difference. "We get a lot of thank-yous afterwards," Fausta explained. In fact, some of the people whom they have escorted in as patients have subsequently joined Fausta and Pat's group as escorts. As Fausta told us, "This is one of the most rewarding things that I do. You can immediately feel what you're doing is helping. It's almost magical, and it's just super satisfying."

CLINIC INGENUITY

Beyond escorts, there are other strategies clinics employ to help soften the blow of protesters for patients entering the clinic. For those who have the ability to do so, strategically choosing the location of the clinic can be key. Donna Sullivan chose the new location for her clinic intentionally, locating it in "the bluest neighborhood in the blue dot" that is her city in the midst of an extremely red (conservative) state. There, the neighbors watch out for the clinic and support them and their patients. Neighbors don't mind when patients or staff are on their property and, on the flipside, are not accommodating to the protesters.

Jennifer Pride explained a related strategy—moving to a neighborhood that the protesters wouldn't want to come to. The protesters in the city where her clinic is situated are older white people. When the clinic chose a location, it chose a working-class Hispanic area of town. There were many factors that went into this choice, such as the fact that there aren't a lot of sidewalks near the clinic, thus limiting protester access. Additionally, Jennifer certainly considered that while the clinic staff and patients would feel comfortable being in this area of the city, the protesters might not. The clinic where Deborah Levin escorts benefits from a similar dynamic. When the clinic moved to a poorer, majority–African American part of the city because of more affordable rent, some of the clinic's protesters were afraid to follow.

Providers also can help the situation by choosing properties that are far from public spaces. One of the clinics that Judith Casella works with has a large private parking lot in front of it, so it's impossible for the protesters to get anywhere near the front door. Rebecca Moore is a fan of the "wide open space" of her parking lot as well. Not only does this space provide the protesters no protection from the extreme temperature swings where the clinic is located, but it also means that the protesters are far enough from the clinic that they can barely be heard.

One of Frances Easton's clinics was on the verge of moving when we talked with her. She said that the "amazing thing" about the new location is that "there's no sidewalks, so there's nowhere for the antis to stand." She said the driveway leads the patients to the back of the building, "so it's a really secure private entrance for patients to come in." This was a very intentional choice for Frances, as the old location's layout allowed the very disruptive protesters to be almost right up to the clinic door.

Another way that clinics have been able to limit the effect of protesters is to have space inside a busy multiuse building. The idea isn't complicated—if many different businesses use the space, the protesters won't be able to target patients because so many people using it for different purposes will be coming and going from the building. Linda Johnston took this approach after a "very, very thoughtful exercise in planning out where our clinic locations would be." All of the other tenants in the building are medical offices, so "whether the patients are going to a dentist or a pediatrician or our clinic, it's more challenging for the protesters to identify."

Abortion providers can also help the situation with their scheduling. Some have to have a regular schedule, given their patient population and volume. But others find that an irregular schedule can help thwart the protesters. Jennifer Pride's clinic has an "unpredictable" abortion care schedule, especially as the clinic integrates other services such as transgender health care into its care model. As a result, the protesters "have absolutely no idea when the patients are coming in, if it's going to be an abortion day or a day when it's just our employees." She said the protesters have sometimes mistakenly yelled at trans women about keeping their baby.

When clinics have protesters on a regular basis, one thing many do is warn patients beforehand. Hannah Miller talked about this at the beginning of this chapter, expressing concern about walking the line between warning patients and scaring them. Nonetheless, many providers include information about the protesters in the standard discussion they have with patients on the phone before their first visit. Pat Earle gets very specific, telling her mainly African American patients to ignore the "middle-aged white guy standing on the sidewalk" that they'll see upon approaching the clinic. She tells them that he will pretend to be with the clinic but that "if he doesn't have on an orange vest that the escorts wear, he's not with us."

Sometimes all a clinic can do to help patients deal with protesters is talk with them after the patient has already encountered them. As part of her counseling session, Kendra Farrell talks extensively with patients who are feeling upset by the protesters:

> The first thing I usually just say is "This is your choice, your body, your choice, your right. You are the owner of your uterus. Those people do not know you so you don't give them that kind of power. It's okay to be upset and disappointed that somebody you don't know is trying to judge you. But at the same time, they don't know you, so just ignore it. You know, we don't know what's going on in their lives." I say all kinds of stuff, to be perfectly honest, but usually just do my best to make them feel better about their choice, even if I have to go into talking about myself. You know, because I have been a patient. I've been on the other side so I know what it feels like to be met with the protesters' ridiculous judgment. But I know it's easier said than done, but I tell them, "Smile at them, ignore them. That's what they need. If you respond or engage, that's what fuels them. So just ignore it like you don't hear it." That's usually how we get through it.

Perhaps the most interesting thing that helped the situation for patients happened at Billie Taylor's northeastern clinic. After years of protesters holding up bloody gory signs outside, a children's bookstore moved in across the street. With so many children constantly in the area now, the city's code enforcement unit told the protesters to change their signs to something less offensive. Miraculously, the protesters complied without suing the city. Billie told us that this has made a big difference for patients coming into her clinic, and she is now a big fan of the bookstore.

With all of the harassment they face entering a clinic, it may seem like a wonder that abortion patients endure it. But they do, and to Jada Curry this makes sense. "Patients, they want an abortion so whatever they have to do to make that happen, I mean, they're troopers. They do it."

But just because women will walk through throngs of screaming protesters to get basic medical care doesn't mean they should have to endure this behavior. Unfortunately, for now, the legal resources available to protect patients only help so much, and anything more is left to volunteers and abortion providers to undertake on their own.

The result is a situation that is unlike what confronts patients entering a medical office for any other form of health care. Erica Valverde summed this up perfectly when she said to us, "I would not stand outside a plastic surgery clinic and say, 'Breast augmentation is for the devil,' because what do I know about someone who has body dysmorphia and issues about their breast size and the breast augmentation would actually help them feel better and live a happier life. Who am I to judge?"

6 Counseling at the Clinic

GOVERNMENT-MANDATED DECEIT

Curtis Boyd, a veteran provider in the South and West and a pioneer in the field of abortion care, captured what has long been an article of faith in the abortion-providing community: "Every woman who comes through is different. Every experience is different. Her counseling is different, her pain management is different. With one you may tell jokes, with one you tell stories, with another you cry." In other words, abortion care is not a one-size-fits-all proposition. Ideally, each woman "should be met where she is at," to cite another common sentiment shared by abortion providers around the country.

Once a woman overcomes the hurdle of getting into the clinic, she will meet with clinic staff about her procedure. If this were any other medical procedure, the medical staff would use their professional judgment to obtain the informed consent of the patient. Informed consent, according to a 1982 Presidential Commission for the Study of Ethical Problems in Medicine and Biomedical and Behavioral Research, must include three elements: "1) patients must have the capacity to make decisions about their care; 2) their participation in these decisions must be without coercion or manipulation; and 3) patients must be given appropriate information germane to making the particular decision." Depending on the nature of the medical procedure, this can be a quick process or quite involved—a tooth extraction or cataract surgery probably being on the quick end of the spectrum, and something like bypass or brain surgery being quite involved.

For any procedure other than abortion, the counseling process would certainly hew to the requirements of the generally applicable law, but beyond that, the judgment of the medical professionals involved would guide the interaction. Some medical professionals might feel that their job is to do nothing more than obtain this informed consent before proceeding, while others might feel that they should probe patients more deeply about the circumstances of their life that affect the decision, their life after the procedure, and anything else relevant to their physical or emotional health. Again, in almost all medical settings, how much more the medical care professional does will be left to their or their employer's best professional judgment It is certainly not regulated by legislators who know nothing about that particular field of medicine.

As with other medical procedures, counseling about abortion takes place before the procedure and involves, at a minimum, obtaining informed consent. In its *Ethical Guidelines for Abortion Care*, the National Abortion Federation, the leading professional association of abortion providers, explains this basic principle:

> The decision whether or not to have an abortion must rest with the patient. The provider must ascertain before providing an abortion that the patient ... is prepared to do so and has not been coerced in any way.... The informed consent process must give the patient an opportunity to learn and/ or discuss whatever information she or her provider believe is relevant to her treatment decision. The process must include a description of the abortion procedure; any medically accepted alternatives that might be appropriate for the patient; and the medically accurate risks and benefits of the abortion to be provided and its alternatives.

During counseling, providers have the opportunity to acknowledge each patient's unique circumstances and needs and to talk with her about these things based on the provider's medical judgment. However, here as elsewhere in abortion care, state restrictions governing counseling and several other factors have imposed barriers that challenge providers' ability to implement best practices in this realm and make it difficult for patients to get the best possible information and assistance they need before having an abortion.

BEYOND INFORMED CONSENT

To be sure, even among abortion providers there is not universal agreement as to what abortion counseling should entail. Providers disagree among themselves about such matters as what content should be addressed, which clinic personnel should do the counseling, how much time should be devoted to this activity, how extensively the provider should delve into the patient's personal life, what format should be used (group or individual, live, or via phone or video recording), and more.

This situation is further complicated by the fact that abortion *counseling* can be easily conflated with the *informed consent* that abortion provision, like all other medical procedures, requires. Informed consent is certainly an essential part of counseling, but from the perspective of most of the abortion providers we spoke with, counseling of some patients ideally involves more and should be open to addressing the feelings women have about the forthcoming procedure as well as their related needs. Sadly, however, this idea of quality, personalized counseling has been hijacked by the necessity of delivering state-mandated propaganda.

Because of these state mandates around informed consent, what is a fairly routine process elsewhere in medicine becomes a more complicated affair. The first two of the elements of informed consent from the Presidential Commission listed above—patient capacity and noncoercion—are not usually problematic in abortion care. As discussed in chapter 2, all the providers we spoke with about counseling explained how scrupulous they are about evaluating the abilities of patients to make decisions and, in particular, about ascertaining that no coercion is involved.

The providers we talked with explained how they ask multiple times whether the patient is certain because sometimes when they ask a second or third time the patient indicates that she isn't so certain and doesn't want the abortion. Several told us stories of being supportive when that happens because choice has many components, not just choosing abortion. Barbara Pierce, a counselor with a clinic in a midwestern state, said that she's been in this position and that the patient is sometimes surprised when Barbara supports her decision not to have an abortion. Barbara understands that some people hold the stereotype of abortion providers as "heartless monsters" who are "just here for the money," so they think providers would never support someone who wanted to continue a pregnancy. But nothing could be further from the truth, and providers would never want someone to have an abortion who does not want one. Barbara said, "I think a lot of people are blown away that we are just regular people trying to help regular people."

One issue frequently comes up for abortion providers around informed consent and noncoercion—counseling patients who bring a partner or parent to the procedure. In the leading textbook on abortion care, experts advise that even though husbands, partners, or parents should be welcomed to participate in preprocedure counseling and discussion, "the woman should initially be questioned *alone* about her decision and afforded an opportunity to disclose coercion."

Jenifer Groves, a clinic director who has worked in almost every aspect of abortion care in two different northeastern states, told us that making sure the decision is the patient's own is just another part of "moral medical care." She said that the "number one" thing that she and her staff must make sure of is that "the patient's not being forced to have an abortion, that she's pretty damn sure that she wants to do this."

It is with the Presidential Commission's third aspect of informed consent—"appropriate information"—that the extreme politicization of abortion becomes a factor. In 2018, the National Partnership for Women and Families released a compendium of state mandates regarding informed consent for abortion procedures. Among its findings related to the counseling and informed consent process, through the beginning of 2018:

- Thirty states require abortion providers to give or offer written information about abortion that was developed by the state, much of which is incorrect or deceptive.
- Thirteen states require providers to tell patients that fetuses can feel pain.
- Eight states require providers to inform patients about negative emotional consequences from having an abortion.

- Four states require providers to tell their patients that abortion can negatively affect future fertility.
- Five states require providers to inform patients that there is a link between abortion and breast cancer.
- Six states force providers to tell their patients that personhood begins at conception.
- Three states require that providers tell patients that a medication abortion can be reversed.
- Twenty-four states require providers to give or offer patients descriptions of the most common abortion procedures.
- Twenty-nine states require providers to give or offer patients descriptions of fetal development throughout pregnancy.

As we will cover throughout this chapter, most of this information is medically inaccurate or intentionally inflammatory (or both). Even the parts that are factually correct are arguably not appropriate for all abortion patients, such as descriptions of fetal development throughout pregnancy when most abortions occur in the first trimester. The necessity to offer this information can be upsetting to patients and frustrating to many providers, who find that the time taken up with offering and then correcting such information is not medically necessary and sabotages other important conversations.

INACCURACIES AND DOWNRIGHT LIES

In the thirty states that require providers to give or offer patients written material, what is actually in the written material varies greatly. Most common are pictures of fetal development along with information about options and abortion risks. The material in Jan Dancy's state includes a glossy book-like brochure with pictures of fetuses and then a separate bound booklet with a guide to clinics in the state that provide maternal health care. Jan explained that the information has not been updated in over a decade, with some of the listed clinics no longer operative.

What upsets Jan the most is that the information is not relevant to what a patient seeking abortion would really need were she to decide to continue her pregnancy. For example, Jan noted that the booklet does not inform patients how to access welfare, legal services, or food assistance. Jan was particularly frustrated by the brochure. "The name of the book, the glossy one that shows all of the fetal development, is called *Abortion: Making A Decision*, but it's all about fetal development and there's no questions about whether you're ready to parent, whether there's an opportunity to co-parent, or someone who would help you if you needed assistance. It's just graphic images of fetal development."

In some states, the provider has to hand the booklet to the patient. Edna Macklin explained that in her state, she must not only hand the booklet to the patient but also have the patient sign a form indicating that she received it. For patients who can't read, Edna has to have available a VCR tape recording of the same material to play for the patients. It has been a "long time" since Edna has had to use her VCR, but she still has it in the clinic in case it's needed.

Edna is in the minority among the people we interviewed because in most states the provider just has to make the written material available to the patient, not actually give it to them. The providers we talked to in these states were all in agreement—when they offer these materials, almost no one wants them. As Jen Moore Conrow, a clinic administrator in a northeastern state, related, "Patients never take them. We basically have to tell them we have copies here, but I think I've only had a person want to read it twice that I know of in the last year."

Not only are these brochures and other written materials a waste of resources and not geared toward what an abortion patient needs, but they are also littered with inaccuracies and downright lies. Professor Cynthia Daniels, a political scientist at Rutgers University, recently led an exhaustive study of the informed-consent materials in twenty-three states, focusing on the materials on fetal development. She convened a panel of seven investigators through the American Academy of Anatomists, asking them to evaluate in particular the accuracy of state brochures given to abortion patients. The scientists were told only that the women received the information in a "reproductive health setting," without making the connection to abortion. The investigators concluded that "nearly one-third of the informed consent information is medically inaccurate [and] that inaccurate information is concentrated primarily in the earlier weeks of pregnancy." North Carolina, the study found, has the dubious distinction of having the greatest amount of misinformation in its informed-consent brochure, with some 46 percent of its mandated information being inaccurate.

The misinformation Daniels and her team found was as shocking as it was central to women's understanding of the procedure. The brochures produced by the states tend to convey fetal development in two-week periods. Among the inaccuracies the investigators cited are the following: from week 2, "the head has formed"; from week 4, "brain activity can be recorded"; from week 6, "fingers, toes, ankles and wrists are completely formed"; and from week 9, "hiccups begin." All of these statements are grossly inaccurate about fetal development and convey to the patient that their fetus is much further along in development than it actually is. Daniels and her team concluded that nationally, 35 percent of women having abortions are given information exaggerating, if not wholly misrepresenting, the development of fetuses and embryos.

MANDATED SCRIPTS

Beyond the fetal development inaccuracies, much of the state-mandated information that providers are compelled to offer contains other problems, like language that can be upsetting for someone presenting for an abortion. For example, many state-mandated scripts repeatedly use the terms *unborn child* or *unborn baby*. Consider, for example, the materials governing informed consent for abortion that the Louisiana Department of Health has developed. In that state, a woman must come to the clinic at least twenty-four hours prior to receiving an abortion (therefore, as explained further in chapter 7, necessitating yet another day of lost wages and child care expenses for many patients), to go over with a staff person a thirty-one-item questionnaire. The questionnaire repeatedly uses the term *unborn child*.

Similarly, several states require abortion providers to tell all patients that they are "terminating the life of a whole, separate, unique living human being." This language, like the language in the Louisiana form, is intentionally designed to undermine a patient's decision. Moreover, it compels providers to use language that they would never, in their best medical judgment, use. Most providers would use the term *fetus*—rather than *unborn child* or *whole, separate, unique living human being*—because that is the medically accurate term and because it will be less likely to upset the patient.

Back to the Louisiana form, where among the items the abortion recipient must certify that she received is information about "the availability of anesthesia . . . to alleviate or eliminate organic pain to the unborn child that could be caused by the method of abortion to be employed." The argument that a fetus, at all stages of development, feels pain has become a major talking point of the anti-abortion movement and has been the rationale for the ban on abortions after twenty weeks imposed in many states. As noted above, twelve other states, in addition to Louisiana, require providers to inform patients of fetal pain. However, the overriding consensus in the medical community is that fetuses are not capable of feeling pain until at least twenty-eight or twenty-nine weeks gestation. Only a minuscule number of abortions in this country take place after that stage of gestation, and providers performing these highly specialized abortions typically cause fetal demise with a chemical agent before the abortion is performed.

Mandates that providers tell patients about fetal pain are just the tip of the iceberg. As noted above, states require providers to tell patients about nonexistent links between abortion and depression, suicide, breast cancer, and infertility. As the 2018 review of the literature from the National Academies of Sciences, Engineering, and Medicine makes clear, none of these connections are backed by medical science except for a connection to infertility in a very tiny subset of women. The report summarized the evidence about physical health effects of abortion: "The committee identified high-quality research on numerous outcomes of interest and concludes that having an abortion does not increase a woman's risk of secondary infertility, pregnancy-related hypertensive disorders, abnormal placentation[,] preterm birth, or breast cancer. . . . The committee did not find well-designed research on abortion's association with future ectopic pregnancy, miscarriage or stillbirth, or long-term mortality." On mental health, the report summarized: "The committee identified a wide array of research on whether abortion increases women's risk of depression, anxiety, and/or posttraumatic stress disorder (PTSD) and concludes that having an abortion does not increase a woman's risk of these mental health disorders." The only risk identified by the report as supported by legitimate research is an increased risk of preterm birth for women with two or more of a particular kind of abortion *if* the time between abortion and conception is less than six months (which is the same for pregnancy spacing in general).

Thus almost every warning that states require abortion providers to give as part of the informed-consent process is not supported by objective medical evidence. Put more bluntly, states with these mandates are forcing abortion providers to lie to their patients.

Informing patients about the possibility of "abortion reversal" is one of the more recent, and to many providers most egregious, requirements imposed by some states. "Reversal" is the idea developed by abortion opponents—and universally rejected by the medical community—that if the second drug, misoprostol, in the medication abortion regime (typically taken some twenty-four hours after the first drug, mifepristone) is not taken, and the patient instead is given high doses of the hormone progesterone, the abortion that was set in motion with the first abortion pills will be "reversed." The American College of Obstetricians and Gynecologists has been clear about this new myth: "Claims regarding abortion 'reversal' treatment are not based on science and do not meet clinical standards." The organization concluded its position statement by saying that it "does not support prescribing progesterone to stop a medical abortion."

Yet several states now require abortion providers to inform their patients about this "option" once they have started the medication abortion process. To Melody Cook, a clinic director in the South, this requirement is "cruel" because it tells patients that if they really are ambivalent they can start the procedure and then make up their mind later. Thankfully, though, in Melody's experience, this information "usually doesn't influence their opinion at all, or their choice, because the patients just want to get it over with."

"THE STATE REQUIRES ME TO READ . . ."

Faced with giving their patients a large amount of false or misleading information, providers are in a tough situation. They are trying to establish a trusting relationship, but at the same time they have to tell their patients things that are completely inconsistent with their sense of professional judgment as well as often plainly false.

Given this predicament, many of the people we interviewed told us about how they "preface the script." Melody Cook described how she manages the requirement to inform her patients about "abortion reversal": "The reversal statement that we prepared for the physician says: 'There is no credible medical evidence that supports reversal of the medication abortion. However, our state requires I tell you, if you want to reverse your medication abortion, there is information available at the state website that you can access.' I think we do a good job of explaining that we really don't think this is true and that patients shouldn't count on this information. And if they don't want to do this, decide it now. Don't decide it after taking the first medication." Robin Flynn, who works closely with Melody at the same clinic, told us that she has never seen a patient who cares about abortion reversal. "It usually doesn't influence their opinion at all or their choice." What matters most, and what Robin conveys to every patient, is that "if you're unsure, wait. You can always come back. If you're then too far along for medication abortion, have the surgical procedure."

Offering misinformation or outright lies to patients puts providers in a very difficult position. Erica Valverde, a physician in a western state, explained how she handles this misinformation and what it means for her sense of professionalism:

> When I read the state-mandated script to the patients, I preface it with "The state requires me to read this to you. Fortunately, this is all information I would have given you anyway. There are a few exceptions where I am going to say something and it is not true. If that is the case, I will stop. I will look up from the paper. I will say, 'That is in fact not true,' and then I will resume reading." So that is what I do, and it's just such—it's just a waste of taxpayer money. It is a waste of legislature time, and it is condescending to human beings.

Erica went even further and discussed how such mandated misinformation violates the ethical guidelines of the American Medical Association. In her state, she must not only talk about "abortion reversal" but also inform patients about "postabortion syndrome," another favored talking point of the anti-abortion movement that has also been repeatedly rebutted by mental health professionals. Contrary to this myth, psychological research has shown that that the best predictor of a woman's psychological state after an abortion is her state before the procedure.

Nonetheless, Erica is required by law to tell her patients about the syndrome and the risk it puts the patient at for depression and even suicidal ideation as a consequence of having an abortion. As she told us,

> As per the AMA, informed consent is giving factual, medically accurate information. And there's a whole paragraph outlined in the AMA code about this. Well, my state cites that code as what they mean by informed consent. But that informed consent is violated by another legislative code! It is violated when I have to tell my patients that there is a risk of postabortion syndrome. Postabortion syndrome is not a thing. It does not exist. It is a made-up term. So for me to say to my patients that this thing is a risk, and then I have to backtrack and say to my patients, "Except that's not true," that is extremely confusing, because on the one hand you've got a doctor holding a piece of paper in front of you, reading off of it as if they don't know what they're talking about, that the state makes them read. And then the doctor tells you that the state is wrong. So now you've got a citizen who is wondering, "Do I trust my doctor, do I trust the state? The state is lying to me, but the doctor's reading from the piece of paper! Who do I trust?" It undermines not only the doctor-patient relationship, but it also creates a complete distrust in the government.

While providers carefully follow the letter of the law, they also, as Erica explained, frequently make clear to patients their disagreement with both the requirement to give patients the material and some of the contents within it. In Melody Cook's state, she is compelled to offer patients a list of anti-abortion crisis pregnancy centers. She explained how she does so while remaining true to her relationship with the patient. "We're very honest about [our disagreement with the requirement] and just say, 'Listen, this is another piece of paper that the state is requiring us to give you. Take it if you want. It's right here.'" Another southern provider, Van May, who is an administrator at a large clinic, explained that there are many inaccuracies in the printed material they are required to hand to patients. In her clinic's brochure, there is a "disclaimer" that says that the material is required by the state but that the clinic disagrees with the information.

However, this tactic used by providers—prefacing the script by making clear their disagreement with the information being offered—may be at risk. In 2018, South Dakota, so often a leader in ever more extreme abortion laws, passed a measure prohibiting a very particular disclaimer before delivering the state-mandated script. In particular, South Dakota prohibited abortion providers from prefacing the mandated script with the phrase "Politicians in the state of South Dakota require us to tell you that. . . ."

The purpose of this measure is clear—to further confuse and pressure patients into choosing to continue their pregnancies. According to the law itself, letting patients know that providers are legally required to make certain statements "is antithetical to the purpose and effectiveness of the disclosures, and evidences a hostility to the required disclosures and signals to the pregnant mothers that the required disclosures, to the extent they are made at all, should be ignored." In other words, South Dakota is restricting abortion providers' speech because the state wants its attempts to stop abortion to be more effective. This law will inevitably be challenged because it violates the providers' First Amendment rights but might nonetheless spread to other states that want to try to blunt providers' attempts to discredit state-mandated lies and misinformation in the counseling and informed-consent process.

"IF IT'S NOT MEDICALLY TRUE, THEN WHY DO YOU HAVE TO SAY IT?"

Let's step back here to the frame of this entire book. Imagine once again that you are getting a tooth pulled or having cataract surgery. It's inconceivable that the state would require your dentist or eye surgeon to inform you about medical risks that the leading organizations in health care and science have concluded are not based on evidence or, even worse, are known to be outright lies. Never would you be faced with the situation of your doctor or dentist reading you a script from the state and then telling you not to believe it.

However, abortion patients encounter this every day in many states throughout the country. As a general matter, abortion patients find counseling helpful, and nearly all find that clinic counselors are supportive of whatever decision the patient makes. However, the Turnaway Study's interviews with over one thousand abortion patients across the country indicate that those who receive counseling in states that mandate the type of scripts discussed in this chapter are less likely to find counseling helpful than those in states that do not have this requirement.

Instead, as our interviews show, in these states patients are often scared or confused or both. Frances Easton works in one of the five states that require providers to falsely inform patients about the links between abortion and breast cancer. At her clinic, staff have to deal with women's reactions first to the upsetting message and then to the fact that they have been told untrue statements. Frances explained the patients' confusion. "I get the question all the time like, 'If it's not medically true, then why do you have to say it?' We go through and explain what's not medically correct and explain that our state is conservative and they have a lot of anti-choice politicians who make laws."

Over and over, providers like Nellie Baker told us the material they were forced to offer patients, either verbally and/or in writing, unnecessarily frightened their patients. Where Nellie works, the state requires that the doctor tell the patient that abortion can cause hemorrhage and death. As Nellie explained, "These are all true but it's very out of context. It doesn't talk at all about the maternal mortality rate [which is about fourteen times that of an abortion]. That this is an extremely safe procedure is not a part of that statement at all." Jennifer Pride made a similar observation about her state-mandated information. "We have to read all of the medical risks, but it doesn't talk about frequency. Yes, technically you could die from a medication abortion, but it doesn't talk about how likely that is, which I think is a deliberate tactic to scare patients."

Other things providers are required to say scare patients into thinking they're doing something illegal. Lynn Thompson, a clinic administrator who does a little bit of everything for a small midwestern clinic, explained that she doesn't mind running through the medically legitimate risks, such as infection, hemorrhage, uterine perforation, anesthesia reactions or, for medical abortion, cramps, nausea, vomiting, or diarrhea. To her, "It makes sense to inform them." But Lynn works in one of the states that requires providers to tell patients that they are "terminating the life of a whole, separate, unique living human being." To Lynn, this is "gross" because "you just feel awful that you have to tell them that." She's even had patients who hear that statement and ask, somewhat understandably, "So this is legal?" Lynn has to explain that abortion is legal but that the state requires her to say this. "It sounds ridiculous to the patient, and it's just hard to even explain, but the required stuff is really shaming."

Even when the mandated information is not frightening or confusing, both providers and patients find much of it irrelevant at best and emotionally disturbing at worst. For example, a number of states require that the woman be informed that the man who impregnated her is liable to pay child support if she continues the pregnancy. As noted throughout this book, three-quarters of abortion patients are poor or low income and therefore tend to have sex or be in a relationship with men of similar income levels. As a result, many patients scoff at this announcement, and providers bristle at the necessity to convey it. As Jen Moore Conrow said, "I don't think any physician would bring that up in conversation with a patient who said to them, 'I want an abortion today.'"

"I AM REQUIRED BY LAW TO DESCRIBE THE DEVELOPMENT I SEE BASED ON THIS ULTRASOUND"

Nearly all abortion facilities routinely perform ultrasounds on patients in order to precisely date the gestational age of the fetus, rule out an ectopic pregnancy, and determine if there are twins (or more). Nonetheless, despite this relatively universal standard of care among providers, a large minority of states have begun to require that ultrasounds be a part of the mandated-counseling aspect of the abortion experience. Seventeen states require that patients be offered to view their ultrasounds. The most invasive laws are in three states (and blocked by courts in another three) that *compel* viewing the ultrasound. In these states, ultrasound technicians are now required to place the ultrasound screen directly in patients' line of sight and also to describe any viewable features of internal organs of the pregnancy. Patients are legally permitted to turn their heads away and "avert their eyes," as these laws put it.

Researchers who have studied the impact of such mandated ultrasound viewing in Wisconsin, one of the three states where the law is in effect, have concluded that these laws have minimal impact on the abortion decision, leading to a very small number of women who decide to continue their pregnancies. These women changing their mind, not surprisingly, tend to be those who already have ambivalence about their abortion.

But as our interviews with providers revealed, even if mandated ultrasound viewing does not lead to changes in the abortion decision, this law can be confusing and upsetting to patients. Kathaleen Pittman runs a clinic in a southern state that requires clinics to display and describe the ultrasound image. She explained how her clinic implements the law. After going through the state-mandated script, the sonographer says to the patient: "I have to have the machine towards you. You don't have to look, but I have to have it set up. If you are far enough along that there's a heartbeat, I have to turn the sound on for you to hear it, unless you tell me you don't want me to. You're free to have a copy of the ultrasound at no additional cost. I am required by law to describe to you the development I see based on this ultrasound while I'm doing this."

Under the law, the sonographer has to describe everything. As Kathaleen explained, "You have to be descriptive about the fingers, toes, you know, everything you're seeing." The patients often have very strong reactions to this. Kathaleen said that the most common patient reaction is "You've got to be fucking kidding me? For real?"

The absurdity, if not cruelty, of these ultrasound display requirements was brought home to us by Andrea Ferrigno, who also practices in a southern state with mandated viewing and listening. She told us that an option for patients who don't want to view the ultrasound and listen to the heartbeat is to sing or cover their ears:

> The patient has the option to say, "No, I don't want to see the image," but they do have to listen to the explanation, whether they want to or not. So if somebody says, "I don't want to know anything about this ultrasound. Just tell me how many weeks and that's it. That's all I want to know," we have to say, "Unfortunately, we do have to explain a few more things about the ultrasound, because it's mandated by the state." The patient can start singing or covering her ears or whatever, but we have to tell them; we have to do that.

For some patients who are forced to look and listen to the ultrasound the experience is very upsetting. As Van May, who also practices in a southern state with mandated viewing and listening, said: "Whenever they're played the fetal heart sounds and are forced to view the images of the ultrasound, it's just when some women start crying, they start questioning themselves, they start—you know, they come in so certain, but then when you have to turn the ultrasound image to them and play the heartbeat, it's a very visceral reaction for many women." Given that research shows that only a very small number of women change their mind after the ultrasound viewing, the only conclusion to draw from this requirement is that it is intentionally cruel.

Not every patient gets upset. Some react by becoming angry at the clinic staff. Andrea Ferrigno explained that these patients "get annoyed and they look at us like we're crazy, kind of like, 'I already told you no. Why are you doing this? That makes no sense.' They get frustrated. Or they feel patronized. And we explain, 'It's not really us. We're the messengers.' But they don't really care. They're just annoyed that that's happened."

Another worrisome aspect of the ultrasound mandate in some states is the requirement that a copy of each ultrasound be returned to the state health department, with information that could possibly be used to identify a patient, even though her name was redacted. In Millie Johnson's state, the ultrasound sent to the health department includes the patient's vital statistics—home city, level of education, previous abortions, method of abortion, and reason for abortion. Millie worried that in her rural state of very small towns, it was not inconceivable that a woman could be identified and her information passed on to anti-abortion activists.

Finally, with respect to ultrasound viewing, it bears restating that providers themselves are aware that for *some* women, seeing their ultrasound can be a positive thing, whatever the impact on their ultimate decision to have an abortion or not, and that the woman's wishes should be honored. In the spirit of the "one size does not fit all" ethos generally governing abortion care, providers, even those in states that do not require such viewing, offer the option to patients. As a California-based study found, without an ultrasound viewing requirement over 42 percent of the almost sixteen thousand patients studied opted to view the ultrasound image. Abortion providers understand this desire, and some even suggest to patients that they view their ultrasound. Edna Macklin explained:

If any patient who wants to see the ultrasound, especially an early patient, I'm going to try to encourage them to do that because I think patients when they come in, they've been subjected to six-foot posters out front of a fetus and then they come in and they have no concept as to what a six-week embryo looks like. And so there are times that, you know, I obviously don't ever insist, but I talk to the patient and say, "Look, okay, you're early in the pregnancy, and I think this might make you feel better if you just looked at the image." Because I think they sometimes have this image that there's this baby in diapers with a pacifier in its mouth. And that's just not the case. It's not this horrific thing that the picketers will make it out to be out front.

HOW CAN THIS BE ALLOWED?

Abortion providers are required to regularly lie to their patients and give them information that is not consistent with best medical practices. As a result, they cause their patients fear and confusion. Some patients even leave the interaction wondering how abortion could possibly be legal. How can this be consistent with a woman having a constitutional right to have an abortion and with abortion providers having a constitutional right to freedom of speech?

The main issue in the litigation that has sprung up around these mandates is whether the requirements are "truthful" and "non-misleading." This standard comes from the 1992 Supreme Court decision in *Planned Parenthood v. Casey*. In that case, Pennsylvania required abortion providers to inform patients about the nature of the procedure, the health risks of abortion and childbirth, the probable gestational age of the pregnancy, and the availability of the state-mandated brochure. The Supreme Court approved this requirement because "the giving of truthful, non-misleading information" is consistent, in the Court's view of the issue, with the government's interest in potential life. The Court further explained that this information should be welcomed by the patient. "In attempting to ensure that a woman apprehend the full consequences of her decision, the State furthers the legitimate purpose of reducing the risk that a woman may elect an abortion, only to discover later, with devastating psychological consequences, that her decision was not fully informed. If the information the State requires to be made available to the woman is truthful and not misleading, the requirement may be permissible."

Under this standard, the courts have struck down some requirements as unconstitutional but upheld others. For instance, one federal appellate court upheld the requirement that South Dakota abortion providers tell their patients that they are terminating a "whole, separate, unique, living human being" under the rationale that the requirement is truthful because "human being" is defined by the statute as including a fetus. The same court also approved the state requiring providers to inform patients about an increased risk of suicide. The court mistakenly credited studies that were put into evidence by anti-abortion groups, studies that the National Academies of Science, Engineering, and Medicine and others have found not reliable on the topic.

Other courts have found that these requirements violate the Constitution. For instance, a federal court in Nebraska struck a law that required abortion providers to inform patients about several of the erroneous health risks mentioned in this chapter because it would require the providers to give "untruthful, misleading, and irrelevant" information to their patients.

In a separate strand of cases, some providers have challenged these laws as a form of compelled speech. Basic First Amendment law prohibits states from requiring people to speak, as in saying the Pledge of Allegiance or putting a state motto on a license plate. Courts have been unpredictable when applying this principle to abortion providers. The federal appeals court covering Texas ruled that the state's ultrasound law was constitutional because providers are giving patients truthful information under the standard from *Casey*. But the federal appeals court covering North Carolina struck down that state's ultrasound law because it was a form of compelled speech. The court said nothing about whether the information was truthful or not but instead focused on the requirement that abortion providers describe the fetus to the patient, which was a form of unconstitutional state-mandated speech.

The Supreme Court hinted at a resolution of this issue in a 2018 case involving crisis pregnancy centers, and it wasn't good for abortion providers wanting to be free from lying to their patients. In that case, the Supreme Court said that a state cannot force crisis pregnancy centers to convey information about abortion and contraception because that would be a form of compelled speech, violating the First Amendment. Preempting the argument that this ruling should also apply to abortion clinics that are forced to speak in ways that they don't like, the five-Justice majority of the Supreme Court wrote that this rule doesn't apply to abortion providers. Unlike crisis pregnancy centers, abortion providers perform a medical procedure for which they must obtain informed consent beforehand, so states can constitutionally require certain things to be said as part of that informed-consent process. Over pleas from the dissenters that the law should apply the same to both crisis pregnancy centers and abortion clinics, the majority answered clearly: abortion is just different.

The result of this legal landscape, as explained throughout this book, is a patchwork of informed-consent and counseling laws throughout the country. Some courts have been very permissive about these state mandates, while others have been much more skeptical. Without the Supreme Court stepping in and addressing any of these particular requirements, this varied landscape for abortion counseling mandates will continue.

THE BETTER APPROACH: LISTENING TO PATIENTS

When providers are able to carve out time for more extended counseling and are not burdened by the state mandates discussed above, the counseling experience is entirely different. Without the irrelevancies and inaccuracies, they can tailor their interaction with the woman in front of them and explore her feelings about her forthcoming abortion on the basis of what she needs. Consider these two stories told to us by longtime abortion providers, both located in the Midwest. The first comes from Suzie Carter, a clinic owner and director who works many different roles within the clinic:

> A patient came to our clinic, and while she was having her ultrasound done, she requested to use our phone to call her home country in Asia. We started to download an international-call app and the patient began to tell her story. She was a woman in her late twenties and stated that she had a good job and life back home in Asia. She worked for a corporation and was working her way up the corporate ladder. The entire time the patient was telling this story, she had her legs and arms crossed very tightly. She said that she was

here in our state due to an arranged marriage. She was pressured heavily by her family to marry this man. She relented, and they married. She stated that she had not seen her passport or her phone since arriving in the US about five weeks ago. This is why she was so desperate to call her home country. I asked her if her husband had ever harmed her and she replied, "Not yet." She said that her husband wanted the abortion, that her family wanted her to have the abortion, but that she just wasn't sure what to do.

She then said she was going to tell me something, something that would make me not like her, something shameful. I told her that there wasn't anything she could tell me that would make me dislike her. She then revealed that the pregnancy was not from her husband, but rather her lover from Asia. She said that being with this other man was the happiest time of her life. She wanted to speak to him about the abortion. The app was done downloading at this time and as the patient educator and I started to get up to give her privacy on the call, she reached out and asked me to stay in the room, because she stated she felt safer with me in the room. Her husband was also out in the waiting room and even though he could not see down the hall to where she was, I believe she thought he would see us emerge from the education room without her and think something was amiss. She made the call and the man answered. We could hear street sounds from her home country—lots of horns honking, motorcycle sounds, lots of voices. She spoke to him in her home language interspersed with English, so we caught bits and pieces of the conversation.

We watched the patient unwind physically, her shoulders relaxed, she cried tears of joy in hearing her lover's voice and she uncrossed her arms. Her foot was not as tightly wound around her other leg. She spoke to him for approximately fifteen to twenty minutes. While she was on the phone, the educator stepped out of the room and wrote down phone numbers and addresses for a shelter, police station, and support services in the city she lives in. When she got off the phone she stated that she definitely wanted the abortion and had her partner's support. I said, "You finally got to talk to the one person whose opinion mattered." The patient cried and said, "YES." The patient thanked us profusely for helping her make the call.

We then addressed the other issues the patient had brought up, namely her phone and passport. I asked her if she was in the United States legally, and she said "yes." I asked her if her husband left her alone during the day while he went to work, she said "yes." We informed her that women, even married women, in the United States have rights and that their husbands do not get to keep their passports and phones away from them. She asked us over and over if this was really true. We assured her it was. We told her that women in the United States have rights the same as their husbands. We gave her the referral numbers and she wrote them down in a book she had in her bag over multiple pages so as to hide the information from her husband. I told the patient that she should just walk out the front door when he leaves for work and go to the police station. I told her that the police would also be able to help refer her to resources. We discussed the patient getting her passport back and going back to her home country.

The patient could now look us both in the eye at this point in the session. Earlier, she had been mostly looking at the floor or at her lap. I told her that if she had lived here where the clinic is that I would have had her come back to the clinic tomorrow when he left for work and taken her to a shelter myself. I told her that there were others in her city that would help her.

I then left and the educator completed the session, explaining the abortion and home care. I happened to see the patient as she was exiting the bathroom after being in the recovery room. She hugged me and thanked me for all the help. She stated that she felt stronger and more sure of her rights now. The nurse told me later that the patient had said that she expected her husband to ask for her medical records and she didn't want him to have them, as he would then know that the pregnancy was not his because of how far along she was. The patient and her husband did return to the clinic about five minutes after leaving and asked for a copy of her records. We were able to say that the doctor was not yet finished with the charts for the day and they left. We have not had a request for them since.

I think of this patient often. I know that I cannot reach out to her because the only phone number we have is her husband's. I do know that we saved her life that day by her coming to our clinic. She now knows her rights and has resources she didn't have access to before. Her visit to our clinic was truly transformative.

Discussing the tiny number of patients who change their mind after coming to a clinic for an abortion, another provider who is also a midwestern clinic owner, Rebecca Salam, shared with us how she keeps letters from patients who appreciate the counseling she and her colleagues provide. Rebecca paraphrased one of those letters for us. "I just gave birth to a baby boy or a baby girl. It wasn't the right time for me to have an abortion, but I was too upset or angry to figure it out, and you helped me see that having a baby was the right thing for me."

In another case, a woman Rebecca knew had a daughter who became pregnant in her first or second year of college. The woman brought her daughter to the clinic because she wanted Rebecca to talk her into having an abortion. Rebecca told the woman, "We don't talk anybody into having an abortion. We'll talk to your daughter, but she's already been in here once. She came in for options counseling and she's told you that. She doesn't want an abortion. She wants to have a baby." Both the daughter and her mom came back for more counseling, but the daughter never had the abortion. Eventually, Rebecca said, "The patient's mother wrote me a letter, and she sent me a picture of her grandson. And she said, 'What a blessing he is to everyone. Thought you would enjoy a note of thanks for your interest and your help.' That's the kind of thing that happens when somebody takes the time to listen to patients."

The common element in these stories is that both Suzie and Rebecca were able to take the time to listen to what the person in front of them needed and then were able to act on those needs. As Jan Dancy explained this role to us, it is one of being a "patient advocate." Jan elaborated: "My job is really just to listen to what someone needs on the day of their abortion and try to make that happen." For Jan, that can mean "anything from finding resources for housing, to acknowledging that the decision is not right in this moment for them to have a termination, to setting up an adoption plan, to holding their hand through a fifteen-week abortion, to working with our finance people and with our outside resources for financial support for patients to make sure that money is not a reason that someone wouldn't be able to obtain an abortion."

As with any specialized field, different approaches are taken by different people to accomplish these goals, thus the variety of names for these positions—some are called "counselors"; others, as in Suzie's story, are called "educators"; while others, like Jan, prefer "advocate." One reason for the different titles is a long-standing debate in the abortion community over the degree to which a focus on the patient's emotional state should constitute a central part of abortion counseling. From as far back as the first generation of abortion counselors, one faction argued that the counselor's role was "support" and not "therapy"; this group's position can be summarized as "Women have thought about it and know they want an abortion; they don't need to talk about it with us." The other, more dominant faction felt that putting a patient's feelings at the center of the abortion experience was appropriate, not only to identify those who were being coerced, but also because the abortion decision raised other important issues in patients' lives, for example, the quality of their personal relationships and their life goals.

As abortion became a more and more politicized issue, some providers felt the need for more in-depth work with certain patients. As Claire Keyes, a veteran abortion counselor and clinic director said, contrasting the patients she counseled in the early days after legalization and those she saw later, starting in the 1990s, "Our patients are not coming to 'exercise their constitutional rights.' They want to talk about prayer and forgiveness." Moreover, this type of counseling can help patients work through the feelings of shame and stigma as a result of choosing to have an abortion in a society that is so polarized over the issue. As one well-regarded book about abortion counseling explains, "Many women are vulnerable to the toxic effects of anti-abortion propaganda in their families and communities. Furthermore, many women who have abortions consider themselves anti-abortion and are struggling to make sense of the conflict between their beliefs and their behavior as they find themselves choosing abortion to resolve a pregnancy."

Floyd Moore, one of the doctors we interviewed, explained to us how he addressed these issues in his group counseling sessions with his mainly African American patients in the South. One of Floyd's main objectives is "dignity restoration"—that is, to counter the shaming his patients have received both from the protesters outside the clinic and from some conservative religious elements within their own communities. Floyd explained: "I just wanted them to walk out with their heads up and to have a sense of this day not of disrespect but indifference at the least and disdain at the most for the protesters and others who would shame them. I found for some, just being able to put them in the frame of mind that they didn't have to ask permission for the care that they were entitled to and that they didn't have to consult anybody about a situation that they were intellectually, morally and emotionally capable of deciding about was reassuring." Given that nationally 13 percent of abortion patients describe themselves as evangelical and 24 percent as Catholic, it is reasonable to assume that some portion of patients have conflicting emotions about their abortions, even if they are determined to obtain the procedure.

The challenge for clinics is to be able to figure out which patients might benefit from talking about these emotions with a sympathetic counselor. As providers explained to us repeatedly, there is not enough time at most clinics to offer all patients extensive counseling, and more importantly, not all abortion patients need this. As discussed in chapter 2, a landmark study of "decisional certainty" among a large sample of women at abortion clinics found that the "level of uncertainty in abortion decision making is comparable to, or lower than, other health decisions." This study ultimately questioned the necessity of laws—such as many of the laws discussed in this and other chapters in this book—that imply that most women have not made up their minds when they enter a clinic.

To tackle this problem, some providers have tried a needs assessment form to be given to abortion patients when they present for an abortion, which would identify those most in need of in-depth counseling. An example of such a form from a midwestern clinic includes the following multiple choice questions (options are "true," "kind of," and "false"): "I want to have the baby and keep it instead of abortion"; "I want to place the baby for adoption instead of an abortion"; "At any stage of pregnancy, it's [abortion] the same as killing a baby that's already born." The form also includes questions about all those in the patient's network who know of the abortion and whether or not they are supportive; previous mental health diagnoses the patient has received; and, if the patient indicates she believes in God or a higher power, whether she is afraid of not being forgiven for having an abortion.

Those patients whose answers raise red flags about their prospects for postabortion health are offered more extended counseling. In some cases they are told to take more time to consider their decision, either by delaying for several hours or by being offered the option to come back another day. In other cases, they are given a series of guided exercises that help them explore their own feelings, their anticipated reactions to abortion, how having a child (or another child) might fit into their current life and future plans, how to find adequate adoptive parents, if that is their ultimate decision, accurate information on fetal development, and more. In rare but periodic cases, as in Rebecca's story told earlier in this chapter, some of those flagged for further counseling decide to forgo the abortion, with the active support of counselors.

There is no adequate body of research that has systematically examined the impact of more in-depth counseling. However, as two experts in the field of abortion counseling have written, "Clinical experience shows that when fear and other emotional distress surrounding an abortion are not addressed, patients can experience heightened anxiety and intensified pain during and after the abortion, misdirected anger toward the provider, or dissatisfaction afterwards."

While the approaches to abortion counseling may vary, everyone in this counseling role needs the same thing, the same thing every medical professional needs: the opportunity to customize the care they give to the person in front of them. One of the main reasons that all abortion clinics don't have this opportunity is the necessity for clinic staff to spend time imparting state-imposed "counseling" mandates and then correcting for both the misinformation contained in them and the emotional turmoil and lack of trust caused by this misinformation. This task can take up all the time that a clinic can allocate for counseling.

But state mandates are not the only reason that clinics are prevented from always providing customized counseling. The steady closure of many clinics discussed in chapter 3, particularly since 2010, has meant that some of those clinics that do manage to stay open can have very large patient loads, and there simply isn't time to do the quality counseling many providers would like to do and keep the "clinic flow" operating smoothly. The Supreme Court recognized this difficulty in the 2016 *Whole Woman's Health* decision when it wrote that, because of clinic closures, patients seeking abortion services would be "less likely to get the kind of individualized attention, serious conversation, and emotional support that doctors at less taxed facilities may have offered. . . . Surgical centers attempting to accommodate sudden, vastly increased demand may find that quality of care declines."

Also, as we discussed in chapter 5, some patients come to clinics so shaken by their encounters with aggressive protesters that all the time allotted to counseling is used up with calming the patient. When these factors are combined with invasive and inaccurate state-mandated scripts, which they often are in the most hostile states for abortion care, counselors are hard-pressed to have time with patients for the open and honest conversations that might be needed.

It may seem that the actions and information that abortion counselors are offering to some patients are very similar to what we have criticized when required by some states: suggested viewing of the ultrasound, offering information on fetal development and adoption, making sure a patient is certain of her decision, and waiting before ultimately choosing (discussed more in the next chapter). But the key word here is *required*. To return to the beginning of this chapter, abortion providers firmly believe that abortion care is not a one-size-fits-all proposition; by definition, state mandates around counseling are exactly that. The removal of the barrier of these mandates would allow providers to meet the needs of all of the women who come before them—from those women who can most benefit from in-depth counseling to those who need very little.

7 Waiting Periods

Twenty-six years old and recovering from an addiction to prescription painkillers, Sarah was eight weeks pregnant and knew she wanted an abortion. During a relapse in her treatment, she'd had sex with a man who was no longer a part of her life. Already the mom to a three-year-old, Sarah knew that she needed to focus on getting clean before having any more children, so she called to schedule an appointment at the abortion clinic in Knoxville, Tennessee, only about a forty-five-minute drive from where she lived.

If Sarah had needed any other kind of nonemergency medical procedure, such as if she were further into her pregnancy and needed an amniocentesis or, unrelated to her pregnancy, needed to have a tooth pulled, she could have called a medical provider and gotten an appointment based on that office's availability. As anyone who has ever needed medical care knows, appointments are not always immediately available, and Sarah might have had to wait before being seen. However, once the office had availability that matched Sarah's schedule, she would have been able to schedule her appointment and receive her medical care.

But Sarah wanted an abortion, and as we've seen throughout this book, the rules for abortion are different. The clinic Sarah called had availability for her on a Monday. However, even though the clinic had the staffing and time to give Sarah the care she wanted that day, state law prohibited it from doing so.

Instead, Sarah had to show up in person at the clinic on Monday and then leave without getting the care she wanted, care the clinic was prepared to give her. Tennessee had recently passed a law requiring women to wait forty-eight hours before having an abortion. This law was particularly burdensome, as it required Sarah to have two in-clinic appointments—the first for the state's version of the mandatory counseling discussed in the last chapter and the second for the abortion.

For Sarah, the waiting period was rough. It did nothing to change her mind, as she knew what was best for her without added delay. "They're just telling you to sit there and think about what you're about to do. Do people think it's not hard enough as it is?" The waiting period made an already difficult situation worse. Even though the state-mandated waiting period is forty-eight hours, the earliest the clinic could see her for the second appointment was Friday, ninety-six hours later. Sarah was suffering from intense morning sickness, so the law meant four extra days of nausea for her.

Along with the nausea, the waiting period also caused Sarah serious stress. Her drug treatment program had strict attendance rules, so missing both Monday and Friday—and additional sessions because of her morning sickness—subjected her to extra scrutiny from her counselors. They warned her that if she missed any more days of the program without a valid excuse she would be kicked out.

On Friday, Sarah again managed to find care for her daughter and again make the forty-five-minute trip to the abortion clinic. She was just under the clinic's limit for a medical abortion, so she chose that less invasive procedure. Had the waiting period been longer or had the clinic been unable to see her on Friday, she would have been pushed beyond the limit and been forced to have a different kind of procedure than what she wanted.

Even with the less invasive procedure, Sarah's body reacted poorly to the medicine. She had intense pain and threw up multiple times. But because she had already missed two days of rehab from having to visit the clinic twice, she could not afford any days off to recover. Instead, she had to force herself to go to rehab so she wouldn't lose her spot. Months later,

Sarah was still sober, but she fixated on what could have happened if the hoops she'd had to jump through had caused her to leave her treatment program. "I don't know where I'd be," she said.

State-imposed delay like Sarah faced is common for women across the country who want an abortion. For some women, the wait is merely inconvenient. For other women, the delay is stressful and expensive and causes medical problems that could have been avoided. What's clear from our interviews as well as other published research on the issue is that these waiting periods do not deter most women from getting an abortion. Instead, they are a useless obstacle thrown in the path of women choosing to terminate their pregnancy.

MEDICAL CARE WAIT TIMES

Almost everyone can relate to the issue of wait times for medical care: Trying to find a primary care physician and being told that the office is not taking new patients until next year. Calling your doctor and finding out that the next available appointment is in two months. Showing up for an appointment or at the emergency room and sitting in the waiting room for an hour or three, only to then move to an exam room where you have to wait yet again before you are seen. Having blood drawn or some other medical testing conducted and then waiting nervously for days or weeks to find out the results. If you haven't experienced these waits, you have somehow avoided using medical care in the United States.

These problems are endemic to modern American health care, which is why the Institute of Medicine has identified timeliness and efficiency as two of the pillars of an improved health care system. In 2001, the Institute of Medicine (now called the National Academy of Medicine), a subunit of the National Academy of Sciences, published a report outlining six ways to improve the quality of health care in the United States. According to the exhaustive report, American health care should strive to be safe, effective, patient centered, timely, efficient, and equitable.

Relevant to waiting periods, the Institute of Medicine wrote that timeliness is "an important characteristic of any service and is a legitimate and valued focus of improvement in health care and other industries." The report noted that health care that is not timely can result in emotional distress from having to live with the uncertainty of untreated illness, physical harm from delaying treatment or diagnosis, and a sense of lack of respect for the patient's well-being. Regarding the other relevant factor—efficiency—the report explains that health systems should avoid waste. In other words, health systems should use resources to benefit "the patients a system is intended to help."

The Institute of Medicine published a subsequent report in 2015 that specifically looked at the issue of timeliness. The report surveyed existing data about wait times across medical fields, finding significant variation across medical areas as well as in different regions of the country. Summarizing the literature on the effects of these wait times, the Institute's conclusion is familiar to anyone who has waited for health care, which is almost everyone "Long wait times may be associated with poorer health outcomes and financial burden from seeking non-network care and possibly more distant health care. Long wait times may also cause frustration, inconvenience, suffering, and dissatisfaction with the health care system." Not surprisingly, Sarah's story that started this chapter featured many of these problems.

MASTERS OF TIMELINESS AND EFFICIENCY

Abortion is a time-sensitive medical procedure. As a woman progresses in pregnancy, she can lose the opportunity to have a medication abortion, which is available generally through ten weeks gestation. Later in pregnancy, the type and length of surgical procedure change, the cost of the procedure goes up, the availability of providers goes down, and state gestational limits for abortion can come into play. Furthermore, although abortion is safe at all gestational ages, with every week further into pregnancy, the minimal risk of complications increases. Abortion providers, of course, understand all of this, so they do their best to be efficient with scheduling appointments and see patients as quickly as possible.

For the most part, they succeed. According to data from the Guttmacher Institute, the average wait time for an abortion appointment in the United States is just over seven days, with over three-quarters of abortion patients able to see a provider within seven days of calling for an appointment. Digging deeper into this number, only a small portion of women experience delays because a clinic is not able to see them earlier; most delays are caused by other factors associated with the woman's life circumstances or decision-making. Compared to the other medical specialties surveyed in the Institute of Medicine reports discussed above, abortion providers are masters of timeliness and efficiency.

The abortion providers we talked with who were able to see patients on the same day they called or first visited the clinic were proud of this capability. "It's great," said Andrea Ferrigno, an administrator at clinics in the South and Midwest. At her clinics in states that have no waiting period, "if someone comes in and they say, 'I want to have an appointment to have an abortion. Do you have anything today?' we can see them today. It's really great to be able to do that." The only restriction is the availability of the medical professional staff, but if they can fit the patient in, they will.

Andrea recognizes that some people might be queasy about women not taking more time to think through their decision but says that anyone who feels that way misunderstands abortion patients. "Of course nobody wakes up one morning saying, 'I'll just have an abortion today.' It's stuff that they've thought about for days. We don't have to regulate that or police when they decided they were going to have an abortion. They just happened to walk in today, and if we have the availability to do it, we will."

Mary Lofton, who also works at a western clinic that can see patients on the same day they make their appointment, emphasized this point. "Occasionally, a woman will come in for a pregnancy test and she finds out that it's positive and she's already thought it was positive and she's already thought about all of her options and this is 100 percent what she wants to do. We're obviously very careful about women making decisions that they feel confident in, and if they are, frequently we are able to accommodate that."

That abortion clinics have figured out a model of care that quickly sees patients contributes to patient satisfaction. Many studies have consistently found that abortion patients have a very high level of satisfaction with their abortion experience. Women tell researchers who study this issue that being able to have an abortion quickly once their mind is made up is important to their overall experience. One woman explained why to researchers, saying that "once you have made up your mind to have the abortion you want it over as soon as possible." Abortion providers who are able to do that reflect the essence of the National Academy of Medicine's aspirational goals of timeliness and efficiency.

STATE-MANDATED DELAYS

What Andrea and Mary can do for their patients is not the norm, though. The majority of states have laws that require delays in abortion care, like the law that Sarah had to navigate in the story that started this chapter. Of the twenty-seven states with laws that require delay, most require a twenty-four-hour waiting period between initial counseling and the abortion procedure. Only Indiana has a shorter requirement, with an eighteen-hour mandatory delay. Three states—Alabama, Arkansas, and Tennessee—require a forty-eight-hour wait, while five states—Missouri, North Carolina, Oklahoma, South Dakota, and Utah—go even further and require a seventy-two-hour wait. South Dakota's delay law has the unique feature of excluding weekends and holidays from counting toward the seventy-two hours.

While the difference between no mandatory delay and a delay of seventy-two (or more) hours is substantial, the length of the delay alone doesn't tell the full story. Mandatory delay laws also vary in two other ways that determine the true burden placed on women. First, while some states with delay laws allow the initial counseling to be done over the phone or online, fourteen require that it be done in person, which means that the patient has to make two separate visits to the clinic. Second, states vary with regard to who has to conduct the initial counseling. Some states allow anyone working at the clinic to do so, others require a physician to do it, and the strictest require that the same physician performing the abortion be the one who delivers the initial counseling.

At their most basic, these mandatory delay laws present logistical difficulties for patients and providers alike. Even the least invasive of these laws—a twenty-four-hour requirement that allows the initial consult to take place over the phone or internet by someone other than the provider performing the abortion—creates all sorts of problems that other health care providers do not face. For many clinics, the mandatory delay, even if it is not a two-visit requirement, means that the clinic has to hire new doctors, nurses, or other staff to deliver the required information before the procedure day. For instance, Charlene Tipton told us with dismay that the impact of a short ten-minute mandatory script being read twenty-four hours before the procedure was that she had to hire an entire new staff member—a licensed medical professional.

In some states, the twenty-four-hour clock starts when the patient reads a notice on the internet. As both Veronica Gordon and Emily Webb recounted to us, what seems like an effort by the legislature to make the law less burdensome—by allowing people to access the information at home and online—is difficult for some people, especially those who are living in poverty or who can't risk someone in their life knowing about their abortion. Veronica, the medical director of a group of southern clinics, explained that her patients have to use their own computer or go to the library to access the state website and then print out a date- and time-stamped verification. The problem is that "not everyone has the internet or a printer, and not everyone wants to print something like this at the library." Her patients can come to her clinic to read the material online and use the clinic's printer, but then that turns the state's law into a two-visit requirement.

Emily also explained the difficulty with the computer-based system for her patients, many of whom live in poverty:

> In our city, many people don't have access to computers. So, especially now with smartphones, their main access to the internet is through their phone, but the fact that you have to print out the information form is a barrier. There's at least one patient every single day that we have to reschedule because they didn't get the twenty-four-hour waiting period information in time, or they screenshot it on their phone because it had a date and time stamp, and they think that's okay. But the state requires it be printed on a piece of paper.

When this happens, Emily has to explain to the patient that "it's not us doing this, it's the state." But this is difficult to explain to a frustrated patient. Without the printout, the clinic usually conducts the consent process in person or lets the patient print out the form using the clinic computer, but the delay clock starts from that new point in time, not when the patient originally viewed the website. Ultimately, "they have to reschedule and sometimes that's a real problem."

In states where providers can give the initial information over the phone, providers do what they can to accommodate patients' lives and fit the initial counseling into their schedule. Vivian Walker regularly makes phone calls in her spare time to patients who need to start the twenty-four-hour clock in the midwestern state where she works. Sometimes, this means that patients sign up for calls at odd hours of the day. She told us one story of making the initial calls on Halloween when patients were out trick-or-treating with their children. Vivian said, "So they're on the phone and I could hear the kids giggling in the background and trick-or-treating, with the mom saying, 'Get in line,' as I'm reading. She's obviously ignoring me, which is okay. It's her choice. I ask if they have any questions. Some people are interested in hearing the information and asking questions. Other people just jump through the hoop and they're not listening."

Halloween informed-consent calls were a first for Vivian, but she regularly makes these phone calls at all times throughout the day. "Sometimes it's in the middle of the day or after dinner because that's the only opportunity. They may be working and trying to do it on their lunch hour. This is private information, so I don't know how they successfully tell their boss about it without giving up some privacy."

Two-visit requirements up the ante for clinics and patients. At their core, they pose problems because, as Kathaleen Pittman put it, "for some women, they struggle to get here the one time, never mind the two times," especially those living in poverty or those for whom there are privacy reasons that they can't share their abortion with others. Gabrielle Goodrick, a doctor in a western state, expressed the same sentiment: "The worst barrier they face is the twenty-four-hour wait, in terms of transportation, getting off work, child care, and just the hassle of coming in twice."

At Donna Sullivan's clinic, because of the newly enacted two-visit law, clinic flow has completely changed. "Two days of office visits are now taken up with these initial consult appointments, which are valueless because our patient educators reiterate a lot of it and most of it's on our website. So they've probably read it, they've heard it, then they get to hear it again." Donna's doctors are required by law to provide the consults, which means that their valuable time is taken up doing these in-person sessions when they could be providing actual medical care. "We need the doctors to be doing other things, and of course they hate it. They just have to say the same thing a million times and they feel like they don't have value. It's a drag for them, for the patients, for everybody." In exchange for this "valueless" consultation, Donna has had to add about $150 to $200 to the abortion price for her patients in order to pay for the doctor's time.

The most burdensome form of mandated delay is the two-visit requirement along with a requirement that the same doctor provide the initial consult and the abortion. Douglas Laube, a doctor in the Midwest, said that where he practices, this requirement is "particularly onerous for women who want to have a medication abortion because I have to be the one on the schedule that they can come back and see." If he is not scheduled for another week or two, the patient might be pushed out of the window for having a medication abortion. If he is the doctor who did the initial consult, Douglas said, "I have to then literally break the bubble pack and push the pill into the palm of their hand and then watch them swallow it. And then make sure it stays down and give them instructions on taking the next pill at home." He has to watch the clock carefully when he is doing the initial consultation so that he doesn't finish so late that he won't be working the next day at that exact time. To Douglas, who has been an abortion physician for several decades and has practiced in multiple states, this new aspect of the law is "a charade really. It's just a total waste of time."

As Douglas's story suggests, abortion practices with multiple physicians have the hardest time under a same-provider law. At Elena Hunter's office, there is only one physician, and he works six days a week. When her state passed a same-provider mandatory delay law that required a doctor to do the initial consult in person, the physician's schedule became even more crowded than it already was, but the patients didn't feel the brunt of the law as much as they could have.

Elena compared her office to another abortion provider in the same city that has many different doctors. At that practice, the state's twenty-four-hour mandatory delay can result in a delay of multiple weeks. If a doctor who does the initial consent is not on the schedule for another week or more, either because she has limited availability, travels to provide abortions, or has an emergency and has to change her schedule, the patient will have to wait for her return or get a new consent. "There's almost more of a burden from waiting periods when you have multiple physicians," Elena told us. As many providers explained, flexibility is key in dealing with these kinds of laws, but not every practice or provider has that luxury.

Some states have exceptions to their mandatory delay laws, such as when the pregnancy will threaten the life of the patient, the pregnancy is the result of rape or incest, or the patient is facing a medical emergency. Jen Moore Conrow said that her clinic uses these exceptions only on rare occasions. She and her colleagues fear that the state might not see the case the same way as they do. "Is it really worth risking our license and the practice to help one person, versus knowing that we're still going to be able to provide abortions for more people?" When her clinic has waived the requirement, it's only been for patients facing extreme time-sensitive emergencies, such as this patient Jen told us about:

> We had a cancer patient who flew here from out of the country to start her cancer care. She had a really rare cancer, and there's a hospital in this city that is one of the only places in the world that can do this treatment. But when she gets to the hospital, she is diagnosed as pregnant. Her emergency cancer surgery is tomorrow. So we need to do this abortion today; otherwise, everything's thrown off. Like if she doesn't have this surgery tomorrow, she can't start this other fancy-pants proton therapy radar cancer treatment, so she needs to have this abortion right now. So that was an instance where we waived the twenty-four-hour consenting rule.

Given her concerns about state oversight, Jen assured us that she and her colleagues "documented all of that."

ARBITRARILY HARMING PATIENTS

"Most people," Hannah Miller explained, "when they call the clinic, do not know about this rule about waiting. They're hoping to get in on a particular day that they are off from work or have child care or transportation. They call us, and we have availability, but they can't be seen on the day they want to." This delay has serious consequences.

At their worst, mandatory delay laws can prevent women from obtaining abortions altogether. Floyd Moore explained how this happens at his southern clinic. The law requires an in-person consultation at least twenty-four hours beforehand. Because of the difficulty the clinic faces finding doctors in this very conservative state, the clinic provides abortion services only two days a week, but those two days change on the basis of the two different out-of-town doctors' schedules. If the other doctor performed the consultation on a Friday, Floyd could provide the patient's abortion on Monday with the delay covering only the weekend.

However, not all patients are so lucky. If a patient first came to the clinic on a Tuesday that Floyd was working and he had already worked Monday, "it was luck of the draw" in terms of when she would have her abortion, based on the other doctor's schedule the following week. If the patient was close to the state's gestational age limit, the patient might be denied an abortion even though Floyd was perfectly capable of providing the patient's abortion when she appeared at the clinic the first time.

"What made this totally arbitrary," Floyd told us, "was that I could do an abortion in the same day. If there wasn't that twenty-four-hour waiting period that woman could have had her procedure done that day." Patients who have faced this situation are devastated. They "beg and plead" with Floyd, who told us he is "moved by the sense of vulnerability that women felt because it was like I had the power of their future in my hands but couldn't use it, and the whole process felt arbitrary to them." In those situations, Floyd "would take time with them to explain why I couldn't bend the rules or break the law because I needed to make the access available to everybody, even though I felt deeply for them and their situation."

Even for patients who are not delayed past the gestational limit at that clinic, these laws increase the difficulty of getting an abortion. One of Melody Cook's patients stood out in her mind in this regard. She was a mother to three children who came to Melody's clinic because the clinic in her home state could not see her. "She was trying to work out being off work, being away from her children, her partner trying to watch her children, and then also to have a driver drive her twice to stay overnight here." The planning was even more difficult because the patient not only had to come to the clinic twice in person while waiting forty-eight hours in between visits but also had to have a two-day procedure because of how far along she was in her pregnancy. "To make the logistics happen took her two weeks or more, which then made her further in gestation, made her procedure cost more, increased her risk, all just for her to logistically make it happen with the two-visit requirement."

The empirical research studying this issue confirms how burdensome mandatory delay laws really are. While there does not appear to be any evidence that short mandatory delays that do not require two clinic visits result in substantial delays or affect overall access to abortion, in-person requirements do. Two states have been studied in depth on this point, and both point to the substantial impact these delays have on patients.

Mississippi was the first state to implement an in-person mandatory delay law, passing a twenty-four-hour, two-visit law in 1992. Researchers who studied the law found that, even though it required only a one-day wait, the practical effect was that patients had to wait, on average, four days between initial counseling and abortion. The law also resulted in an increase in women traveling out of state for an abortion as well as a substantial increase in the number of women who had second-trimester abortions. Perhaps most concerning, the studies found that, like the women Floyd Moore described above, between 11 and 13 percent of women who wanted an abortion in Mississippi were not able to obtain an abortion at all because of the new law.

Edna Macklin experienced some of these issues with patients at her clinic, though in an even worse way because her state had recently transformed its twenty-four-hour waiting period into a forty-eight-hour in-person one. Her clinic performs abortions only on Fridays, and all procedures begin before 8:00 a.m. Patients come in for first visits Monday through Thursday. But now, if someone comes in on Wednesday or Thursday, that person has to wait until the Friday of the *following* week. So, as Edna said, "The reality is an eight- or nine-day waiting period."

Delaying patient care was one of the chief concerns that Van May had when we talked to her about her state's in-person twenty-four-hour mandatory delay that requires the same physician to deliver the state-mandated information in a private setting. Van said that "whoever helped the legislators write this law had intimate knowledge about abortion services" in order to have maximum effect. Her clinic sees a large number of patients and has many rotating physicians. "It requires major manipulation of the schedule to get patients in to comply with this requirement." The same-physician law can result in wait times of almost two weeks because Van doesn't have the same physician every single day.

Delays in patient care can have the serious effect of pushing patients beyond the gestational limit or pushing patients into a different type of medical procedure. Erica Valverde, a doctor in a western state, explained that the mandatory delay law, which in her state is seventy-two hours, "may cross a gestational age where the price increases, sometimes even double." As an example, she said that "if someone first comes to see me at twelve weeks and six days, the next day they are thirteen weeks. Because of fetal development, that's a completely different procedure with a differ-ent price, which can be very burdensome as well."

Forced delay can be disruptive to patients' lives in other ways. Jan Dancy explained that patients sometimes wind up sitting in the waiting area of the clinic solely because of the state law. If the patient completed the counseling session the day before at 11:00 am, the procedure can't start until 11:00 am the next day, even when "we are in clinic and things are moving and rocking and jamming and the doctor's here and it's 9:30." That ninety-minute wait might not seem like much, but Jan has seen many patients for whom that little amount of time makes a difference. Patients have, for instance, deadlines for picking up their child from a bus stop or, for the flight attendants on layover that Jan has cared for, getting back on a plane. For these patients, waiting for no reason other than that the state requires it is "gut-wrenching." It also can be physically uncom-fortable because patients aren't allowed to eat after midnight before their procedure. "They're not waiting because of a part of their medical care. They're waiting for the state to give them a blessing about their own fam-ily care and decisions."

The other state that has been studied in depth is Utah. In 2012, it enacted the nation's first law requiring a seventy-two-hour delay between initial counseling and the abortion. With the state's accompanying in-person counseling requirement, Utah had the strictest mandatory delay law on the books. Because it was unique at the time, several researchers studied the law. The overall conclusion was that, despite the law's stated goal of giving women time to reconsider their abortion, nine out of ten women became more certain or did not change how certain they were about their decision, while only 8 percent of women became less certain. The researchers found that the small number of women who became less certain were already conflicted at their initial appointment, which would have alerted the abortion provider to further counsel the patient, encouraging her to take more time or even come back another day. In terms of women actually changing their mind, the study found that 2 percent of patients changed their minds from unconflicted to continuing the pregnancy because of the waiting period, a number that is in the same range as the number for those changing their minds about abortion in states without a waiting period.

However, despite the law not significantly changing how certain women are about having an abortion or how many change their minds, it does increase the burden on patients. As in Mississippi, where the twenty-four-hour delay became, on average, a four-day delay, the Utah seventy-two-hour delay was associated with about eight days of delay. It also increased women's anxiety because they had to wait even longer for a procedure that they wanted. One woman told researchers that "knowing that I had to wait after deciding what I wanted to do and not having control over my own life and my body made me mad."

The delay's impact was broad. Costs associated with the procedure went up by about 10 percent because of logistical and financial difficulties. Among the other ways that women were affected by the new law were taking more time off work, missing more school, losing wages, incurring increased child care and transportation costs, having friends or family members miss work or spend money, and being forced to tell someone about the abortion that they would not have otherwise wanted to tell.

Millie Johnson told us she was gravely concerned about these effects for her patients. Her clinic is in a very large, sparsely populated state. It has limited days each month when it provides surgical abortion, so patients often have to drive long distances twice—once for the in-person consent and then again for the procedure. If the patients are lucky, they can stay with family in the area or afford a hotel room during the required delay. But for her patient population, "it's a lot of low-income women who can't afford a hotel, so we have people sleeping in our parking lot." Cindi Cranston has seen the same thing at her clinic, which also has a two-visit requirement. "Every year I've worked here, at least once we've opened up on a day where we will find a car that's been parked in our lot overnight with people spending the night in their car waiting for the next day to actually get their procedure."

The Utah law explored by this research allows the medical care provider who delivers the seventy-two-hour consent to be a different person from the one who provides the abortion. In the state neighboring Nellie Baker's midwestern clinic, the law requires two visits, a seventy-two-hour delay, and the same physician to deliver the consent and perform the abortion. Nellie, who doesn't perform abortions in this state but does practice other forms of medicine there, told us that this law creates scheduling nightmares for the clinic. On a regular basis, Nellie fields calls from doctors in that state who send patients to her so that they can be seen without the burden of the delay. Nellie recognizes how challenging this is for patients who start at one clinic in one state but then wind up traveling to another clinic in another state just to have their procedure without any further delay.

In one of the states where Vivian Walker performs abortions, patients are also required to wait seventy-two hours, make two in-person visits, and see the same physician. The delay can potentially be even longer under some circumstances required by law. In this large rural state that often has bad weather, there is one abortion clinic, so the patients already have to travel long distances, often in treacherous conditions. Vivian is one of multiple doctors who travel by plane to the clinic, which means she and the patients she cares for need perfect luck to see each other again:

> So if we successfully see each other on Monday and if anything happens to either one of us on Thursday, whether there's a snowstorm and my plane was cancelled or let's say a snowstorm in the western half of the state, they can't get out, they can't drive, or a flat tire or just the same barriers that we all have successfully getting out of the house, getting in the car, and getting somewhere. There's things that can go wrong, whether the car doesn't start, whether the friend doesn't pick them up. Those variables are just multiplied by the fact that it would have to be the same physician. So if something goes wrong they can't just come back the following Monday when there's a different doctor there and have the abortion. They have to wait and they would have to reschedule starting the whole process over again the next week.

Reflecting on this tight schedule and her patients' travel challenges, Vivian said, "Abortion care is important work anyway, but it's especially important in places like this, so making sure that I can get there, and I am there for those patients is vitally important, because there isn't anyone else. If I can't get through the snow, these patients aren't having an abortion this week because of the waiting period, and who knows if they can have one next week?"

WITH THE SUPREME COURT'S BLESSING

Despite these burdens, the Supreme Court has upheld a twenty-four-hour mandatory delay and only a small number of state courts have struck down similar laws. In 1992, before most of the research about the burden of mandatory delays had been published, the Supreme Court upheld Pennsylvania's twenty-four-hour waiting period. The Court had previously struck down a similar Ohio law in 1983, reasoning that the mandatory delay would not make the procedure safer or the woman's decision more informed and was thus "arbitrary and inflexible." In 1992, with several new Justices on the Court, the result was different. In the Pennsylvania case, the Court said that its 1983 decision was wrong because "the idea that important decisions will be more informed and deliberate if they follow some period of reflection does not strike us as unreasonable."

The Court was aware of the burdens the waiting period caused but dismissed them as inconsequential. It recognized that the law would cause a delay longer than just one day, increase the costs associated with abortion, subject women to greater harassment from anti-abortion protesters, and risk women having people in their lives find out whom they didn't want to, such as employers and relatives. Nonetheless, the Court said that while these might be "particular burden[s]," they were not so serious and such a risk to health that they amounted to unconstitutional "substantial obstacle[s]."

That the US Supreme Court upheld the twenty-four-hour waiting period in Pennsylvania in 1992 does not mean that, barring the Supreme Court overturning that decision, every waiting period will be found constitutional. That decision was based on the particulars of that case, so in another case in another state the exact same law might constitute an unconstitutional substantial burden. For instance, in a case that may ultimately be reviewed by the Supreme Court, in 2018 the federal appeals court covering Indiana struck down that state's eighteen-hour mandatory delay that required an ultrasound at the first visit, saying that the law's "only effect is to place barriers between a woman who wishes to exercise her right to an abortion and her ability to do so." Moreover, that the Supreme Court has previously approved a twenty-four-hour mandatory delay does not mean that forty-eight- or seventy-two-hour delay laws are constitutional, especially those with two-visit and same-physician requirements.

Plus, as is always the case, state courts can strike down identical laws as violating their state constitutions, as Florida's Supreme Court did in 2017 with its twenty-four-hour delay law. The reasoning the court used to conclude that the law violated the state constitution's right to privacy is consistent with the basic premise of this book. As the Florida Supreme Court wrote, "No other medical procedure, even those with greater health consequences, requires a twenty-four hour waiting period in the informed consent process." In Iowa, the state supreme court struck down a seventy-two-hour mandatory delay after reviewing all of the studies discussed here. As the court wrote about the studies, "In truth, the evidence conclusively demonstrates that the [seventy-two-hour delay law] will not result in a measurable number of women choosing to continue a pregnancy they would have terminated without a mandatory 72-hour waiting period. Moreover, the burdens imposed on women by the waiting period are substantial, especially for women without financial means."

The absurdity of the US Supreme Court's logic allowing at least a twenty-four-hour mandatory delay is that, as everyone we talked with made clear, no one wants a woman to have an abortion who does not want to have one. Or, to use the pithy language already quoted in this book, "There's no do-over." Almost every provider we interviewed voluntarily shared this concern, which is why as part of normal care, abortion clinics regularly assess certainty in their patients and encourage women who are not certain to take more time in making their decision.

Other medical care providers also make sure patients are certain about their choices, but unlike other medical care providers, abortion providers and patients are singled out in more than half the states in the country in this regard. Legislatures concerned with the twin myths that abortion clinics pressure women to have abortions just to make more money and that women seeking abortions haven't already thought carefully about their decision treat abortion patients differently from other patients, requiring them to wait a state-mandated period of time.

With these laws having no benefit and being all burden, Erica Valverde summed up the feelings of everyone we talked with about mandatory delays: "For the government to be so bold as to say this is the time you need to think about your decision, I mean I can't think of anything more condescending, especially when someone has probably already made their decision and thought about it before even getting pregnant. So it's an arbitrary rule." The landmark 2018 study from the National Academies of Sciences, Engineering, and Medicine agrees with Erica, concluding after extensive research about the practice of abortion in this country that mandatory delay laws are inconsistent with the goals of timeliness and efficiency in health care.

These requirements also deliver a very clear message about patient agency that Jan Dancy captured perfectly: "Every day I have to explain why someone was told by the state to wait to be able to obtain an abortion. That is, to me, an egregious barrier because the assumption is that someone's not capable of making a decision or the decision is going to be spur of the moment and not actually a true thought." Or, in the words of the federal appeals court covering Indiana, these laws contradict the basic notion that "women, like all humans, are intellectual creatures with the ability to reason, consider, ponder, and challenge their own ideas."

8 The Procedure

POLITICS OVERRIDES MEDICAL EXPERTISE

In 2017, a young woman in Maine found herself pregnant—and far from any of the large, sparsely populated state's abortion clinics, which are mainly clustered on the coast. She wanted an abortion and had her mother's support. Instead of making the drive to one of the state's clinics, which would have been difficult for her family because of various challenges in their life, this teen had her abortion at home, receiving abortion pills in the mail.

She was able to do this through one of the state's abortion clinics that was taking part in a five-state experimental study conducted by the research organization Gynuity. After the teen and her mother went to a local doctor for an ultrasound and bloodwork, she and the abortion clinic's doctor talked via video conference to go over any questions the teen had and to enable her to sign the appropriate documents. Once that was completed, she received the pills in the mail the next day and completed her abortion in the comfort of her own home.

The ease with which this Maine teen, far from the state's abortion clinics, was able to have the abortion procedure that was both best suited for her particular circumstances and backed by evidence-based medicine can be contrasted with the experience of women in many other states where the procedure itself is much more highly restricted. For instance, women who find out late in their pregnancy that they are carrying a fetus with a lethal anomaly often have a very difficult time finding an abortion provider because most states prohibit abortions at that stage of the pregnancy.

Kate's story is emblematic of these women. Kate and her husband already had one daughter and were eager to have another child. After three miscarriages, Kate finally made it through the first and second trimester of her fourth try and eagerly awaited the new arrival to her family. Nonetheless, given the miscarriages, she still worried. "At seven months, I tried to think positively. I picked up my knitting needles and began a tiny sweater for this next baby girl. I was working the final rows of that sweater at an ultrasound, which my midwife hoped would ease my relentless worry. When she saw me knitting, the doctor's eyes welled with tears."

The doctor had devastating news. The ultrasound revealed that there were holes in the fetal brain consistent with Dandy-Walker malformation, an anomaly often diagnosed only late in pregnancy. Based on the severity of the diagnosis, Kate was told that if she carried her pregnancy to term, it would be a high-risk birth for her and her baby, and that, if the baby somehow survived, she would need heavy medical intervention and have a very short life filled with suffering.

Kate and her husband were distraught, but they knew what they had to do. "I could not subject my child to that kind of suffering. I wished for a miracle, but I would not risk my daughter's wellbeing. My heart sang clearly: I would give my daughter peace. Abortion was the choice to meet our family's values and our daughter's needs—it was the option we could live with."

The trouble for Kate was that abortion at this stage of pregnancy is outlawed in most states, including where she lived. Only a few states allow abortion in the third trimester, and even fewer doctors openly perform such procedures. As a result, Kate was faced with the very difficult situation of having to fly two thousand miles across the country to a doctor who charged thousands of dollars for the complicated and rare medical procedure. Luckily, she was able to raise the money with the help of family and had the support from them to make the trip. Once she was at the clinic that could legally perform her abortion, she received "kind, legal, compassionate, and, most importantly, safe" care that terminated her pregnancy.

Looking back, Kate has "never once regretted" her decision because she "did the best I could for my daughter" and was able to "give her the gift of peace." She was fortunate to be able to do so despite laws making the medical procedure she needed illegal in her home state and most others.

Once a woman makes her decision, finds and gets to a provider, arranges payment for the procedure, gets inside the clinic, listens to state-mandated misinformation as part of the counseling process, and waits the required period of time, in an ideal world a combination of her personal preferences and evidence-based medicine should determine the medical procedure she receives. However, as with every other step on a woman's path to obtain an abortion, at the point of receiving the procedure itself, abortion exceptionalism is very much present. In other areas of medicine, medical expertise determines the procedure performed to treat a patient. Not so in abortion. What procedures are permissible, who is legally allowed to perform an abortion, and how late in her pregnancy an abortion can be performed—all these matters have been subject to a level of regulation by anti-abortion politicians that is not present in other areas of medicine. In other words, when it comes to the actual abortion, legislatures are dictating the procedure rather than what should be the driving force—a combination of the patient's desires and evidence-based medicine.

TRYING TO QUASH MEDICATION ABORTION

Medication abortion, an increasingly common form of abortion in the first trimester, has always been embroiled in abortion politics. This method involves two different drugs—mifepristone, which causes the fetus to stop developing, and misoprostol, which causes uterine contractions and the expulsion of the fetus. This method is typically used in the United States through the first ten weeks of pregnancy. The most common protocol is that mifepristone is administered in an abortion clinic. Then patients are given misoprostol to take at home at a specified time. While the protocol for this method was approved in France in 1988, it was not approved in the United States until 2000. It is impossible to assess that gap in time when a safe abortion procedure that would improve accessibility existed without pointing to the impact of anti-abortion politics on best medical practices.

Medication abortion has been highly regulated by a number of states in spite of its excellent safety record. Following evidence-based medical research on the procedure, many clinics modified the original 2000 Food and Drug Administration protocol, which required four patient office visits and a high (and thus expensive) dose of mifepristone, to a lesser dose and fewer office visits. When they did so, the clinics found no difference in patient outcomes.

But although it is common for FDA-approved protocols in other branches of medicine to be modified by clinicians on the basis of further research and actual clinical experience, several states have passed legislation requiring clinics to return to conformity to the original protocol. Not surprisingly, researchers found that the number of medication abortions dramatically decreased under this requirement, in part because some clinics just stopped offering the option to their patients on account of the state requirement that clinics use the old protocol. In 2016, the FDA changed the sixteen-year-old protocol and made it consistent with the practices at most abortion clinics. This change meant that the clinics that chose to stop performing medication abortions under state law could once again offer this option to patients.

Nonetheless, there continue to be ways that states restrict the provision of medication abortion. For instance, delivering medication abortion via telemedicine is currently one of the most promising ways to facilitate abortion, as this chapter's opening story about the experimental project in Maine demonstrates. Telemedicine, which involves the use of new technologies to offer health care services to patients at an offsite location (either another health care office or the patient's home) has grown exponentially in recent years, with one estimate suggesting that some 70 percent of all health care providers in the US utilize telemedicine to some degree.

In the most common form of abortion via telemedicine, a patient who lives at some distance from an abortion facility comes to a general health care clinic for an intake appointment, including an ultrasound. An abortion provider at an offsite location, usually an abortion clinic but possibly the provider's own office or even home, reviews her ultrasound and her medical history. After videoconferencing with the patient, if the provider determines that the patient is an appropriate candidate for a medication abortion, the patient is given the first drug in the presence of the provider watching via video and an onsite clinician (usually a nurse) who is in the same room as the patient. The patient is then instructed when to take the second drug at home and is told to return to the local clinic in two weeks to ensure that the abortion has been successfully completed. As with in-clinic medical abortions, the patient then goes home to complete the abortion on her own by taking the final doses of medicine.

Millie Johnson is a doctor in a western state that allows telemedicine for medication abortions. She described at length to us the value of being able to provide abortions in this way. In her state, patients can be hundreds of miles away from physicians, but with the ease of telemedicine they can still get their abortion. Millie said that a patient can be at a health center in a rural part of the state while Millie is "sitting wherever I happen to be on that day," and she can still "provide the abortion care to the patient in the more rural site." In theory, Millie laughed, the doctor "could be sitting in their pajamas in their living room" and provide the care, but her office has, to date, always had the doctor in the office. This bow to the threat of anti-abortion criticism "limits use a little bit," but overall Millie explained that this system greatly increases access in her state.

The safety of medication abortion via telemedicine has been well established. Iowa has been at the forefront of telemedicine abortion. Researchers there examined the records of twenty thousand medication abortion patients and found that a telemedicine procedure was as safe as an in-patient one. This research was instrumental in convincing a state court to reinstate telemedicine abortion in Iowa after the state legislature had banned it. Researchers also found that those patients who had received their abortions via telemedicine tended to have earlier procedures than those who had received them in abortion clinics. Furthermore, they found that telemedicine abortions were somewhat more effective than in-clinic abortions, though all the medication abortions studied had high rates of effectiveness. An issue that the researchers of the Iowa experience did not address was how much time and money women save by having the option of telemedicine, but common sense suggests that, given all of the issues addressed in chapter 3 of this book, not having to travel long distances and not having to pay for child care, gas, and, perhaps, lodging lead to considerable savings and greater accessibility.

Telemedicine abortions are, obviously, most helpful in states that are large and have few clinics. However, seventeen states ban abortion via telemedicine, including Texas, where the state's huge size would make this a very helpful option for women. Notably, telemedicine is widely used in other branches of health care in that state, but consistent with the central claim of this book, patients cannot gain its benefit when they seek abortion care. The experience of Hawaii, in contrast, is very different, as the state does allow abortions via telemedicine. This has proved very beneficial, as the only abortion facilities in Hawaii are in Honolulu and Maui, and women living on other islands who are eligible for medication abortion are spared the necessity of flying in order to receive their health care.

ONLY DOCTORS?

Perhaps one of the restrictions that has the greatest potential to reshape the abortion landscape has to do with who can perform an abortion. Can only doctors perform abortions or can other medical professionals, such as nurses, midwives, and physician assistants (generally referred to as advanced-practice clinicians or APCs for short)? The reason this is so important is, as Monica McLemore, a nurse at a hospital-based clinic in a western state, explained, "The big elephant in the room is that there's so many more advanced-practice clinicians than there are physicians." With those numbers, Monica told us that broadening who can perform abortions, in particular medication abortions, to include APCs would result in much greater access for women.

However, the reality on the ground is that states have limited who can perform abortions. Some states limit abortion provision to physicians only. Mississippi is alone in going a step further and limiting provision only to obstetrician-gynecologists, even though ever since *Roe* physicians in other specialties, especially family medicine, have safely provided abortions.

Peculiarities of state laws, and not only abortion politics per se, play a part in determining who can perform abortions. Vermont and Montana, for example, have a long history of permitting physician assistants (PAs) to perform numerous medical functions, including abortion, that other states limit to doctors. In both these states, the abortion safety record of PAs has been comparable to that of doctors. Indeed, the safety record achieved by PAs in both these states was so strong that in 1990, at a symposium cosponsored by the American College of Obstetricians and Gynecologists (ACOG) and the National Abortion Federation, the participants concluded that "under physician supervision, appropriately trained midlevel clinicians, including physician assistants, nurse practitioners, and certified nurse midwives, offer considerable promise for expanding the pool of qualified abortion providers." The symposium's final report included recommendations for the APCs' training and for their integration into abortion provision.

Currently, seventeen states and the District of Columbia permit abortion provision by APCs, while the other thirty-three states have physician-only laws governing abortion. Mainly this APC provision involves medication abortion. This method, many argue, is ideally suited for APCs because the skills involved are heavily dependent on counseling, as well as taking a medical history and ascertaining the length of a pregnancy. Rebecca Moore, the director of a network of clinics in western states, enthusiastically described to us how important medication abortion provision by nurse practitioners was in facilitating abortion access in one of the large states her clinics serve:

> We're doing medical abortions with nurse practitioners all over the state, and it's particularly important in the mountains. If you think about it, if you're in one of our small-town mountain communities and you find out you're pregnant, you can go in that same day if the nurse practitioner is there. It's fabulous. We've been providing in one particularly remote part of the state for years, but we did it with a circuit-riding doctor, and so if the doc was there on Tuesday and you came in on Wednesday, you had to wait another week or two, which meant that it might get you out of your time frame. And then you'd have to drive over two mountain passes to get to the big city. So now you can come in on the day the nurse practitioner is there, which is almost every day, and be taken care of. I love it. I'm so, so proud of this work. It's at least a dozen health centers where we are doing this.

In spite of her satisfaction that her organization is able to facilitate this access in a dozen health centers, abortion politics are never far from Rebecca's mind. "I kind of hold my breath that this won't be reversed by the legislature."

Pam Monroe, another clinic director in a western state where nurse practitioners are permitted to provide medication abortions, spoke of the scheduling ease this permitted. Her clinics don't need a special day or series of days dedicated to abortion because "if it's medication abortion, those are just mixed in the regular family planning schedule." And because abortion patients are mixed with family planning patients and those receiving other forms of health care, "nobody really knows what anybody's there for." As a result, anti-abortion extremists cannot target abortion patients.

In five states currently, APCs are also allowed to perform the other dominant form of first-trimester abortion, "aspiration abortion." Aspiration abortion has traditionally been done via a vacuum suction machine. In this method, the provider first dilates the patient's cervix, then inserts a medical instrument called a cannula into her uterus, and finally suctions out the contents of her uterus using a pump. The safety record of APCs doing aspiration abortion has been definitively established in a large-scale research project conducted at the University of California, San Francisco. Under a waiver granted by the state of California, clinicians trained forty-seven APCs to competency in early aspiration abortion. The nearly nine thousand abortions completed by this group were compared to about eight thousand completed by physicians, and both groups had very similar—and very low—complication rates. The results of this research led the state legislature in 2013 to pass a bill expanding APCs' authority to perform abortions in the state from just medication abortion to aspiration abortion as well.

Jen Castle is a nurse practitioner who works in a northeastern state that allows her to perform both aspiration abortions and medication abortions. To her, this "makes a huge difference for access." The clinics where she works are staffed every day of the week with APCs, which means that patients always have access to both types of abortion. "It's not like we have to bring in a doctor once a week who is familiar with our center and our ways and our patients." This not only increases access for patients but also normalizes abortion care. "It's just an extension of caring for our patients," Jen said. "Being able to integrate abortion into family planning services that I can provide is fantastic."

While APCs in California and Jen's state are allowed to perform early aspiration abortions, Andrea Hillman, a nurse practitioner in a northeastern state, is not. Andrea received training in early aspiration abortion care at the same institution that trained the California APCs who have achieved such a positive safety record. However, the law in her home state is such that she is permitted to use the same technique as an aspiration abortion *only* on a patient whose fetus is already dead—known as "miscarriage management"—but not if the fetus or embryo is alive. As she told us, "It's the exact same procedure. The difference is that the fetus is alive or the fetus is not alive."

Andrea spoke wistfully of the special element she feels that nurse practitioners bring to abortion care, which she is currently prohibited from providing: "There are clients that really need a little bit more intensive psychosocial type of support, and that's kind of a cornerstone of what nursing brings to practice, you know, the education and counseling piece. We're trained in that. We go a little bit more in depth than physicians do and it's often said about me, 'Andrea takes care of the nuance.'" Monica McLemore agrees. On the basis of her training and experience, she knows that the "nursing model of care" would allow "a more holistic way to be able to provide care" to abortion patients. Monica cautioned that she didn't want to paint too rosy a picture because she understands that some nurses can be "stigmatizers" around abortion care. But she believes that with the appropriate training nurses can at a minimum provide the same quality of care for most early abortion patients and, for some patients, provide even better care.

Monica also explained another advantage that APCs have over doctors. Along with greater numbers, APCs practice in more geographically diverse locations. Doctors in rural areas are in short supply in many areas of medicine. Nurses and physician assistants deliver more service outside urban areas. Monica told us that "we know that there are nurse practitioners who are the primary people who are providing care in a lot of rural areas, so it would simply be adding to their skill set and being able to get them trained to be able to provide things like medication abortion. This would allow individuals who go work in rural areas to be able to provide comprehensive sexual and reproductive health care."

Janet Cook is an example of just how powerful a relaxed requirement for who can perform abortions can be when coupled with advances in telemedicine. Janet is a physician assistant who is allowed in her large western state to perform first-trimester abortions. As Janet sees it, travel time is the biggest obstacle to abortion access in her state. She has long been able to perform abortions, but only recently has she begun also using telemedicine. The combination has made a huge difference for her patients. Sometimes from several hundreds of miles away, Janet is able to "talk to the patient. She's in the exam room. She sees me, I see her, and we chat and sometimes we get into other things." Without the need for a doctor or for the patient to be in the same physical space or even the same part of the state, Janet is able to provide her with a safe, quality abortion experience that would have been almost impossible without these more accessible laws.

Laws that prohibit APCs from performing abortions have begun to be challenged across the country. So far, there has not been an appellate court ruling on the issue. In the meantime, the comprehensive 2018 report on abortion safety and accessibility from the National Academies of Sciences, Engineering, and Medicine has chastised states for restricting APCs from performing abortion care, arguing that these prohibitions hinder the accessibility of abortion care while doing nothing to promote safety.

LEGISLATING HOW SURGERY CAN BE PERFORMED

Beyond medication abortion, legislators have taken aim at surgical abortion procedures as well. The congressional ban of so-called "partial birth abortion" represents the most dramatic and broadly sweeping case to date of political interference in the medical performance of a surgical abortion—or, arguably, any medical procedure. Partial birth abortion, a term made up by anti-abortion strategists that exists nowhere in the medical literature, refers to a procedure known in the medical world as "intact dilation and extraction," or "intact D&E."

This procedure had been used fairly infrequently for abortions later in the second trimester. In contrast to a standard D&E, which involves dilating the woman's cervix and then using forceps to remove the fetus piece by piece, a physician performs an intact D&E by, after dilating the cervix, removing the fetus intact until only the skull remains in the uterus (because it is too large to pass through the cervix), then partially collapsing the skull so it can pass through the cervix safely for the woman. In some situations, physicians feel this method is safer because the doctor has to pass a medical instrument into the uterus fewer times than with the standard D&E procedure, and therefore there is lessened risk of blood loss and perforation. Because the fetus is removed intact, there is also less of a risk of leaving fetal tissue in the uterus and, according to those who used this method before it was banned, more of an opportunity for grieving parents to hold their child's body after the procedure to say farewell.

By the early 2000s, more than half the states in the country and the federal government banned this procedure. As a result, the laws were challenged in court by abortion providers who used the procedure and believed it was the safest and most medically sound way to terminate some of their patients' pregnancies. At the numerous court trials in those challenges, these abortion providers enumerated various conditions in which intact D&E may be safer, for example for women with a history of bleeding disorders or uterine scars. ACOG also chimed in, adding to the reasons that this procedure can be the most appropriate and safest for some patients by explaining the value of its shorter length: "The shorter the procedure, the less blood loss, trauma, and exposure to anesthesia." ACOG concluded that the "intuitive safety advantages of intact D&E are supported by clinical experience."

Even though this comparatively rare procedure had safety advantages for the patient, it came under national attack by the anti-abortion movement in the mid-1990s. The campaign to ban intact D&E had its roots in the realization by elements within the anti-abortion movement that actually *describing* abortion procedures, rather than focusing on abstract arguments about fetal rights or the immorality of abortion, would sensationalize abortion and help turn public opinion against it.

Though abortions in the second trimester represent only about 10 percent of all abortions, and those after twenty weeks only about 1.5 percent, anti-abortion forces made "partial birth abortion" their key talking point starting in the mid-1990s. The movement correctly guessed that the "gross-out" factor would work and that a description of abortion procedures, out of context, would be upsetting to many. The campaign was also successful in promoting the false idea that many abortions take place late in pregnancy. When the federal government took up a bill banning the procedure, senators opposed to abortion launched lurid attacks on intact

D&E on the floor of the Senate, armed with charts showing what appeared to be several-months-old babies with a scissor at the back of their necks. Noticeably missing from the graphic depictions of the procedure was the woman having the abortion. After President Clinton twice vetoed federal bans on the procedure, the House and Senate once again passed a ban on intact D&E in 2003. With a Republican now in the White House, this version was signed into law by President George W. Bush.

The Supreme Court twice considered bans on this procedure. The first case, involving a state ban from Nebraska, struck down the law because it contained no exception for women's health, an unprecedented omission in abortion jurisprudence. However, the second case, just seven years after the first, upheld what was essentially the same ban—again without a health exception—though this time it was a federal law instead of a state law. Simply put, the difference between the two cases can be explained by a change in the composition of the Court—Justice Sandra Day O'Connor, who had voted against the ban in 2000, was no longer on the Court in 2007, and anti-abortion conservative Justice Samuel Alito had taken her place.

In justifying the Court's willingness to uphold the federal ban, Justice Anthony Kennedy wrote that providers would still have access to the most common method of second-trimester abortion, the standard D&E method described above D&E is the method used in over 96 percent of the approximately 140,000 second-trimester abortions performed annually in the United States. However, in recent years, a number of state legislatures have moved to ban this method as well. Taking a page out of the playbook of the successful "partial birth" campaign, anti-abortion opponents have given a grotesque-sounding nonmedical name to an established, safe medical procedure. This time, they are calling D&E abortions "dismemberment abortions."

Ten states have passed bans on D&E, but only the laws in Mississippi and West Virginia are, at the time of this writing, in effect. Both of those states have one remaining abortion clinic, neither of which has challenged the law in court. In seven of the other states (excluding North Dakota, whose ban will not take effect until a court approves the law), clinics have attacked the laws as unconstitutional and, so far, have won. States have tried to defend these bans by saying that doctors could perform the procedure a different way by inducing fetal death prior to performing the abortion, a practice that has not yet been studied for earlier second-trimester procedures. Along the lines of one of the central themes of this book, one federal judge that struck down Alabama's law noted that if abortion patients were treated in this manner, they "will be unique: there is no other medical context that requires a doctor—in contravention of her medical judgment and the best interests of the patient—to administer a procedure that delivers no benefit to the patient."

These lower federal court decisions that have all struck down these bans might not be the final say in the matter. The Supreme Court has so far declined to review these decisions striking down procedure bans, but many people think the Supreme Court is likely to eventually rule on these bans. Should the Court uphold such a ban, the only methods available for second-trimester abortions would be those that are not supported by the best currently available medical evidence, such as inducing fetal death before the abortion in certain cases, or the induction method. Labor induction, which providers strongly feel is a lesser option in most instances at this stage of pregnancy, used to be a common form of second-trimester abortion until doctors developed the safer, shorter, and medically preferable D&E procedure. Banning the standard D&E would turn the clock back on medical advances.

The prospect of a ban on D&Es is of tremendous concern to abortion providers, including those we interviewed for this study. Foremost among their concerns is that they do not want to be forced to practice unsafe medicine, but they also understand the slippery slope. As Shelley Sella, a doctor in the West, explained to us, if one procedure can be banned, then why not others. She predicted that if a D&E ban is allowed, states will next ban drugs that bring about fetal death. And from there, there will be no real stopping point.

The ramifications of the vilification of particular abortion procedures go beyond abortion providers. Gabrielle Goodrick, one of a handful of abortion providers in the state of Arizona, recently wrote publicly about a disturbing incident that occurred in a large urban hospital in Phoenix. The story, told to her by a colleague, concerned a patient hospitalized for a miscarriage in process. The patient "was in the second trimester, still well over a month before even the cusp of fetal viability, and rapidly bleeding out. A D&E procedure could have quickly ended her ordeal, but that was a procedure no one currently on staff at the hospital could perform. Instead, they induced labor, giving her blood transfusion after blood transfusion as the process continued for hours. Throughout the entire process, the patient begged the staff not to let her die. She survived, but her life never should have been at risk. Never."

D&E is not only the most common form of second-trimester abortion but also the recommended method by experts for addressing miscarriages in the second trimester. The failure to use this method in the Phoenix case is, yet again, an illustration of how politics can override medical expertise in the provision of abortion care. The fact that no one in this hospital knew how to perform a D&E reflects how limited training is for abortions later in pregnancy, particularly in red states. But the incident also suggests that no one in that hospital's leadership thought it a priority to have a qualified D&E practitioner on staff because of the way the procedure has been stigmatized and shunned.

INCONSISTENT, ARBITRARY RULES

Among the saddest and most frustrating stories we heard from providers in the course of researching this book were their efforts to meet the needs of patients whose pregnancies exceeded their state's (or their facility's) gestational limits. As discussed throughout this book, the landmark Turnaway Study has estimated that roughly four thousand women are turned away from abortion facilities each year, and thus have to continue their pregnancy until birth, because they arrived at a particular clinic too late and were unable to get themselves elsewhere. The Turnaway research demonstrated that those women who are turned away end up poorer and more susceptible to domestic violence than those who receive the sought-after abortion. Significantly, the study also found that the children born to those denied an abortion suffer poorer maternal bonding than the subsequent children born to women who received a requested abortion. When the providers interviewed for this book are faced with would-be patients whom they are unable to treat, they, along with allied and volunteer groups, undertake the herculean efforts described in chapter 3 to find care for these women elsewhere—sometimes successfully, often not.

One question the people we interviewed are often posed about women who present at clinics after the first trimester is "Why did they delay?" After all, the thinking behind this question goes, reliable pregnancy tests are readily and cheaply available in drugstores. People should be able to find out they are pregnant quickly so they can make a decision early in the pregnancy. The answers to this common question are several: Some women, particularly obese ones, young women, or those with irregular periods, simply do not recognize their pregnancies for some time; some adolescents, afraid of parental and others' reactions, are simply in denial; others don't receive news, such as a medical diagnosis, that changes their view of their pregnancy until months into it; still others have so much going on in their life—jobs, family, finding housing and food, and other responsibilities—that they get to the point of deciding about their pregnancy later than other people might.

However, consistent with what we described in chapters 3 and 4, researchers who have studied this issue have found that "the most common reason for delay was having to raise money for travel and procedure costs." Chloe Hebert, who supervises the National Abortion Federation Hotline Fund, a national hotline that both helps women with referrals to clinics and helps with the cost of the procedure and travel, gave some context to this research as she talked about the complicated path to find care in those situations. "Because a lot of patients are managing their care and trying to collect resources, sometimes it takes them a lot longer than they anticipated and then they're pushed over the state limit, and then their opportunities for care become very, very minimal and require a lot of logistical resources that sometimes they aren't up to or can't manage regardless of the assistance that's provided to them." Among related factors causing delay that Chloe frequently encounters on the hotline are promised financial help from relatives being withdrawn, intimate partners giving mixed signals to the woman about whether to continue the pregnancy or abort, and scheduled rides to a clinic simply falling through or being sabotaged. All these occur against the backdrop of, as she put it, "women racing the clock" in order to get to a provider before they are too far along in the pregnancy.

Chloe pointed to abortion stigma as something that also leads women to seek help later than desirable. "There's the internal stigma that patients suffer of just guilting themselves so thoroughly, which delays decision-

making. It creates barriers to asking for support because they're weighing
the fact that 'if I feel this ashamed about this, who can I tell who would
understand?' And because there's so much moralizing around abortion,
the isolation and stigma can be what deters patients, especially when
there are things they have to comply with—like with any other like medical procedure that requires sedation—such as having someone who can
drive you there and pick you up." Chloe explained further: "But then
women feel that they can't ask anybody in their life to go with them to
have an abortion or there are people who say they will and then sabotage."
She added sardonically, "I don't know that that happens with people going
to the eye doctor or to get their wisdom teeth removed."

Chloe also cited the "fear factor." Some women calling the hotline repeat
incorrect concerns about later abortions that they've heard elsewhere,
concerns that lead them to fear, and therefore delay, the procedure that
they are ultimately seeking. "It's interesting that when we talk to patients,
even when they're choosing abortion, they're still using anti-abortion
rhetoric and myths, like 'I know I might not be able to have children anymore,' or 'I know this is probably illegal, but I need to do it anyway,' or 'I
know this is a really, really dangerous procedure.'"

The situation facing women needing abortions after the first trimester
is further complicated by the fact that there is no uniformity across the
states as to how late in pregnancy abortion facilities are legally able to
provide. Seventeen states, for example, prohibit abortions after twenty
weeks. These twenty-week bans can be particularly problematic because
some fetal anomalies are only discovered around eighteen weeks of pregnancy or later. But even in places where there is no gestational prohibition, some clinics have their own limits—such as only through the first
trimester or early in the second trimester—because of a lack of available
providers who are trained to perform later abortions.

Yet another complicating factor in later abortions is the lack of clarity
in medical circles as to what constitutes an actual threat to the life or
health of the woman, or when an anomaly is "lethal," so that an exception
to the state's gestational limit can be used. These are subjective judgments
in many instances, where, hardly surprisingly, physicians' views on the
acceptability of a particular abortion often reflect their larger views on
abortion. As an exasperated ob-gyn in South Dakota said at the time the

state banned the intact D&E procedure, which did permit an exception in the case of a threat to a woman's life: "If someone has a 10 percent chance of dying, is that what they mean? Or is it 30 percent or 50 percent or 80 percent? By the time you figure out that somebody is at a high risk of dying, they're probably going to die."

Given the subjectivity inherent in determining medical risk, there is considerable variation across states, and even across different cities within states—particularly in light of different local medical and political cultures—as to what chances doctors are willing to take. In other words, providers often make these difficult decisions as much on the basis of their calculations as to whether performing a certain abortion will bring unwanted attention from anti-abortion colleagues and/or legal authorities as they do on the basis of their best medical judgment.

In some communities more friendly to abortion, even sometimes in states with twenty-week bans, maternal fetal medicine (MFM) specialists, doctors who treat women with high-risk pregnancies, quietly perform post-twenty-week procedures on patients—often euphemistically referred to as "terminations" and not "abortions"—even when the woman's life is not strictly at risk and/or when the anomalies are serious but not necessarily lethal. But in the very conservative southern state with a twenty-week ban where Van May is the director of a large clinic, the physicians on staff are of necessity extremely cautious when it comes to performing later abortions. She explained, "So the mentality for all physicians here is that 'I don't want to go to jail or lose my medical license for the rest of my life.' So my three physicians, we err on the side of conservatism, that's just a physician choice."

Van went on to tell us how the decisions in her facility to perform post-twenty-week abortions were dependent on the evaluations of other physicians. As she explained, if the genetic counseling notes and the ultrasound record do not state that the patient is dealing with a lethal anomaly, then "our physicians will not proceed." She suggested that these outside evaluations could vary according to the political views of the evaluators, leading to immense frustration on the part of her staff doctors: "They absolutely hate it because, as health care providers, the physicians get so frustrated when they're reviewing these ultrasound records because it's one of those things where it's like, you know how miserable the parents are going to be, you know how miserable the child's going to be, but yet, because it doesn't say 'lethal' on the evaluation, so in order to protect yourself and your ability to help more women, you have to turn this one patient away." Van conveyed how wrenching it is for her to be a part of turning women away in such a difficult situation: "It's hard. As health care providers we know that there's not going to be any quality of life. We know that and we have to turn these women away and unfortunately, for these women who are in such sensitive situations, they blame us for turning them away when it's the state's fault. We frequently get told, 'You're making me have a baby!' You would not believe how many times we're told that."

Van pointed out to us that the disparity in health care access that characterizes American health care in general exists, in this situation, in a particularly cruel way. "If you are a woman of means with private insurance, the children's hospital will do in utero surgery for some of these conditions. So that does not help poorer women at all because sometimes MFMs and the genetic counselors actually use this coded phrase in the notes, writing something like 'In utero surgery to repair the anomaly is an option.'" As Van suggested, documenting the possibility of addressing the anomaly via an expensive surgery—even though her patients could never afford this procedure—further increases her doctors' wariness about possible legal prosecution were they to proceed with the abortion.

We heard similar stories from other facilities where what was legally permitted often stood in tension with providers' fears of political controversy. This was especially true of complex, medically challenging cases that might bring unwanted attention. Vanessa Barrett directs a northeastern clinic in a state that permits abortions up to twenty-four weeks gestation. Because of general concerns about abortion politics, the clinic's policy was to go to only twenty-two weeks, though there were sometimes exceptions when the clinic thought there wouldn't be controversy. As Vanessa said, "Occasionally, we'll get somebody that comes in over twenty-two and the doctor will be like, 'Oh, you know what, that's okay. It doesn't look like it's going to be a complicated case, so it will be fine.'"

In many cases, when providers were unable to take care of women who were too far along in their pregnancy for their clinic or state, they themselves scrambled to get these women to places that could care for the patient, making efforts similar to those already discussed in chapter 3. Andrea Ferrigno, who oversees several clinics in a southern state that recently imposed a twenty-week ban, spoke of the aftereffects of this ban. "It was very difficult. Knowing that we had been doing those cases perfectly fine and safely before, and now we have to consider: Okay, how do we get you to a nearby state that performs abortions after twenty weeks? We are dealing with people that haven't really ever left their communities, and now we have to get them to go to a different state. And then the logistics of the finances as well." Andrea told us: "We have actually bought plane tickets for people. I remember this young woman that needed an abortion. We ended up having to buy a plane ticket for her to go to California so that she could get the care there. I mean, talk about fund-raising! That was hard, but we did it."

Unfortunately, in some cases, as the mere existence of the Turnaway Study indicates, providers are simply unable to undertake this fund-raising and logistical support and lose contact with the women they have had to turn away. Frances Easton, who works at a midwestern clinic in a state with a twenty-week ban, spoke candidly of her fears about the desperate women she is unable to help and her frustration at not knowing what becomes of them. "Every time something happens on the news, I am looking at the person's name. So if there is a story about somebody killing their baby, you know, I'm looking at their name and praying that it's not somebody we had to turn away. It's rough."

Although some state courts have upheld twenty-week bans, the only federal appeals court to have considered them has struck down both Arizona's and Idaho's. The reason is simple. As the Ninth Circuit Court of Appeals wrote, a ban at twenty weeks is "directly contrary to the [Supreme] Court's central holding in *Casey* that a woman has the right to 'choose to have an abortion *before viability* and to obtain it without undue interference from the State.'"

Courts have reached the same result for even earlier bans on abortion that a small number of states have passed. Mississippi passed a ban at fifteen weeks, Arkansas at twelve weeks, and North Dakota was the first state to ban abortion at six weeks. All of these laws were easily struck down as unconstitutional because, as the Ninth Circuit recognized, the Supreme Court has, so far, left no wiggle room about banning abortion before viability.

Nonetheless, as we have seen particularly in the first half of 2019, states continue to pass laws banning abortion earlier and earlier in pregnancy—

Missouri at eight weeks; Georgia, Ohio, Kentucky, and Mississippi at six weeks; and Alabama at conception. It's no mystery why states pass these clearly unconstitutional laws that will not take effect anytime soon because they will be struck down by every lower court judge in the country. As a federal judge in Mississippi recognized in late 2018 when he struck down the state's fifteen-week ban, the real reason states pass these early bans is not to test the limits of *Roe* but rather something more nefarious: "No, the real reason [behind the law] is simple. The State chose to pass a law it knew was unconstitutional to endorse a decades-long campaign, fueled by national interest groups, to ask the Supreme Court to overturn *Roe v. Wade.*"

SKITTISH HOSPITALS

Hospital-based abortions account for only about 4 percent of the abortions occurring each year in the US. But hospitals are where some of the most difficult abortions take place: difficult medically, because hospitals are where the clinics send their sickest patients, often in emergency situations, when an outpatient procedure is not suitable; and also difficult emotionally, because hospitals often care for patients carrying wanted pregnancies that have been found, late in pregnancy, to have lethal or severe anomalies.

But it is no simple matter for very sick women to obtain the care they need in hospitals. Eleven states have laws prohibiting abortion care in public hospitals, making exceptions only if a woman's life is in danger (with some of these states permitting abortions also in cases of rape and incest). However, as suggested earlier in this chapter, it is highly subjective—and deeply contested—as to what actually constitutes a threat to a woman's life. As Chrisse France, the director of an independent clinic in Ohio, told a reporter, getting a patient too ill to be seen at her clinic admitted to a hospital is extremely difficult: "She cannot be seen at our public hospital unless pretty much she's going to die today or maybe tomorrow." These difficulties put providers working in clinics in the deeply frustrating situation of either denying women care altogether or proceeding with the abortion in not entirely ideal circumstances. As one provider commented, "Because access is so restricted and there are so few places for people to go, we practice at the brink of what we find safe." Cruelly, only two of these eleven states permit abortions in situations where the woman is healthy but her fetus can't survive, leading women in the other states to continue a pregnancy that they know will end in a stillbirth.

Moreover, despite the emotional pull of these abortions, many hospitals, in both red and blue states, are very skittish about abortion care and often have unclear or ever-changing policies that are very frustrating to providers and patients. In a national study of teaching hospitals with ob-gyn residencies conducted by a team of researchers at the University of California, San Francisco, 56 percent of the hospitals surveyed had gestational limits that were more restrictive than what state law permitted. The study also found that doctors seeking to perform an in-hospital abortion later in the second trimester or beyond typically needed approval from some combination of the MFM specialists in the hospital, the chair of the ob-gyn department, the hospital ethics committee, a special abortion committee, and/or senior hospital administrators and lawyers. Similarly, a researcher from a liberal northeastern state told us that the rule of thumb among doctors in her community was not to do even medically necessary abortions in a hospital after the twenty-four-week cutoff "unless you are prepared to defend it in court."

The reasons for this hesitation to approve abortions among hospital personnel are familiar ones. According to the UCSF team, a hospital's ultimate decision to approve or forbid an abortion winds up being based on some combination of the decision makers' personal beliefs about abortion, the desire to avoid controversy and protesters, and concerns that the hospital might lose funding from donors or the state legislature if too many abortions are performed.

Alondra Becerra, a researcher who works with clinics in a remote location, is very familiar with this situation. At the university hospital she is affiliated with, doctors will perform second- and third-trimester abortions if necessary but will do so only in very specific circumstances. "The availability is very bureaucratic and restrictive," she told us. "They only do it for medical reasons, but those medical reasons have to be in the list that they have. The hospital is quite limited in which procedure it will do too, because we face a huge boycott from nurses and some physicians as well for doing a D&E, so the way they do second- and third-trimester abortions is through inductions. They don't do D&Es in the hospital because the nurses boycotted them."

In contrast to Alondra's situation, in Fariba Rahnema's western state, hospital practice is much easier. Fariba explained that hospital-based abortion care has been provided there for decades, so to everyone who works in the hospital it's just a part of routine care. "I don't ever see nurses that say they're uncomfortable, that they don't want to scrub. The anesthesia groups, same thing. It's kind of part of regular practice here." Fariba attributes this to "the long-standing culture here of abortion care being part of regular hospital practice," as well as the doctors being "very well integrated into the medical community. Everyone knows them, and everyone loves them."

The challenges of in-hospital abortions are exacerbated in Catholic hospitals, even when seriously ill women are admitted. In her landmark research into the issue, Lori Freedman offers harrowing accounts of what becomes of a patient who is in the process of miscarrying but whose fetus still has a heartbeat: under some hospitals' interpretation of the directives governing Catholic health care, providers are forbidden to end the doomed pregnancy because it would be considered an abortion. These cases often result in quite sick patients being transferred to non-Catholic hospitals, a practice some refer to as "patient dumping." In one case that Freedman relates, a patient whose membranes had ruptured (putting her at risk for infection) was transferred ninety miles to a secular hospital.

In other cases, Freedman tells of doctors who took matters into their own hands because they were so fearful that their patients would die. This was the situation with a doctor she interviewed who failed to get the hospital's ethics committee to approve a termination of a patient he believed to be dying. "And so I went in to examine her, and I was able to find the umbilical cord through the membranes and just snapped the umbilical cord and 'Oh look. No heartbeat. Let's go.' And she was so sick she was in the ICU for about ten days and very nearly died." This experience left this doctor so shaken that he left his job at the Catholic hospital.

Providers we interviewed for this book had similarly frustrating experiences trying to assist their patients who required a hospital abortion. Jada Curry, a clinic staff person in the Midwest, told us of a particularly difficult case of a woman being denied an abortion because of the state's twenty-week ban, a case that still haunts her. The patient had come to Jada's clinic just on the cusp of the twenty-week limit, and clinicians there determined that her health status necessitated an in-hospital abortion. "She wanted this abortion because she was faced with fetal anomalies that were not at all compatible with life. Like there was a 1 percent chance of survival after birth, and she did not want to continue the pregnancy. However, she didn't have the funds. So I worked really, really hard with this patient. I mean, I even got on the phone with the medical director of the insurance carrier at home. I mean, I just kept going and going until I got them to try to cover her procedure, and still it was declined." Jada related a crucial detail: "But the patient had no funds for transportation to another state to be seen in an inpatient facility." As a result, Jada explained, even though the patient wanted an abortion, the difficulty and expense of procuring an in-hospital abortion meant that she ended up having to carry the pregnancy to term.

Though most providers are unable to follow up with patients they cannot help for later abortion, in this case, Jada was. "I actually was in touch with her physician because I had to refer the patient to a high-risk obstetrician when she was forced to continue. And I just wanted to know, what she was going to be going through? And then, most importantly, was she going to be okay, both physically and mentally after now being forced to make this decision to continue the pregnancy?" What Jada learned about the patient, unsurprisingly, was that she experienced postpartum difficulties. "When she delivered, of course, the child didn't survive and she ended up really having a lot of mental frustration with the system and with the delivery. And then her insurance spent so many more dollars and resources in trying to now sustain life for this incompatible pregnancy that ended up dying." The sad irony of the situation was not lost on Jada. "It would've been much less mental anguish for the patient—as well as financially it would've been cheaper—for her to get an abortion. That's all she wanted."

Even in one of the better settings for women who need later in-hospital abortions that we encountered in our research—the hospital-based clinic where Jen Moore Conrow works, which routinely offers abortions up to twenty-four weeks—it can be very challenging to integrate later abortion care into a hospital's routine. Jen's institution has one operating room for which the clinic has blocked time for one day a week, but the clinic is in a state that requires a twenty-four-hour waiting period. As Jen explained:

If we get somebody on the phone who is being referred to us—often these much later patients are typically being referred to us by a maternal fetal medicine physician or even another freestanding clinic, but often a patient's private ob-gyn. If it's somebody who's twenty-two weeks and six days pregnant and we don't have an opening until next week, then she's going to be twenty-three and four, five, six, really pushing to that twenty-four-week gestation limit. If that happens, our patient coordinator will talk with the physicians about, can we phone-consent this person? Can we get them in sooner? Can we add them onto an operating room schedule somewhere else? So we do a significant number of these kinds of add-on, ad hoc cases where maybe she calls on Tuesday, we phone-consent her on Tuesday, and she comes in on Wednesday for dilators, and we do an add-on case in the operating room on Thursday.

As Jen said to us, this schedule juggling doesn't always work for the patient. "Occasionally we get calls from people who are so borderline that we can't make that work, or they are legitimately beyond our ability to care for them legally." When this happens, Jen and her colleagues scramble to see if the patient can be treated at one of the clinics in distant states that performs later procedures. "Depending on how severe their complications or their medical history sounds, we may refer them." However, this isn't always possible given the patient's medical condition or her financial situation. When this happens, patients are left without medical care even though they are at a premier medical institution that, outside the context of abortion, routinely provides world-class care for patients in the most desperate medical situations.

Jen told us that exceptions to the state's twenty-four-week limit were rare, even though post-twenty-four-week abortions are permitted when the pregnancy threatens the woman's life or poses a serious health risk. Echoing other providers who have to painfully weigh the needs of one patient against the larger population of potential patients, she said, "We have not granted many exceptions. There's the fear of 'Will that really be acceptable to the state, is it really worth risking our license and the practice to help one person, versus being able to know that we're still going to be able to help more people?'" On top of that, Jen added that "there's also a training issue, which is that beyond twenty-four to twenty-five weeks the procedure really changes, and our physicians aren't trained to see patients that late in gestation. So it's both a training issue and a legal issue."

CRUELTY TO ABORTION PATIENTS, CONTEMPT FOR ABORTION PROVIDERS

The practices described in this chapter—the unprecedented level of restricting, even banning, medical procedures; the arbitrary rules of who can legally provide abortions, which ignore a body of compelling evidence; and the contortions that providers must often go through to enable hospital-based abortions—do not only convey a cruelty toward women, often in desperate circumstances. These practices also display a disturbing contempt for abortion providers and their professional, medical, evidence-based judgments.

This willingness of politicians to override medical authority in the area of abortion is ironic. The text of *Roe v. Wade* has long been criticized by feminists and others for being *too* deferential to physicians and for ignoring almost completely the part women play in the decision to have an abortion. For instance, in the decision's conclusion, Justice Harry Blackmun completely erases the existence of the woman's role in the abortion: "The decision vindicates the *right of the physician* to administer medical treatment according to his professional judgment up to the points where important state interests provide compelling justifications for interventions. Up to this point, the abortion decision in all its aspects is inherently and primarily a medical decision, and basic responsibility for it must rest *with the physician*." Reflecting an almost complete about-face caused by nearly thirty-five years of the politicization and stigmatization of abortion in America, by 2007, Justice Anthony Kennedy's decision in *Gonzales v. Carhart*, the case upholding the federal intact D&E ban, threw even abortion doctors by the wayside. He wrote that "the law need not give abortion doctors unfettered choice in the course of their medical practice, nor should it elevate their status above other physicians in the medical community."

But why not "elevate" the status of medical professionals who provide abortions in *matters pertaining to abortion*? Relatively speaking, there are very few abortion providers in the United States, and only a portion of these perform abortions in the second trimester or beyond. The intact D&E procedure that was banned and upheld in *Gonzales* was infrequently performed, and the complexities of this technique were best known to the small number of doctors who utilized it. At the various trials about the ban, none of the government's expert witnesses had ever actually done an abortion using this method, and at least one of the physician witnesses had never done an abortion by any method. Yet the Supreme Court ultimately deferred to these nonexperts' judgment rather than the judgment of those who best know this aspect of medicine. This doesn't happen in other fields of health care and shouldn't happen with abortion either.

As current political developments point to the likelihood of the Supreme Court soon ruling on the constitutionality of yet another abortion procedure restriction or ban, very possibly this time the ban of regular D&Es, there is reason to fear once again that the evidence-based views of abortion providers—those who are most familiar with the safety benefits of this method—will again be dismissed for political reasons. This extreme politicization of the abortion procedure itself that we have spoken of in this chapter, and indeed throughout this book—politicization and interference that would never happen with any other form of health care—is obviously very disheartening to those who support safe and legal abortion. And it is especially troublesome for pregnant patients who want accessible and safe care from qualified providers, the same they would expect in any other field of medicine.

9 An Alternate Vision

ABORTION AS NORMAL HEALTH CARE

Much of this book, admittedly, has been quite depressing. Politically motived abortion barriers coupled with the poverty of the large majority of abortion patients prevent many women, especially women of color and women far from population centers, from getting the care they need in a timely, dignified, and medically supported manner—or getting this care at all.

In fact, the cumulative effect of all of the barriers described throughout this book would make a reasonable observer believe that only a small number of rich and resourceful women can possibly get an abortion in the United States. However, as we know, almost one million women get abortions every year. Though that number is on the decline, most analysts attribute the decline not to abortion restrictions but rather to more widespread use of effective contraception, the unknown number of women who are self-managing their abortions outside of the medical system, and the similarly unknown number of very poor women who simply lack the wherewithal to reach the declining number of abortion facilities in this country.

So how does this happen—that amid these seemingly endlessly burdensome abortion barriers so many women are still able to obtain the medical procedure they want? Much of the answer is a testament to what has been documented throughout this book—women's commitment to their and their families' dignity and health, providers' creativity and determination to serve their patients, and the tireless efforts of allies and volunteers. That combination is powerful, and it explains how, despite the barriers women face every step of the way, so many do get the care they want and need.

But if one thing is abundantly clear from considering all the obstacles a woman must overcome in this country in order to have an abortion—from the moment she first finds out she's pregnant and has to make a decision about what to do with the pregnancy all the way through the procedure itself—it's that she shouldn't have to have incredible fortitude and her medical care providers shouldn't have to have unparalleled devotion just to get what is usually a short, simple medical procedure that has an excellent safety record. Rather, just like patients who want any other form of medical care, such as a tooth pulled or cataracts removed, abortion patients should be able to make up their minds and then straightforwardly get the care they want. They should be able to do so without targeted government interference and without their health care providers needing superhuman determination.

In states where this happens—where abortion is treated like any other form of health care—we get a glimpse of the promise of normalized abortion care. Consider the story of an anonymous abortion storyteller we'll call Diana who had her abortion in one such state. Diana was seventeen when she realized that her cervical cap had failed after she had sex with her boyfriend. Because of some very obvious symptoms, she quickly realized she was pregnant and knew what she was going to do. "There was no question of whether or not I would get an abortion. I was about to move back east to go to college. And I was not equipped to be a good parent, emotionally or financially."

Both Diana's boyfriend and mother supported her decision and helped her get to the clinic and pay for the procedure. Her mom was worried there would be protesters at the clinic, but on her procedure day there were none, so she was able to walk into the clinic without being harassed. The procedure itself was quick and went smoothly. As Diana summed up her experience, "The fact that I lived in a state with ready access to abortion services, that I had family support, my financial resources, and that there were no protesters physically impeding my way all helped me. The fact that I did not need to wait twenty-four hours to complete a procedure that I had already thought long and hard about also helped me. This was not ever an impulsive decision but one that was very carefully reasoned out." All of these factors created an abortion experience for Diana that was exactly what it should be—based on her choice and without government interference. Unfortunately, as Diana recognized, the degree to which her experience differs from so many other people around the country makes her "lucky."

The people we interviewed for this book who work in states like Diana's agreed. They told us encouraging stories about better ways of offering abortion care now taking place in some localities, where anti-abortion politics are not a hindrance. Plus, where allowed by government, researchers are exploring some promising and innovative scenarios for improved abortion access that could take place more widely in the future, should the political environment improve.

There is a better way, and what's heartbreaking about the current situation in this country is that it's painfully obvious that this better way already exists. When abortion is regulated just like other medical procedures, we know that women are able to access the procedure the same way they access any other medical care—on the basis of their own choices and the availability, skill, and professional judgment of the medical providers they see. That doesn't mean abortion care would suddenly be perfect, as there are still countless issues that all patients face in accessing medical care in the United States. But it does mean that patients would be able to shed the unique barriers associated with abortion.

IS THERE A "BEST" WAY TO DO ABORTION CARE?

For the sake of argument, what if abortion did become depoliticized in the United States and the various restrictions we have discussed in this book were overturned? What would then be the best way to provide abortion? The most important parts of what we visualize have already been stated: abortion should be geographically accessible; affordable, which means including Medicaid coverage; and without restrictions that serve no purpose other than to delay the procedure and/or to burden and stigmatize the patients. In other words, abortion should be like what we want for all other health care.

Stated differently, our view of the ideal way for abortion care to proceed in the United States is, simply, that states and the federal government let patients and providers determine the best form of care for the diverse needs and preferences of the approximately one in four American women who will have an abortion in their lifetimes. For the foreseeable future (assuming that *Roe* is not overturned), most women—especially those who have been subject to misinformation and shaming about the choice of an abortion—will prefer the counseling and comfort available in free-standing clinics. Other women will prefer the privacy, convenience, and often lower cost of having an abortion on their own, or a "self-managed abortion," as it has come to be called. Still others will want an abortion from an already-trusted medical provider, such as the gynecologist or family doctor that they have been seeing for years. And then another group of women, for instance those who have certain health conditions or who discover fetal anomalies late in pregnancy, will require an abortion in a specialized clinic or hospital setting. Our vision of the best way for abortion provision to proceed is for all these models—and others not mentioned or yet to be conceived—to flourish without unnecessary legislative interference.

There are states around the country where this ideal is already bearing fruit. When we interviewed them, providers in those states made clear what reasonable abortion policies look like. There are places in the country that do not interfere with patient decision-making, including decisions of minors; where there is an ample supply of clinicians available to work in abortion care and providers do not have to be flown in from out of town at great expense to everyone involved; where the state not only pays for the abortions of Medicaid recipients but also subsidizes their travel to the clinic, just as these states help with travel for Medicaid patients seeking other medical services; where women can enter clinics without battling through a war zone; where medical professionals can obtain informed consent without lying to patients while tailoring the process to the individualized needs of the person before them; where women can be offered care the same day they contact the clinic without any unnecessary delay; and where medical professionals in conjunction with their patients make the ultimate decision about what procedure will best treat the patient.

In particular, the difference when states allow Medicaid dollars to be used for abortion is hard to overstate. This means that patients and providers alike are not forced to desperately try to raise funds before the woman is too far in gestation to permit a legal abortion. Medicaid coverage often alleviates travel concerns as well.

Another huge difference maker, in terms of timely access to abortion care, is when states allow advanced-practice clinicians (APCs) to offer this service. This is especially true in larger states where many women live far from urban centers. Moreover, when APCs and doctors can offer care without being encumbered by waiting periods, parental notification and consent laws, and other unnecessary restrictions, abortion patients are more likely to get quality and safe health care. This is consistent with the National Academies of Sciences, Engineering, and Medicine's conclusion, in its recent landmark 2018 report on abortion, that unnecessary barriers that cause delay imperil the safety of the procedure.

The stories in this book also revealed the importance of telemedicine, especially in less populated areas with few clinics and little public transportation. Seeing this positive impact of telemedicine on abortion access in states where it is permitted, a practice supported by research showing no difference in safety when this method is used, is proof that the states that currently ban telemedicine abortion care are harming access for no medical reason, especially considering that they permit it for other health care services.

Compare these stories of easy, safe access to medical care in states that do not interfere with abortion with the stories about lengths that providers and committed allies and volunteers have to go to in order to help abortion patients in hostile states. Their innovation and dedication are inspiring, but these stories would be less necessary in a just world. For instance, in chapter 3 we told the story of Pat Earle, who helped create a house for patients and their families immediately next door to the southern clinic where she also works. The clinic is one of the small number that remain in the state because of the burdensome laws there. As a result, patients travel long distances to get to the clinic. The house, staffed by volunteers, is a place for those patients and the people who travel with them to rest and, if necessary, stay the night because of the state's waiting period and to have their children watched during the procedure. In a world where poverty still exists, perhaps extraordinary interventions like this one will always be needed, but it is impossible to ignore the way that unnecessary abortion barriers exacerbate the need for Pat's efforts.

But while the extensive efforts of abortion allies and volunteers in helping women pay for a procedure, get to a clinic, and find overnight lodging are deeply moving, in the better world we envision here where abortion is treated like all other medical procedures, the need for these efforts—whose availability varies greatly around the country—would be drastically reduced. While there will always be a place for volunteers in the abortion-providing world, access should not depend on the availability, ingenuity, and dedication of allied organizations and volunteers.

Only if abortion is normalized as a routine part of reproductive health care will equitable abortion care become closer to a reality. What this means is clear—policies that trust people's decisions to have an abortion; easy access to nearby facilities; Medicaid coverage for poor women and no insurance bans for all others; depoliticized entrances to clinics; accurate and medically relevant information given to patients based on what the provider determines the patient needs; no state-mandated waiting periods; increased use of APCs and telemedicine; and the freedom of medical professionals to determine the best procedure for their patient. All other fields of medicine have these things. Abortion care should as well.

INNOVATIONS IN ABORTION CARE

When abortion is treated like all other forms of medicine, the creativity of medical care providers, researchers, and patients can flourish and help make abortion even more accessible. Even in the midst of the hostile national environment we are currently living in, some of these creative projects are already under way and are showing promise in greatly improving access. Some of these projects are taking place in experimental pilot programs, while others are still in a more preliminary state of research. We have no doubt that in the better world we envision here, the projects we briefly describe below would be accompanied by others that could help provide abortion in a more equitable and just manner.

Abortion by Mail

As described at the start of chapter 8, Gynuity Health Projects, a reproductive health research organization based in New York, is pioneering the direct mailing of mifepristone and misoprostol to the home of a woman wishing to have an abortion. As of 2019, this is being done on an experimental basis in only five states. In this model, the patient directly contacts an abortion clinic from her own phone or computer, speaks with a physician at the clinic, and then has orders for an ultrasound and blood test sent to a general, nonabortion health care clinic near her home. Once the patient gets the ultrasound and blood test and an abortion provider reviews the results, the medication abortion drugs, along with instructions, are sent to her home, where she takes them as instructed. The patient subsequently has a virtual follow-up visit with the provider.

For women who live far from an abortion clinic, this option is obviously less costly and more convenient. And for patients who don't want to deal with what can often be a tense environment outside their local abortion clinic, this option is more private. Dr. Beverly Winikoff, president of Gynuity, told us that of the patients who have participated in this project to date, the abortion success rates are comparable to in-clinic procedures, and participants report high degrees of satisfaction. A 2019 published review of the program found that it was "safe, effective, efficient, and satisfactory. The model has the potential to increase abortion access by enhancing the reach of providers and by offering people a new option for obtaining care conveniently and privately."

Mifepristone at Pharmacies

Researchers at the University of California, San Francisco, under the direction of Dr. Daniel Grossman, are exploring the feasibility of making mifepristone available at pharmacies. The other drug used in the medication abortion regime, misoprostol, is already available at pharmacies, by prescription, for use in other medical conditions. If mifepristone were also available at pharmacies, medical care providers could write prescriptions for the drug rather than having to stock it themselves, currently a barrier for some doctors and APCs providing medication abortions.

As it stands now, mifepristone must be stocked at clinics and cannot be sold at pharmacies. This is because in 2000, when the Food and Drug Administration initially approved mifepristone for use in the United States, it imposed stringent requirements, stipulating that mifepristone must be ordered directly from the American distributor of this drug. This requirement was made under the REMS program of the FDA. As the FDA website explains, "Risk Evaluation and Mitigation Strategy (REMS) is a drug safety program that the U.S. Food and Drug Administration (FDA) can require for certain medications with serious safety concerns to help ensure the benefits of the medication outweigh its risks."

The pro-choice medical community has long argued that this requirement of ordering directly from the distributor is unnecessarily cumbersome and inhibits some potential providers from performing medication abortions. For example, doctors in private practices cannot easily predict what the demand for such abortions will be and hesitate to order drugs that might not be used before they expire. Furthermore, given the excellent safety record that mifepristone has achieved after nearly twenty years of use in the United States, abortion providers also convincingly argue that there is no credibility to the claim of "serious safety concerns." In making the case for the availability of mifepristone at pharmacies, the researchers point to the recent implementation of this practice in pharmacies in Australia and some provinces of Canada. This change has improved access to medication abortion in those countries by increasing the number of medication abortion providers, particularly in rural areas.

Preliminary evidence indicates that the same would be true in the United States. According to one study, if physicians were able to write prescriptions for mifepristone to be filled at a pharmacy, the number of medication abortion providers among ob-gyns in the United States would likely increase from less than one-quarter of these physicians to 31 percent. Currently, these restrictions are being challenged in a federal lawsuit in Hawaii. The lawsuit argues that the restrictions are unconstitutional because they are not supported by science and because they harm patients in the state who would otherwise have easier access to the medicine.

Advance Provision and Over-the-Counter Availability

Two other ideas, still at the "thought experiment" stage, involve advance provision of mifepristone by clinicians to nonpregnant patients and provision of this drug on over-the-counter status at pharmacies. Though at the present political moment these innovations are far from being actualized, researchers are actively involved in investigating their feasibility and the level of interest among potential abortion patients.

For example, as part of a 2017 national study of reproductive-aged women, UCSF researchers asked participants about their response to the above two possibilities. Of the seven thousand women who responded to the survey, nearly half supported, and about one-third expressed personal interest in, these models. Support for these options is highest among women who support legal abortion or who themselves have undergone an abortion. Unsurprisingly, among the women who have previously had an abortion, support is highest among those who have experienced barriers in obtaining their procedures. For example, when the results are narrowed to women in states with very restrictive policies, support of advance provision for themselves is 78 percent and for others is 86 percent. If these models were ever implemented, public education would be essential, as among the main hesitations expressed about these ideas is the lack of in-person involvement with a provider and the possible lack of safety.

In making the case for these models, the study authors point to existing research showing that women are able to take mifepristone and misoprostol safely and effectively outside of a clinic setting and that most women can correctly date the gestation of their pregnancies. By convincingly making these cases and showing that there is substantial interest in these two options among potential abortion patients, researchers are laying the groundwork for what they hope will be an expansion of abortion access in the future once there is a changed political environment.

Self-Managed Abortion

Another possibility for the future that has been of intense interest to researchers, especially in this current political environment, is what has come to be known as "self-managed abortion" (SMA)—that is, people who are pregnant attempting an abortion on their own outside of the medical system. This model, unlike advance provision and over-the-counter accessibility, is already a reality for many women in the United States and globally who order mifepristone and misoprostol online or obtain misoprostol alone. Women also use other less safe and effective methods, including herbs, high doses of Vitamin C, and, disturbingly, blows to the abdomen, either self-inflicted or inflicted by others. But the focus of the current SMA discussion is medication abortion, which is a safe and effective option for some women when the drugs are used correctly. As noted previously, the combination of mifepristone and misoprostol is 96 percent effective, and misoprostol alone is 85 to 90 percent effective.

It is of course impossible to know precisely how many women attempt their own abortions or how successful these attempts are, but several studies have estimated the extent of this practice. A 2014 national study of abortion patients by the Guttmacher Institute found that about 2.2 percent of abortion patients had previously tried to end their pregnancy. Predictably, the figure reported was considerably higher in states where abortion access is more challenging. For instance, a Texas study of abortion patients around the same time reported that 7 percent had attempted SMA with their current pregnancy. The same team of researchers also concluded, in a representative survey of Texas women of reproductive age, that at least one hundred thousand women in that state had attempted SMA at some point during their lives. A startling indicator of the growing interest in SMA is that there were a reported seven hundred thousand Google searches in 2016 in the United States using this and similar terms.

For some time, various nongovernmental organizations have attempted to make medication abortion drugs available to women in countries where abortion is illegal. One of the best known of these efforts is Women on Web, led by a Dutch physician, Rebecca Gomperts. Women on Web grew out of an existing project led by Gomperts, Women on Waves, which consists of a ship docking in waters off countries that are hostile to abortion, taking passengers on board, and, once the ship returns to international waters, having medical personnel provide abortion and other services. Though this ship still makes periodic journeys, much of Gomperts's work currently is making mifepristone and misoprostol available to women who contact her organization online. After doing an online consultation and establishing that the woman is an acceptable candidate for medication abortion, Gomperts and her colleagues arrange for the two abortion drugs to be shipped to the woman. Gomperts estimates that she has helped facilitate seventy thousand abortions in this manner in the past twelve years.

In the past, Women on Web did not make its services available to women in the United States, arguing that women here have access to legal abortion. However, after being inundated with requests from American women, and in light of the worsening access situation in the United States, much of which is documented in this book, Gomperts recently changed this policy. As she told a reporter, "I got an email from a woman who was living in a car with two kids. Something had to be done." She established a new offshoot of Women on Web called Aid Access, which is specifically oriented for women in the United States. As with Gomperts's work in other countries, after American women are deemed acceptable candidates for medication abortion, Aid Access sends them the drugs along with detailed instructions for their use for a cost of ninety-five dollars. Between October 2018 and March 2019, twenty-one thousand American women sought the services of Aid Access, and between a third and half of those women were sent the pills by mail.

Given the worsening state of abortion access in the United States, the possibilities of SMA—specifically by using mifepristone and misoprostol, or misoprostol alone—are intriguing to many in the abortion rights community. This is because, in sharp contrast to the pre-*Roe* era, when many thousands of women died or were injured from illegal abortions, medication abortion, even when taken outside of a medical setting, is far safer than the methods used in the past.

However, the level of legal scrutiny that SMA may receive in coming years, especially as the practice increases, is not clear and is worrisome. In another contrast with the pre-*Roe* era, when there was, relatively speaking, little crackdown on women who attempted their own abortions or on those who helped them, we may see a very different situation in the future. Following the well-known pattern of social movements creating countermovements, the modern drive to legalize abortion, culminating in *Roe,* in turn led to the emergence of a very effective anti-abortion movement, whose impact has been evident throughout this book. Among law enforcement, this movement has a strong presence at the national level, including the vehement anti-abortion records of Trump's several attorneys general. At the state and local level, there are powerful law enforcement officials in many jurisdictions who have similarly anti-abortion views.

What this means is that, even though the American College of Obstetricians and Gynecologists has called for the decriminalization of SMA because of the risk of negative health consequences if women fear going to providers and because of the way it would interfere with the doctor-patient relationship, the legal response to SMA in this country could be very troubling, especially if the experience in other countries is any indication. Michelle Oberman, a legal scholar, has extensively documented the situation of women in El Salvador, a country where abortion is absolutely banned. She contends that events happening there could possibly foreshadow what occurs in America. Oberman describes a society in which the reproductive behavior of poor women in particular is highly scrutinized, as women are routinely jailed for long sentences if they have attempted an abortion, either from others or by themselves. Moreover, since medical professionals are unable to distinguish between a miscarriage that occurs naturally and one that is induced by misoprostol (which is widely used in Latin America), Oberman tells of cases of women who arrive at hospitals in the midst of a natural miscarriage and who are falsely accused of abortion and then jailed. As she chillingly puts it, "When abortion is a crime, the emergency room can become the scene of a criminal investigation, and doctors the detectives."

It is not far-fetched to think this kind of scrutiny could happen in the United States. There had been reports of the FDA raising issues about the legality of importing mifepristone from abroad, and in March 2019 the agency sent warning letters to Aid Access and to another online provider of medication abortion drugs. Most concerning, however, is that over twenty women in the United States have already been arrested, and in some cases imprisoned, for attempting their own abortions. Just as Oberman saw in El Salvador, there are also cases in the United States of women undergoing miscarriages—such as a pregnant woman who accidentally fell down a stairway—who are now subject to legal scrutiny. And, as usual with almost every use of the criminal justice system, these punishments have disproportionately fallen on women of color.

These seemingly disparate events—arrests for SMA and suspicion by authorities of naturally occurring miscarriage—have as a common thread the vigorous attempts by the anti-abortion movement to establish the "personhood" of fetuses, that is, the claim that fetuses have the same rights as pregnant women. Were this claim of fetal personhood to be eventually recognized by the Supreme Court or federal law, abortion—and quite possibly IVF treatment and various forms of birth control—could be abolished everywhere in the United States.

It's not just pregnant women who could be arrested for SMA but providers as well. Though no providers have, as of yet, been arrested for aiding women attempting SMA, this could change, especially if abortion were to become illegal in some states and the rates of SMA in those places were to significantly increase. Even among those in the abortion-providing community who are convinced that SMA can be safe and effective for most women, there is widespread agreement that those attempting an abortion on their own should have access to a trusted provider if questions arise. For example, some women will need advice as to how much bleeding is normal versus how much warrants a trip to an emergency room. If providers who offer this advice are also anxious to protect the woman from prosecution, they may suggest that, if the woman does go to an emergency room, she not tell the personnel there that she has used medication abortion drugs but rather say she is undergoing a natural miscarriage. What liability will exist for the provider in such cases is unclear. One thing that is clear, though, assuming increasing rates of SMA, is that emergency room doctors and nurses will need to be educated by their abortion-providing colleagues and convinced not to report women suspected of SMA.

Arguably, the demedicalization inherent in the very phrase "self-managed" seems at odds with the notion suggested throughout this book as the best option for abortion care—normalizing abortion within existing health care provision. However, that view is a very narrow understanding of SMA for three reasons. First, advocates and researchers who support SMA also firmly support the principle that women using this option have access to medical authorities for consultation. Second, only because the safety of SMA using mifepristone and misoprostol, or misoprostol alone, has been proven through traditional medical science are so many people excited about the option as such a breakthrough possibility. And third, mainstream health care providers regularly rely on people using widely available medicine outside the context of in-office care in order to treat conditions. The most obvious example is the flu—some people go to their provider to treat it, while others go to the pharmacy, with or without consulting a provider.

To offer an analogy from the field of reproductive health, many health activists have decried what they consider the excessive medicalization of pregnancy and birth in the United States, in particular pointing to the much higher rates of Caesarean section deliveries compared to other countries. These activists have also called for more use of midwives (as opposed to obstetricians); for less use of high-tech equipment, such as fetal monitors; and for deliveries to take place in a birth center or at home, as opposed to a hospital. A tiny group in the United States and elsewhere even advocate "off the grid" birth, that is, labor and delivery apart from any medical assistance whatsoever. But virtually all who promote these demedicalizing measures also support the idea of medical backup, including hospitalization in the event of a problem labor that may be putting the mother and/or baby at risk.

Moreover, no one is suggesting that SMA is a cure-all for abortion access. Medication abortion—by far, the safest method of SMA—is considered most effective only through ten weeks or so of pregnancy. Abortions after that are most safely and effectively done in a clinical setting, which means that all of the reforms written about in this section will not affect post-ten-week abortion care. While most abortions happen before that point in pregnancy, a significant number of people need abortions at that point or later, and any attempts to reform abortion provision in the future need to also address these patients.

Moreover, many women will still choose or need to have an abortion at a medical office with trusted medical care professionals assisting them, even if SMA becomes widely and easily accessible. Plus, SMA presents the complex issue of how freestanding clinics can survive if SMA becomes more prevalent. After all, if enough first-trimester procedures eventually take place as self-managed ones, many clinics will be forced to close because of decreased revenue, and as a result those needing abortions after ten weeks or wanting abortions before ten weeks in a clinical setting will have an even harder time accessing services. In other words, the promise of SMA does not come without challenges that need to be resolved by smart minds in the future.

IS CHANGE POSSIBLE?

Is this vision for abortion care in the United States that we outline above, a variety of models allowed to operate without inappropriate abortion-specific regulation, remotely feasible? Writing these words in the midst of the Trump presidency, with a presumed 5–4 anti-abortion majority on the Supreme Court that could get even worse depending on possible retirements by liberal Justices, and with some state legislatures continuing to pass ever-more draconian laws, it is, to be sure, challenging to find grounds for optimism. The Supreme Court's 2016 *Whole Woman's Health* decision, which offered so much promise in insisting that abortion restrictions have actual medical benefits that outweigh the real burdens they impose on women, sometimes seems like a distant memory.

Nonetheless, there are some possibilities for an improved future for those needing abortions and those providing them. Several things contribute to this very cautious optimism. First, the Democrats' decisive victory in the 2018 midterm elections can be understood partly as a backlash against the threats to abortion that have marked the Trump era, and specifically to the controversy over the appointment of the strongly anti-abortion Brett Kavanaugh to the Supreme Court and the risk to *Roe* that he represents. In that election, Democrats gained forty seats to retake the House of Representatives, with nearly all of the newly elected congress-people identifying as supporters of abortion rights.

Moreover, the political polarization that has been generated by the Trump presidency led to an unusually high turnout for that midterm election. Given that this polarization shows no signs of abating, the 2018 election may spell the end of low turnout elections, in both midterm and presidential contests. If such a pattern of increased voting, especially by younger people, does indeed take place, there is consensus that this would favor Democrats generally, and by extension abortion rights. In short, the present moment in American politics and culture might be understood as one in which there is not only heightened awareness of the threat to abortion but also a sense that the only way to truly stop the threats to abortion is to participate in democracy en masse.

Second, it seems that the more people learn about abortion and the ways in which it is regulated, the more they reject extreme anti-abortion policies and the politicians that promote them. A May 2019 Reuters/Ipsos poll released in the wake of 2019's wave of extreme abortion bans confirms this. Support for abortion being legal in all or most cases has risen 8 points from 2018 to 2019, with 58 percent of Americans now believing it should be broadly legal. Furthermore, total abortion bans are extremely unpopular, with no state—not even the most conservative ones—having more than a quarter of its population supporting a total ban.

A 2018 poll by the PerryUndem firm, which is unusual in the depth in which it explored respondents' thoughts on abortion, gives even more support to this view. The poll contains the views of over one thousand voters, aged eighteen and up, in a nationally representative survey that included diverse political views. Like other polls concerned with abortion, this one found a strong majority of Americans want abortion to remain legal—72 percent of respondents did not want *Roe v. Wade* overturned.

But the PerryUndem survey went well beyond issues of legality and queried people on their views of what the *experience* of abortion should be. Notably, strong majorities stated they wanted the abortion experience for a woman to be informed by medically accurate information (96 percent), to be nonjudgmental on the part of staff (80 percent), without added burdens such as waiting periods (81 percent), available in her community (80 percent), and covered by insurance (67 percent). In other words, virtually all of the barriers to abortion that we have discussed in this book are decisively rejected by a cross section of the public—once they have been informed of these restrictions. Similar large majorities answered that they would want someone who had decided on an abortion to feel supported by her loved ones (88 percent) and to be without shame (75 percent) or guilt (73 percent), and that they themselves would give support to a friend or family member who had an abortion (88 percent).

The poll also asked respondents their views on who should be making decisions about the procedures used for abortion. In another lopsided response, only 4 percent stated that politicians at the state or federal level should be making such decisions, and only 9 percent were in support of the Supreme Court doing so. The majority stated some combination of the woman, her partner, and her doctor should decide this question. But, as discussed in chapter 8, it is precisely politicians and judges who are in the midst of deciding the fate of D&E abortions as well as how medication abortions are to be administered. In general, 78 percent of respondents (including 68 percent of self-identified Trump voters) agreed with the statement, "I don't think this issue should be so political or politicized."

This poll also revealed that American voters—even those supportive of abortion rights—are not very well informed about important aspects of abortion, such as the laws, the types of abortion, and its safety. But simply feeding the public facts about abortion will not necessarily lead to changed minds. What the PerryUndem survey and other work have shown is how important *context* is for the public's sympathy for women receiving abortions. Real women's stories, as opposed to abstract discussions of abortion, have the capacity to move people's attitudes. In this vein, the various abortion storytelling ventures that have emerged from within the pro-choice community, including the training of abortion patients in storytelling techniques, are potentially powerful game-changers.

Third, in another encouraging development for abortion rights supporters, in a review of abortion legislation passed by the states during 2018, the Guttmacher Institute reported that an increasing number of states are passing laws to expand abortion access. The report explained that "more than half of all states adopted measures to expand or protect access to sexual and reproductive health care," eighty measures in all. And, looking even more granularly, many cities continue to take steps to protect or even expand abortion and reproductive health care access, showing that the frequently repeated mantra that "all politics is local" could have increasing importance for abortion rights going forward. To be sure, these initiatives do not erase the difficulties faced by those in other locations. However, these proactive state and local reforms can still help many people access abortion while also serving as a model for a saner national abortion policy in the future.

In contrast, in 2018, only fifteen states enacted twenty-three restrictions on abortion, the lowest number of new restrictions enacted in at least a decade. It would be a mistake to overstate the significance of this disparity, especially considering the rush in many states to pass extreme abortion bans and restrictions that we've seen through the summer of 2019 (when this book is being finalized). Beyond the numbers, all it takes is one restrictive law to be challenged to then become the case that goes before the Supreme Court and culminates in an overturning of *Roe v. Wade*. In the meantime, laws like 2019's bevy of six-week bans or the Alabama near-complete ban on abortion will be blocked by the lower courts, delaying the time when they take effect (if they ever do). On the other hand, laws that expand abortion access are taking effect immediately. Thus, in looking at the practical reality of these various laws, *for now*, the proactive push that has continued into 2019 gives both needed encouragement and real, practical impact in expanding reproductive health services.

Fourth, not all of these eighty proactive measures passed in 2018 address abortion. These measures also involve contraception, testing and treatment for sexually transmitted diseases, reproductive health care for minors, infertility coverage, pregnancy discrimination, and comprehensive sex education. It is precisely this broader reproductive agenda that may offer the best hope for the eventual recognition of abortion as one necessary point on the spectrum of reproductive health services to which all people need access.

One of the most important political developments that has occurred regarding abortion in recent years is the gradual evolution of the reproductive *rights* movement of the *Roe* era to the reproductive *justice* movement of the present one. The former focused almost exclusively on securing and then defending legal abortion, while the latter—developed by black women and now largely led by women of color—firmly defends the right to an abortion but places it within the broader context of a more comprehensive set of issues regarding reproduction—the right to have a child, the right not to have a child, and the right to parent the children one has in a healthy and safe environment. Or, as Folami Eze explained to us when talking about how her organization, based in the South, which helps with abortion funding, transportation, and housing, differs because it is a reproductive justice organization:

There's a certain realness that we bring when we have this conversation with people and interact with people. It's this continuity of care. So once we've talked about that person's abortion access, we identify how it's related to all of the other issues that may impact their life. Then we're able to have those conversations, talking about, you had your abortion, but also your unemployment and you're trying to find a job or the reason that you wanted to have your abortion was because you want to be able to provide a better life for your child or for the children that you already have. So what would that look like? It looks like having better food options in the community. It looks like making sure that black and brown folks aren't continually criminalized just because of staying in this society. We want to make sure that if you do bring a child into this world, they're not going to end up being a hashtag because of some sort of police brutality. So we're able to bring that kind of realness into the conversations with people and let them know that yes, the work that we do is about abortion but it's also about class and gender and economics and racial justice, all of these things combined. You've had an abortion and now here's how it's related to all these other things and how can we evolve to make the world—to make it like the world that we want. This is not just a single issue.

This expanded platform of the reproductive justice movement makes obvious practical sense, given that around 60 percent of abortion patients are already mothers, the majority of them live in poverty, and they are disproportionately women of color. The reproductive health services that pregnant women need go well beyond access to abortion, and the reproductive justice movement highlights these needs and the racial, class, and gender inequities that prevent them from being met.

But this approach also makes strategic sense because it carries the possibility of new coalition partners because of its broader focus. One example of this possibility is a remarkable organization in Bloomington, Indiana, called All-Options. As the name implies, this organization is a nonjudgmental source of advice and services for pregnant women, whether they wish to have an abortion or remain pregnant and whether they want to parent or pursue adoption. It is also one of the main sources of abortion referrals and funding in the area.

As its founder, Parker Dockray, has described All-Options, "Diapers and abortion funding are the two pillars of our work. But diapers have been a critical entry point for us. We've gotten support and donations from local restaurants, elected officials, and sororities. . . . We've been covered in the local press. Even the local [crisis pregnancy center] refers people to us for diapers! So it's been an important way to build trust and visibility in the community because we are meeting a concrete need for local families." According to Parker, this presents a political opportunity. "All-Options allows us to transcend the stale pro-choice/pro-life debate and invites people to be curious and compassionate about how abortion and parenting needs can coexist."

In a similar vein, one of the people we interviewed for this study, Elizabeth Wolff, a clinic administrator in a southern state, reflected on a similar possibility in her waiting room: "You have a woman who's there for birth control, you have a woman who's there for a prenatal exam, and a woman who's there for a medication abortion, all sitting next to each other—which is exactly how it should be." This integration of abortion with other services can also be found in clinics that have incorporated obstetrical care, transgender health care, and adoption agency referrals. Not all clinics can do this, as many are forced for a variety of reasons to focus entirely on abortion or to segregate their abortion patients from their other patients. But for those that can, the integration of abortion into other health services can be not only an alternative source of revenue in the face of dwindling abortion numbers but also a powerful agent of change.

These potential reasons for optimism cannot erase the many uncertainties and contradictions facing abortion in the United States at this time. In October 2019, the Supreme Court agreed to hear a Louisiana case about admitting privileges that many expect will, given the Court's conservative makeup, chip away at Roe and its progeny, or possibly even worse. We would hope that the research and stories presented in this book would be part of the argument against doing so, but with the current makeup of the Court we are not blind to the reality of the moment. At the same time, the backlash against the Trump presidency and fears of what the Court might do have spurred a revitalized defense of abortion that is increasingly embedded within this growing reproductive justice movement. The movement has drawn in younger and more diverse women, many of whom were not previously affiliated with the older reproductive rights movement, including allies from other social movements such as immigration rights groups, criminal justice reformers, and the labor movement.

But what gives us the most hope is the commitment of the providers and their allies and volunteers to make abortion as accessible and safe as possible given the current legal and social environment. The obstacles that their patients must overcome—around being able to freely decide to have an abortion without interference, finding a place to do so without distant travel and fraudulent interference, paying without sacrificing other life essentials, getting inside without being tormented, being counseled without listening to lies, waiting for no medical reason, and having the most appropriate medical procedure without politicians overriding—are unparalleled in medicine. And yet, because people are so determined to control their own reproductive lives and providers are so committed to helping them do so, abortion care in the United States continues.

Of course, unfettered access to abortion care alone will not solve all of the problems the reproductive justice movement focuses on or all of the issues faced by the mainly poor women whose stories have been told in this book. Nor will lack of government interference mean that everyone who wants or needs an abortion in this country will be able to get one, as the general health care system in the United States has deeply rooted problems that will persist, especially for indigent people. For abortion patients' lives to truly improve would involve addressing the massive income inequality that characterizes American society.

Nevertheless, it is amply clear that people who obtain desired abortions fare better than those who do not, and the children of the former do better than those of the latter. The best way to this end is for politicians in this country to just get out of the way and treat abortion like other fields of medicine. If this were to occur, the herculean efforts of patients and providers to navigate the abortion obstacle course would become a thing of the past. Instead, people seeking an abortion would be what they should be—simply, patients, like all others, obtaining the medical care they need.

Notes

The endnotes that follow are keyed to short phrases that start the paragraph that corresponds to the source(s) used in that paragraph. All citations here, as well as the text throughout the book, follow the *Chicago Manual of Style*.

1. INTRODUCTION

"Yet, consider Talia's story" Emily Rooke-Ley, "Deception and Trickery at a Fake Abortion Clinic: Meet Talia," *Jane's Due Process*, September 17, 2015, janesdueprocess.org/blog/meet-talia/.

"Or take Brittany's story" Liz Welch, "6 Women on Their Terrifying, Infuriating Encounters with Abortion Clinic Protesters," *Cosmopolitan*, February 21, 2014, www.cosmopolitan.com/politics/news/a5669/abortion-clinic-protesters/.

"Now consider what it took for Wandalyn" As told to us by one of the volunteers who assisted Wandalyn, with Wandalyn's permission and additions. Wandalyn is not her real name.

"But what these three stories highlight" Caitlin Borgmann, "Abortion Exceptionalism and Undue Burden Preemption," *Washington and Lee Law Review* 71 (2014): 1047; Linda Greenhouse and Reva B. Siegel, "Casey and the Clinic Closings: When 'Protecting Health' Obstructs Choice," *Yale Law Journal* 125 (2016): 1428. On problems endemic to all health care, see Eric C. Schneider, Dana O. Sarnak, David Squires, Arnav Shah, and Michelle M. Doty, "Mirror, Mirror

2017: International Comparison Reflects Flaws and Opportunities for Better U.S. Health Care," *Commonwealth Fund*, July 2017, interactives.common wealthfund.org/2017/july/mirror-mirror/assets/Schneider_mirror_mirror_2017. pdf; Leiyu Shi and Douglas A. Singh, *Essentials of the U.S. Health Care System*, 5th ed. (Burlington, MA: Jones and Bartlett Learning, 2018); Elisabeth Rosenthal, *An American Sickness: How Healthcare Became Big Business and How You Can Take It Back* (New York: Penguin Books, 2017); Jonathan Bush and Stephen Baker, *Where Does It Hurt? An Entrepreneur's Guide to Fixing Health Care* (New York: Portfolio/Penguin, 2014).

"That abortion is one of the most divisive issues" Elizabeth Nash, "Unprecedented Wave of Abortion Bans Is an Urgent Call to Action," Guttmacher Institute, May 2019, www.guttmacher.org/article/2019/05/unprecedented-wave-abortion-bans-urgent-call-action.

"At the same time" Amelia Thomson-Deveaux, "Abortion Rights Haven't Been a Priority in Blue States—Until Now," *FiveThirtyEight*, June 10, 2019, fivethirtyeight.com/features/abortion-rights-havent-been-a-priority-in-blue-states-until-now/; David S. Cohen and Carole Joffe, "Supporters of Abortion Rights Should Be Energized, Not Demoralized," *Washington Post*, April 29, 2019, www.washingtonpost.com/opinions/2019/04/29/supporters-abortion-rights-should-be-energized-not-demoralized.

"Political attempts to interfere" There is an extensive literature on the anti-abortion movement and its tactics, including Dallas A. Blanchard and Terry J. Prewitt, *Religious Violence and Abortion: The Gideon Project* (Gainesville: University Press of Florida, 1993); James Risen and Judy L. Thomas, *Wrath of Angels: The American Abortion War* (New York: Basic Books, 1998); Center for Reproductive Rights, *Defending Human Rights: Abortion Providers Facing Threats, Restrictions, and Harassment* (New York: Center for Reproductive Rights, 2009); Jack Fainman and Roland Penner, *They Shoot Doctors, Don't They? A Memoir* (Winnipeg: Great Plains Publications, 2011); Emily Lyons and Jeff Lyons, *Life's Been a Blast: The True Story of Birmingham Bombing Survivor Emily Lyons* (Birmingham, AL: I Em Books, 2005); Eyal Press, *Absolute Convictions: My Father, a City, and the Conflict That Divided America* (New York: Henry Holt, 2006); Bruce S. Steir, *Jailhouse Journal of an OB/GYN* (Bloomington, IN: AuthorHouse, 2008); Susan Wicklund, *This Common Secret: My Journey as an Abortion Doctor* (New York: PublicAffairs, 2008); David Cohen and Krysten Connon, *Living in the Crosshairs: The Untold Stories of Anti-abortion Terrorism* (New York: Oxford University Press, 2015); Faye Ginsberg, *Contested Lives: The Abortion Debate in an American Community* (Berkeley: University of California Press, 1989); Ziad Munson, *The Making of Prolife Activists* (Chicago: University of Chicago Press, 2009); Deanna Rohlinger, *Abortion Politics, Mass Media, and Social Movements in America* (New York: Cambridge University Press, 2014); Drew Halfmann, *Doctors and Demonstrators: How Political Institutions Shape*

Abortion Law in the United States, Britain, and Canada (Chicago: University of Chicago Press, 2011); Mary Ziegler, *After Abortion: The Lost History of the Abortion Debate* (Cambridge, MA: Harvard University Press, 2015); Rickie Solinger, ed., *Abortion Wars: A Half Century of Struggle, 1950–2000* (Berkeley: University of California Press, 1998); Stephen Singular, *The Wichita Divide: The Murder of Dr. George Tiller and the Battle over Abortion* (New York: St. Martin's Press, 2011); Patricia Baird-Windle and Eleanor J. Bader, *Targets of Hatred: Antiabortion Terrorism* (New York: Palgrave, 2001); Alesha E. Doan, *Opposition and Intimidation: The Abortion Wars and Strategies of Political Harassment* (Ann Arbor: University of Michigan Press, 2007); Carol Mason, *Killing for Life: The Apocalyptic Narrative of Pro-life Violence* (Ithaca, NY: Cornell University Press, 2002); Dallas Blanchard, *The Anti-abortion Movement and the Rise of the Religious Right: From Polite to Fiery Protest* (New York: Twayne, 1994); Jennifer Jefferis, *Armed for Life: The Army of God and Anti-abortion Terror in the United States* (New York: Praeger, 2011); Marian Faux, *Crusaders: Voices from the Abortion Front* (Secaucus, NJ: Birch Lane Press, 1990); Kerry N. Jacoby, *Souls, Bodies, Spirits* (New York: Praeger, 1998); Frederick S. Jaffe, *Abortion Politics: Private Morality and Public Policy* (McGraw-Hill, 1980); Carol J.C. Maxwell, *Pro-life Activists in America: Meaning, Motivation, and Direct Action* (New York: Cambridge University Press, 2002).

"Legislative efforts to restrict abortion" Guttmacher Institute, "State Abortion Policy Landscape: From Hostile to Supportive," December 2018, www.guttmacher .org/article/2018/12/state-abortion-policy-landscape-hostile-supportive.

"In spite of the extensive literature" Scratching the surface of this voluminous literature, some of the books we have relied heavily on in building our knowledge of this area are Angela Bonavoglia, *The Choices We Made: Twenty-Five Women and Men Speak Out about Abortion* (New York: Random House, 1991); Celeste Condit, *Decoding Abortion Rhetoric: Communicating Social Change* (Urbana: University of Illinois Press, 1990); Ann Furedi, *The Moral Case for Abortion* (New York: Palgrave Macmillan, 2016); Lori Freedman, *Willing and Unable: Doctors' Constraints in Abortion Care* (Nashville, TN: Vanderbilt University Press, 2010); Marlene Gerber Fried, ed., *From Abortion to Reproductive Freedom: Transforming a Movement* (Boston: South End Press, 1990); David Garrow, *Liberty and Sexuality: The Right to Privacy and the Making of Roe v. Wade* (Berkeley: University of California Press, 1998); Linda Gordon, *The Moral Property of Women: A History of Birth Control Politics in America* (Urbana: University of Illinois Press, 2002); Linda Greenhouse and Reva Siegal, *Before Roe v. Wade: Voices That Shaped the Abortion Debate before the Supreme Court's Ruling* (New York: Kaplan, 2010); David Grimes and Linda Brandon, *Every Third Woman In America: How Legal Abortion Transformed Our Nation* (Carolina Beach, NC: Daymark, 2014); Carole Joffe, *Dispatches from the Abortion Wars: The Costs of Fanaticism to Doctors, Patients and the Rest of Us* (Boston: Beacon

Press, 2009); Carole Joffe, *Doctors of Conscience: The Struggle to Provide Abortion before and after Roe v. Wade* (Boston: Beacon Press, 1995); Laura Kaplan, *The Story of Jane: The Legendary Underground Abortion Service* (Chicago: University of Chicago Press, 1997); Kristin Luker, *Abortion and the Politics of Motherhood* (Berkeley: University of California Press, 1984); Kristin Luker, *Taking Chances: Abortion and the Decision Not to Contracept* (Berkeley: University of California Press, 1975); Michele McKeegan, *Abortion Politics: Mutiny in the Ranks of the Right* (New York: Free Press, 1992); Patricia Miller, *Good Catholics: The Battle over Abortion in the Catholic Church* (Berkeley: University of California Press, 2014); James Mohr, *Abortion in America: The Origins and Evolution of National Policy* (Cambridge, MA: Harvard University Press, 1978); Ziad Munson, *Abortion Politics* (Medford, MA: Polity Press, 2018); Jennifer Nelson, *Women of Color and the Reproductive Rights Movement* (New York: New York University Press, 2003); Michelle Oberman, *Her Body, Our Laws: On the Front Lines of the Abortion War, from El Salvador to Oklahoma* (Boston: Beacon Press, 2018); Willie Parker, *Life's Work: A Moral Argument for Choice* (New York: Simon and Schuster, 2017); Rosalind Petchesky, *Abortion and Women's Choice: The State, Sexuality and Reproductive Freedom* (Boston: Northeastern University Press, 1990); Katha Pollitt, *Pro: Reclaiming Abortion Rights* (New York: Picador Press, 2014); Leslie Reagan, *Dangerous Pregnancies: Mothers, Disabilities, and Abortion in Modern America* (Berkeley: University of California Press, 2012); Leslie Reagan, *When Abortion Was a Crime: Women, Medicine and Law in the United States, 1867–1973* (Berkeley: University of California Press, 1997); Carol Sanger, *About Abortion: Terminating Pregnancy in Twenty-First-Century America* (Cambridge, MA: Harvard University Press, 2017); Johanna Schoen, *Abortion after Roe* (Chapel Hill: University of North Carolina Press, 2015); Helena Silverstein, *Girls on the Stand: How Courts Fail Pregnant Minors* (New York: New York University Press, 2007); Rickie Solinger, *The Abortionist: A Woman against the Law* (New York: Free Press, 1994); Lawrence Tribe, *Abortion: The Clash of Absolutes* (New York: W. W. Norton, 1990); Katie Watson, *Scarlet A: The Ethics, Law, and Politics of Ordinary Abortion* (New York: Oxford University Press, 2018); Sarah Weddington, *A Question of Choice* (New York: G. P. Putnam, 1992); Mary Ziegler, *Beyond Abortion: Roe v. Wade and the Battle for Privacy* (Cambridge, MA: Harvard University Press, 2018).

"The interviews with providers, allies, and volunteers" For those interested in methodology, we chose our interview subjects on the basis of a combination of purposive and snowball sampling. The original goal was to obtain a diverse sample of subjects who could talk about how they provided care amid different forms of abortion restrictions. After we had covered a broad enough sampling of states and providers to have a comprehensive picture of some basic background about the current landscape of abortion and how abortion restrictions work in practice, we realized we were only about ten states away from having talked with people providing care in every state in the country. At that point in time, we expanded our interviews to make sure that we covered the entire country. From there, we had the interviews transcribed and then coded the transcriptions using Dedoose software. Consistent with grounded theory, the coding was an iterative process that helped us develop the themes that appear throughout this book.

"To situate the material in this book" Jenna Jerman, Rachel K. Jones, and Tsuyoshi Onda, "Characteristics of U.S. Abortion Patients in 2014 and Changes since 2008," Guttmacher Institute, May 2016, www.guttmacher.org/report /characteristics-us-abortion-patients-2014.

"Additionally, while abortion in this country" Jerman, Jones, and Onda, "Characteristics."

"Overall, the demographic breakdown" Dorothy Roberts, *Killing the Black Body* (New York: Vintage Books, 1998); Jael Miriam Silliman, Loretta Ross, Elena R. Gutiérrez, and Marlene Gerber Fried, *Undivided Rights: Women of Color Organizing for Reproductive Justice* (Boston: South End Press, 2004); Loretta J. Ross, Lynn Roberts, Erika Derkas, Whitney Peoples, and Pamela Bridgewater Toure, eds., *Radical Reproductive Justice: Foundation, Theory, Practice, Critique* (New York: Feminist Press, 2017); Marcela Howell, *Our Bodies, Our Lives, Our Voices: The State of Black Women and Reproductive Justice* (Washington, DC: In Our Own Voice: National Black Women's Reproductive Justice Agenda, June 2017); Loretta Ross and Rickie Solinger, *Reproductive Justice: An Introduction* (Oakland: University of California Press, 2017).

"Though the numbers are declining" Rachel K. Jones, Elizabeth Witwer, and Jenna Jerman, "Abortion Incidence and Service Availability in the United States, 2017," Guttmacher Institute, 2019, www.guttmacher.org/report /abortion-incidence-service-availability-us-2017; Guttmacher Institute, "Induced Abortion in the United States," 2019, www.guttmacher.org/fact-sheet /induced-abortion-united-states. The Centers for Disease Control reports lower abortion numbers, but their totals are incomplete, as they do not have data from every state, including California. Joerg Dreweke, "Abortion Reporting: Promoting Public Health, Not Politics," *Guttmacher Policy Review* 18 (2015): 40.

"Ever since Guttmacher released" Guttmacher Institute, "U.S. Abortion Rate Reaches Record Low amidst Looming Onslaught against Reproductive Health and Rights," 2017, www.guttmacher.org/gpr/2017/01/us-abortion-rate-reaches-record-low-amidst-looming-onslaught-against-reproductive-health#chart2.

"Much more likely to have contributed" Guttmacher Institute, "U.S. Abortion Rate"; Diana G. Foster, "Dramatic Decreases in US Abortion Rates: Public Health Achievement or Failure?," *American Journal of Public Health* 107 (2017): 1360–62. It remains to be seen whether the Trump administration will change this trend with contraceptive restrictions that it has put in place. Robert Pear, "Trump Proposes a New Way around Birth Control Mandate: Religious

Exemptions and Title X," *New York Times,* November 17, 2018, www.nytimes
.com/2018/11/17/us/politics/trump-birth-control.html.

"The decrease in the published abortion rate" Guttmacher Institute, "Abortion
Incidence and Service Availability in the United States," 2017, www.guttmacher
.org/journals/psrh/2017/01/abortion-incidence-and-service-availability-united-
states-2014.

"What is not captured" D. Grossman, K. White, L. Fuentes, K. Hopkins, A.
Stevenson, S. Yeatman, and J. E. Potter, "Knowledge, Opinion and experience
Related to Abortion Self-Induction in Texas," Texas Policy Evaluation Project
Research Brief, November 17, 2015, liberalarts.utexas.edu/txpep/_files/pdf
/TxPEP-Research-Brief-KnowledgeOpinionExperience.pdf.

"Regardless, despite the apparent decline" Nikki Madsen, Jay Thibodeau, and
Dallas Schubert, "Communities Need Clinics: The Role of Independent Abortion
Care Providers in Ensuring Meaningful Access to Abortion Care in the United
States," *Abortion Care Network,* August 2017, 1–12, www.abortioncarenetwork
.org/wp-content/uploads/2017/08/CommunitiesNeedClinics2017.pdf; Esme
Deprez, "Abortion Clinics Are Closing at a Record Pace," *Bloomberg Business-
week,* February 24, 2016, www.bloomberg.com/news/articles/2016–02–24
/abortion-clinics-are-closing-at-a-record-pace; Rachel K. Jones and Jenna Jerman, "Abortion Incidence and Service Availability In the United States, 2014,"
Perspectives on Sexual and Reproductive Health 49 (2017): 17–27.

"As common as abortion is" Whole Woman's Health v. Hellerstedt, 136 S. Ct.
2292, 2315 (2016); Kari White, Erin Carroll, and Daniel Grossman, "Complications from First-Trimester Aspiration Abortion: A Systematic Review of the Literature," *Contraception* 92 (2015): 422; Ushma Upadhyay, "Incidence of Emergency Department Visits and Complications after Abortion," *Obstetrics &
Gynecology* 125 (2015): 175; National Academies of Sciences, Engineering,
and Medicine, *The Safety and Quality of Abortion Care in the United States*
(Washington, DC: National Academies Press, 2018), www.nap.edu/download
/24950.

"The best research" Advancing New Standards in Reproductive Health,
"Turnaway Study," n.d., accessed July 27, 2019, ANSIRH, www.ansirh.org
/research/turnaway-study.

"The central finding of the Turnaway Study" Diana Foster, M. Antonia Biggs,
Lauren Ralph, Caitlin Gerdts, Sarah Roberts, and M. Maria Glymour, "Socioeco-
nomic Outcomes of Women Who Receive and Women Who Are Denied Wanted
Abortions in the United States," *American Journal of Public Health* 108, no. 3
(2018): 407–13; Ushma Upadhyay, M. Antonia Biggs, and Diana Greene Foster,
"The Effect of Abortion on Having and Achieving Aspirational One-Year Plans,"
BMC Women's Health 15, no. 1 (2015): 201.

"Other measures show" Sarah Roberts, M. Antonia Biggs, and Karuna S.
Chibber, "Risk of Violence from the Man Involved in the Pregnancy after Receiv-

ing or Being Denied an Abortion," *BMC Medicine* 12, no. 1 (2014): 144; Jane Mauldon, Diana Greene Foster, and Sarah C. M. Roberts, "Effect of Abortion vs. Carrying to Term on a Woman's Relationship with the Man Involved in the Pregnancy," *Perspectives on Sexual and Reproductive Health* 47, no. 1 (2015): 11–18; M. A. Biggs, U. D. Upadhyay, J. R. Steinberg, and D. G. Foster, "Does Abortion Reduce Self-Esteem and Life Satisfaction?," *Quality of Life Research* 23, no. 9 (2014): 2505–13; Antonia Biggs, Ushma D. Upadhyay, Charles E. McCulloch, and Diana G. Foster, "Women's Mental Health and Well-Being 5 Years after Receiving or Being Denied an Abortion," *JAMA Psychiatry* 74, no. 2 (2017): 169–78.

"Children are also worse off" Diana Greene Foster, Sarah E. Raifman, Jessica D. Gipson, Corinne H. Rocca, and M. Antonia Biggs, "Effects of Carrying an Unwanted Pregnancy to Term on Women's Existing Children," *Journal of Pediatrics* 205 (2019): 183–89; Diana Green Foster, M. Antonia Biggs, and Sarah Raifman, "Comparison of Health, Development, Maternal Bonding, and Poverty among Children Born after Denial of Abortion vs after Pregnancies Subsequent to an Abortion," *JAMA Pediatrics* 172 (2018): 1053–60; Ushma Upadhyay, Evelyn Angel Aztlan-James, and Diana Foster, "Intended Pregnancy after Receiving vs. Being Denied a Wanted Abortion," *Contraception* 99 (2019): 42–47.

"Women who are denied abortions" Lauren J. Ralph, Eleanor Bimla Schwarz, Daniel Grossman, and Diana Greene Foster, "Self-Reported Physical Health of Women Who Did and Did Not Terminate Pregnancy after Seeking Abortion Services: A Cohort Study," *Annals of Internal Medicine* 171 (2019): 238–47; Caitlin Gerdts, Loren Dobkin, Diana Greene Foster, and Eleanor Bimla Schwarz, "Side Effects, Physical Health Consequences, and Mortality Associated with Abortion and Birth after an Unwanted Pregnancy," *Women's Health Issues* 26 (2016): 55–59; Affidavits in Allegheny Reproductive Health Center v. Pennsylvania Department of Human Services (filed January 16, 2019), www.womenslawproject. org/2019/01/16/pennsylvania-abortion-providers-file-state-lawsuit-challenging-medicaid-abortion-coverage-ban/.

"At its most serious, continuing" Nina Martin, "U.S. Has the Worst Rates of Maternal Deaths in the Developed World," *NPR*, May 12, 2017, www.npr .org/2017/05/12/528098789/u-s-has-the-worst-rate-of-maternal-deaths-in-the-developed-world; Centers for Disease Control and Prevention, "Pregnancy Mortality Surveillance System," www.cdc.gov/reproductivehealth/maternalinfanthealth /pmss.html; Nina Martin, "Black Mothers Keep Dying after Giving Birth. Shalon Irving's Story Explains Why," *NPR*, December 7, 2017, www.npr .org/2017/12/07/568948782/black-mothers-keep-dying-after-giving-birth-shalon-irvings-story-explains-why; Ross and Solinger, *Reproductive Justice*.

"The answer to that query" Roe v. Wade, 410 U.S. 113 (1973).

"For almost two decades" Planned Parenthood of Southern Pennsylvania v. Casey, 505 U.S. 833 (1992).

"In the decades after Casey" Gonzales v. Carhart, 550 U.S. 124, 166 (2007); Aziza Ahmed, "Abortion in a Post-truth Moment: A Response to Erwin Chemerinsky and Michele Goodwin," *Texas Law Review* 95 (2016): 198.

"This relaxed standard" Whole Woman's Health v. Hellerstedt, 136 S. Ct. 2292, 2315 (2016).

"As argued by the state" Oral argument transcript, *Whole Woman's Health v. Hellerstedt*, March 2, 2016, www.supremecourt.gov/oral_arguments/argument_transcripts/2015/15–274_d18e.pdf.

"On the other side" J. Alexander Lawrence et al., "Brief for Petitioners in *Whole Woman's Health v. Cole*" (2015), 14–18; Anton Melitsky et al., "Brief for Social Science Researchers as Amici Curiae in Support of Petitioners in *Whole Woman's Health v. Cole*" (2016); Kimberly Parker et al., "Brief for Amici Curiae American College of Obstetricians and Gynecologists, American Medical Association, American Academy of Family Physicians, American Osteopathic Association, and American Academy of Pediatrics in Support of Petitioners in *Whole Woman's Health v. Cole*" (2016).

"With its decision" Daniel Grossman, "The Use of Public Health Evidence in *Whole Woman's Health v. Hellerstedt*," *JAMA Internal Medicine* 177, no. 2 (2017): 155–56; John A. Robertson, "*Whole Woman's Health v. Hellerstedt* and the Future of Abortion Regulation," *U.C. Irvine Law Review* 7 (2017): 623; Mary Ziegler, "The New Negative Rights: Abortion Funding and Constitutional Law after *Whole Woman's Health*," *Nebraska Law Review* 96 (2018): 577.

"And yet, several years" Center for Reproductive Rights, "Virginia Health Care Providers File New Lawsuit Challenging Longstanding Abortion Restrictions," press release, June 20, 2018, www.reproductiverights.org/press-room/virginia-health-care-providers-file-new-lawsuit-challenging-longstanding-abortion-restric; Jessica Mason Pieklo, "Advocates Set Sights on Indiana Abortion Restrictions in New Lawsuit," *Rewire,* June 22, 2018, rewire.news /article/2018/06/22/advocates-set-sights-indiana-abortion-restrictions-new-lawsuit/; David Yaffe-Bellany, "Five Years after Wendy Davis Filibuster, Texas Abortion Providers Struggle to Reopen Clinics," *Texas Tribune,* June 25, 2018, www.texastribune.org/2018/06/25/five-years-after-wendy-davis-filibuster-abortion-clinics/. The start of 2019 has seen an overwhelming number of extreme abortion restrictions, including many states passing laws that would, if they ever take effect, ban abortion at six weeks of pregnancy, before many women even know they are pregnant and also before many clinics even do abortions. Elizabeth Nash, "A Surge in Bans on Abortion as Early as Six Weeks, before Most People Know They Are Pregnant," Guttmacher Institute, March 2019, www .guttmacher.org/article/2019/03/surge-bans-abortion-early-six-weeks-most-people-know-they-are-pregnant. Even worse, Alabama has passed a law that bans all abortions except when the pregnancy poses a serious threat to the woman's health. Kate Smith, "Alabama Governor Signs Near-Total Abortion Ban into

Law," *CBS News,* May 16, 2019, www.cbsnews.com/news/alabama-abortion-law-governor-kay-ivey-signs-near-total-ban-today-live-updates-2019-05-15/. None of these extreme bans will be allowed to take effect unless the Supreme Court overturns *Roe.*

"Furthermore, with Justice Anthony Kennedy" Erica Smock, *What If Roe Fell? The State-by-State Consequences of Overturning Roe v. Wade* (New York: Center for Reproductive Rights, 2019), www.reproductiverights.org/sites /default/files/documents/bo_whatifroefell.pdf.

2. MAKING THE DECISION

"All of these reasons" Lawrence R. Finer, Lori F. Frohwirth, Lindsay A. Dauphinee, Susheela Singh, and Ann M. Moore, "Reasons U.S. Women Have Abortions: Quantitative and Qualitative Perspectives," *Perspectives on Sexual and Reproductive Health* 37 (2005): 110; Antonia Biggs, Heather Gould, and Diana Foster, "Understanding Why Women Seek Abortions in the US," *BMC Women's Health* 13 (2013): 1, 12.

"As it turns out" Corinne H. Rocca, Katrina Kimport, Sarah C.M. Roberts, Heather Gould, John Neuhaus, and Diana G. Foster, "Decision Rightness and Emotional Responses to Abortion in the United States: A Longitudinal Study," *PLoS One* 10 (2015): 1, 10; Lauren Ralph, Diana Greene Foster, Katrina Kimport, David Turok, and Sarah C.M. Roberts, "Measuring Decisional Certainty among Women Seeking Abortion," *Contraception* 95 (2017): 269.

"For example, both Oklahoma and Idaho" Idaho Code Ann. § 5-334; Cailin Harris, "Statutory Prohibitions on Wrongful Birth Claims and Their Dangerous Effects on Patients," *Boston College Journal of Law and Social Justice* 34 (2014): 365, 379.

"Even laws that allow" Wood v. University of Utah Med. Center, 67 P.3d 436 (Utah 2002), 459-60 (C.J. Durham, dissenting); "Utah Legislative Survey—1983," *Utah Law Review* 115 (1984): 224-25.

"Because of these laws" Maya Manian, "Lessons from Personhood's Defeat: Abortion Restrictions and Side Effects on Women's Health," *Ohio State Law Journal* 74 (2013): 75, 104-5; Harris, "Statutory Prohibitions," 365; William C. Duncan, "Statutory Responses to 'Wrongful Birth' and 'Wrongful Life' Actions," in *Proceedings of the Fourteenth University Faculty for Life Conference* (Washington, DC: University Faculty for Life, 2004), 14-15, www.uffl.org/Vol14/Duncan-04.pdf.

"In some places" Ky. Rev. Stat. § 216B.400(5).

"Kentucky is alone" Guttmacher Institute, "State Family Planning Funding Restrictions," 2019, www.guttmacher.org/state-policy/explore/state-family-planning-funding-restrictions.

"However, under the Trump administration's change" Kinsey Hasstedt, "A Domestic Gag Rule and More: The Administration's Proposed Changes to Title X," 2018, www.guttmacher.org/article/2018/06/domestic-gag-rule-and-more-administrations-proposed-changes-title-x; Kinsey Hasstedt, "Trump Administration Looks to Impose 'Domestic Gag Rule,' Continuing Its Assault on Reproductive Rights," 2018, www.guttmacher.org/article/2018/06/trump-administration-looks-impose-domestic-gag-rule-continuing-its-assault; Ariana Cha, "Is It a Gag Rule after All? A Closer Look at Changes to Title X Funding Regarding Abortion," *Washington Post*, May 23, 2018, www.washingtonpost.com/news/to-your-health/wp/2018/05/23/is-it-a-gag-rule-what-changes-to-family-planning-funds-and-abortion-referrals-might-mean; Pam Belluck, "Planned Parenthood Refuses Federal Funds over Abortion Restrictions," *New York Times*, August 19, 2019, www.nytimes.com/2019/08/19/health/planned-parenthood-title-x.html.

"A similar assault" Rust v. Sullivan, 500 U.S. 173 (1991); Department of Health and Human Services, "42 CFR Part 59: Compliance with Statutory Program Integrity Requirements," s3.amazonaws.com/public-inspection.federalregister.gov/2018–11673.pdf. In June 2019, the Ninth Circuit paved the way for the new regulations to take effect, ruling that they were likely to survive a federal court challenge. California v. Azar, 927 F.3d 1068 (9th Cir. 2019). While this is undoubtedly not the final word in this saga (the Ninth Circuit reheard the case in September but has yet to rule), it increases the likelihood of the regulations surviving legal challenge.

"In many places" Sital Kalantry, *Women's Human Rights and Migration: Sex-Selective Abortion Laws in the United States and India* (Philadelphia: University of Pennsylvania Press, 2018); Sital Kalantry, "Sex Selection in the United States and India: A Contextualist Feminist Approach," *UCLA Journal of International Law and Foreign Affairs* 18 (2013): 61, 81–82; Guttmacher Institute, "Abortion Bans in Cases of Sex or Race Selection or Genetic Anomaly," 2019, www.guttmacher.org/state-policy/explore/abortion-bans-cases-sex-or-race-selection-or-genetic-anomaly.

"Issues of race and ethnicity" Guttmacher Institute, "Claim That Most Abortion Clinics Are Located in Black or Hispanic Neighborhoods Is False," 2014, www.guttmacher.org/article/2014/06/claim-most-abortion-clinics-are-located-black-or-hispanic-neighborhoods-false; Seema Mohapatra, "False Framings: The Co-opting of Sex-Selection by the Anti-abortion Movement," *Journal of Law, Medicine, and Ethics* 43, no. 2 (2015): 270–74; Shivana Jorawar and Miriam Yeung, "Wolves in Sheep's Clothing: The Impact of Sex-Selective Abortion Bans on Asian American and Pacific Islander Women," *Asian American Policy Review* 24 (2014): 31–41.

"No court has ruled" Guttmacher Institute, "Abortion Bans."

"The stated rationale" Michael Berube, "This Pa. Abortion Bill Has Nothing to Do with Helping Kids with Down Syndrome or Their Families: Opinion,"

Penn Live, April 6, 2018, www.pennlive.com/opinion/2018/04/this_pa_abortion_bill_has_noth.html.

"So far, the courts" SCOTUSblog, "Box v. Planned Parenthood of Indiana and Kentucky Inc.," n.d., accessed July 27, 2019, www.scotusblog.com/case-files/cases/box-v-planned-parenthood-of-indiana-and-kentucky-inc/.

"A small but not insubstantial percentage" Jenna Jerman, Lori F. Frohwirth, Megan L. Kavanaugh, and Nakeisha Blades, "Barriers to Abortion Care and Their Consequences for Patients Traveling for Services: Qualitative Findings for Two States," *Perspectives on Sexual and Reproductive Health* 49, no. 2 (2017): 95–102; Jenna Jerman, Tsuyoshi Onda, and Rachel K. Jones, "What Are People Looking for When They Google 'Self-Abortion'?" *Contraception* 97, no. 6 (June 2018): 510–14; Katie Woodruff, "Coverage of Abortion in Select U.S. Newspapers," *Women's Health Issues* 29 (2018): 80–86.

"One of the most hotly contested sources" Katrina Kimport, Rebecca Kriz, and Sarah Roberts, "The Prevalence and Impacts of Crisis Pregnancy Center Visits among a Population of Pregnant Women," *Contraception* 98, no. 1 (2018): 69–73.

"For instance, Cherisse" Kimberly McGuire, "I Love My Son, but a Crisis Pregnancy Center Tricked Me into Having Him," *Romper*, January 31, 2018, www.romper.com/p/i-love-my-son-but-a-crisis-pregnancy-center-tricked-me-into-having-him-7928219.

"In 2006, Congressman Henry Waxman" US House of Representatives Committee on Government Reform—Minority Staff, Special Investigations Division, "False and Misleading Health Information Provided by Federally Funded Pregnancy Resource Centers," *Mother Jones*, July 2006, www.motherjones.com/files/waxman2.pdf; Amy G. Bryant and Erika E. Levi, "Abortion Misinformation from Crisis Pregnancy Centers in North Carolina," *Contraception* 86 (2012): 752.

"A copy of one such form" Exposefakeclinics.com, "What Exactly Is a Fake Clinic?," n.d., accessed July 27, 2019, www.exposefakeclinics.com/what-is-a-cpc-2/.

"Unfortunately, in the summer of 2018" National Institute of Family and Life Advocates v. Becerra, 138 S. Ct. 2361 (2018).

"In 2017, the story of 'Jane Doe'" Julie Tulbert, "Maddow's Bombshell That the Trump Administration Tracked Immigrant Pregnancies Also Reveals How Bad Fox's Coverage Was," *MediaMatters* (blog), March 19, 2019, www.mediamatters.org/blog/2019/03/19/maddows-bombshell-trump-administration-tracked-immigrant-pregnancies-also-reveals-how-bad-foxs/223177; Maria Sacchetti and Ann E. Marimow, "Undocumented Teen Immigrant Has the Abortion She Sought for Weeks," *Washington Post*, October 25, 2017, www.washingtonpost.com/politics/courts_law/undocumented-immigrant-teen-has-abortion-ending-weeks-long-court-battle/2017/10/25/9805249a-b90b-11e7-9e58-e6288544af98_story.html.

"Jane Doe's experience" Guttmacher Institute, "Minors' Access to Prenatal Care," 2019, www.guttmacher.org/state-policy/explore/minors-access-prenatal-care.

"Abortion, on the other hand" Guttmacher Institute, "Parental Involvement in Minors' Abortions," 2019, www.guttmacher.org/state-policy/explore/parental-involvement-minors-abortions.

"Regardless of what a state requires" Lauren Ralph, Heather Gould, Anne Baker, and Diana Foster, "The Role of Parents and Partners in Minors' Decisions to Have an Abortion and Anticipated Coping after Abortion," *Journal of Adolescent Health* 54, no. 4 (2014): 428.

"Parental involvement requirements" Lee Hasselbacher, Anne Dekleva, Sigrid Tristan, and Melissa Gilliam, "Factors Influencing Parental Involvement among Minors Seeking an Abortion: A Qualitative Study," *American Journal of Public Health* 104 (2014): 2207; Laurie Zabin, Marilyn Hirsch, Mark Emerson, and Elizabeth Raymond, "To Whom Do Inner City Minors Talk about Their Pregnancies? Adolescents' Communication with Parents and Parent Surrogates," *Family Planning Perspectives* 24 (1992): 148.

"Nonetheless, many minors" Hasselbacher et al., "Factors Influencing Parental Involvement," 2207; Stanley Henshaw and Kathryn Kost, "Parental Involvement in Minors' Abortion Decisions," *Family Planning Perspectives* 24 (1992): 196.

"For these minors" Bellotti v. Baird, 443 U.S. 622 (1979).

"Common sense tells us" Carol Sanger, *About Abortion: Terminating Pregnancy in Twenty-First-Century America* (Cambridge, MA: Belknap Press, 2018), 154–84; Kate Coleman-Minahan, Amanda Stevenson, Emily Obront, and Susan Hays, "Young Women's Experiences Obtaining Judicial Bypass for Abortion," *Texas Journal of Adolescent Health* 64, no. 1 (2019): 20–25.

"Scholars who have studied" Helena Silverstein, *Girls on the Stand: How Courts Fail Pregnant Minors* (New York: NYU Press, 2009).

"With so many obstacles" Lauren J. Ralph, Erin King, Elise Belusa, Diana Greene Foster, Claire D. Brindis, and Antonia Biggs, "The Impact of a Parental Notification Requirement on Illinois' Minors' Access to and Decision-Making around Abortion," *Journal of Adolescent Health* 62, no. 3 (2018): 281–87; Elizabeth Janiak, Isabel R. Fulcher, Alischer A. Cottrill, Nicole Tantoco, Ashley H. Mason, Jennifer Fortin, Jamie Sabino, and Alisa B. Goldberg, "Massachusetts' Parental Consent Law and Procedural Timing among Adolescents Undergoing Abortion," *Obstetrics & Gynecology* 133 (May 2019):978–86, journals.lww.com/greenjournal/Fulltext/2019/05000/Massachusetts__Parental_Consent_Law_and_Procedural.19.aspx.

"Beyond delay and travel" Janiak et al., "Massachusetts' Parental Consent Law"; Caitlin Myers and Daniel Ladd, "Did Parental Involvement Laws Grow Teeth? The Effects of State Restrictions on Minors' Access to Abortion," *IZA Institute of Labor Economics*, August 2017, 1–46.

3. FINDING AND GETTING TO A CLINIC

"But, as this chapter explains" Alice F. Cartwright, Mihiri Karunaratne, Jill Barr-Walker, Nicole E. Johns, and Ushma D. Upadhyay, "Identifying National Availability of Abortion Care and Distance from Major US Cities: Systematic Online Search," *Journal of Medical Internet Research* 20 (2018): e186.

"As this book was being finalized" Melody Gutierrez, "Abortion Medication to Be Available at California's College Health Centers Under New Law," *Los Angeles Times*, Oct. 11, 2019, www.latimes.com/california/story/2019-10-11/abortion-medication-california-college-health-centers-legislation.

"Unfortunately, California is an outlier" Daniel Grossman, Kate Grindlay, Anna L. Altshuler, and Jay Schulkin, "Induced Abortion Provision among a National Sample of Obstetrician–Gynecologists," *Obstetrics & Gynecology* 133 (2019): 477; National Academies of Sciences, Engineering and Medicine, *The Safety and Quality of Abortion Care in the United States* (Washington, DC: National Academies Press, 2018), S-5; Rachel K. Jones and Jenna Jerman, "Abortion Incidence and Service Availability in the United States, 2014," *Perspectives on Sexual and Reproductive Health* 49, no. 1 (March 2017): 20.

"All told, according to the most recent data" Rachel K. Jones, Elizabeth Witwer, and Jenna Jerman, "Abortion Incidence and Service Availability in the United States, 2017," Guttmacher Institute, 2019, www.guttmacher.org/report/abortion-incidence-service-availability-us-2017; Lawrence B. Finer and Stanley K. Henshaw, "Abortion Incidence and Services in the United States in 2000," *Perspectives on Sexual and Reproductive Health* 35 (2003): 6–15; Associated Press, "Abortion Clinics and Crisis Pregnancy Centers Differ," *U.S. News & World Report*, August 26, 2018, www.usnews.com/news/healthiest-communities/articles/2018–08–26/abortion-clinics-and-crisis-pregnancy-centers-differ; Gaby Del Valle, "This Map Shows the Surprising Number of Fake Abortion Clinics in NYC," *Outline*, June 8, 2018, theoutline.com/post/4882/crisis-pregnancy-centers-new-york-pro-truth?zd=1&zi=cilyfpa5.

"Why are there so few abortion-providing facilities" Carole Joffe, *Doctors of Conscience: The Struggle to Provide Abortion before and after Roe v. Wade* (Boston: Beacon Press, 1995).

"But also part of the story" 42 U.S.C. § 300a-7; Angel M. Foster, Jane van Dis, and Jody Steinauer, "Educational and Legislative Initiatives Affecting Residency Training in Abortion," *JAMA* 290 (2003): 1777–78; 42 U.S.C. § 238n.

"Training efforts" American College of Obstetricians and Gynecologists Committee on Health Care of Underserved Women, "Abortion Training and Education" (Committee Opinion), November 2014, www.acog.org/Clinical-Guidance-and-Publications/Committee-Opinions/Committee-on-Health-Care-for-Underserved-Women/Abortion-Training-and-Education. In particular, the Kenneth J. Ryan Residency Training in Abortion and Family Planning is active in over ninety medical schools in the United States. See the website for the Ryan Residency Program, ryanprogram.org/.

"A greater problem" Lori Freedman, *Willing and Unable: Doctors' Constraints in Abortion Care* (Nashville, TN: Vanderbilt University Press, 2011).

"Even when a clinic has its own property" Guttmacher Institute, "Targeted Regulation of Abortion Providers," 2019, www.guttmacher.org/state-policy /explore/targeted-regulation-abortion-providers; Whole Woman's Health v. Hellerstedt, 136 S. Ct. 2292 (2016); Emily Crockett, "Mississippi Gov. Phil Bryant: 'My Goal Is to End Abortion in Mississippi,'" *Rewire,* January 31, 2014, rewire.news/article/2014/01/31/mississippi-gov-phil-bryant-goal-end-abortion-mississippi/.

"Though exact numbers are difficult to come by" Esme Deprez, "Abortion Clinics Are Closing at a Record Pace," *Bloomberg Businessweek,* February 24, 2016, www.bloomberg.com/news/articles/2016–02–24/abortion-clinics-are-closing-at-a-record-pace.

"Finding property for an abortion clinic" Jenny Deam, "Doctor Struggles to Fill Role of Slain Kansas Abortion Provider," *Los Angeles Times,* March 5, 2012, articles.latimes.com/2012/mar/05/nation/la-na-kansas-abortion-20120305; Reena Diamante, "Longtime Austin Abortion Provider's Lease Bought Out by Anti-abortion Group," *Spectrum News,* February 22, 2019, spectrumlocalnews.com/tx/austin/news/2019/02/21/austin-lifecare-takes-over-previous-location-of-whole-woman-s-health.

"A similar story of a disruption" Rachel Wells, "Tennessee City Officials Are Using Zoning Rules to Erode Access to Abortion," *Rewire,* March 15, 2019, rewire.news/article/2019/03/15/tennessee-city-officials-are-using-zoning-rules-to-erode-abortion-access/.

"And if it's hard to find clinics" Guttmacher Institute, "Fact Sheet: Induced Abortion in the United States," January 2018, www.guttmacher.org/fact-sheet /induced-abortion-united-states.

"The experience of an anonymous abortion storyteller" Storyteller, "My Privileged Abortion Experience," *We Testify,* 2019, wetestify.org/stories/my-privileged-abortion-experience/.

"Part of the reason for fewer clinics" Guttmacher Institute, "State Bans on Abortion throughout Pregnancy," 2019, www.guttmacher.org/state-policy /explore/state-policies-later-abortions.

"Patients with pregnancies gone horribly wrong" Amy Littlefield, "'Not Dead Enough': Public Hospitals Deny Life-Saving Abortion Care to People in Need," *Rewire.News,* March 7, 2019, rewire.news/article/2019/03/07 /not-dead-enough-public-hospitals-deny-life-saving-abortion-care-to-people-in-need/.

"At the same time" Joffe, *Doctors of Conscience,* 141–47.

"The recent trend of mergers" American Civil Liberties Union, "New Report Reveals 1 in 6 U.S. Hospital Beds Are in Catholic Facilities That Prohibit Essential Health Care for Women," May 5, 2016, www.aclu.org/news/new-report-reveals-1-6-us-hospital-beds-are-catholic-facilities-prohibit-essential-health-care.

"Given the shortage" Laura Dodge, Sadia Haider, and Michelle Hacker, "Using a Simulated Patient to Assess Referral for Abortion Services in the USA," *Journal of Family Planning and Reproductive Health Care* 38 (2012): 246–51; Melanie Zurek, "Referral-Making in the Current Landscape of Abortion Access," *Contraception* 91, no. 1 (2015): 1–5; Valerie French, Renaisa S. Anthony, Susana E. Berrios, Libby D. Crockett, and Jody E. Steinauer, "A Sense of Obligation: Attitudes and Referral Practices for Abortion Services among Women's Health Providers in a Rural US State," *Clinical Obstetrics, Gynecology and Reproductive Medicine* 2 (2016), doi: 10.15761/COGRM.1000151.

"Referrals to abortion services" Guttmacher Institute, "Trump Administration Looks to Impose 'Domestic Gag Rule,' Continuing Its Assault on Reproductive Health and Rights," 2018, www.guttmacher.org/article/2018/06/trump-administration-looks-impose-domestic-gag-rule-continuing-its-assault; Laura Huss and Katelyn Burns, "What You Need to Know about Trump's Attacks on the Federal Family Planning Program," *Rewire*, February 22, 2019, rewire.news/article/2019/02/22/what-you-need-to-know-about-trumps-attacks-on-the-federal-family-planning-program/; US Department of Health and Human Services, "Consciences Protections for Health Care Providers," 2018, www.hhs.gov/conscience/conscience-protections/index.html.

"Another tactic of fake clinics" Tamar Lewin, "Anti-abortion Center's Ads Ruled Misleading," *New York Times*, April 22, 1994, www.nytimes.com/1994/04/22/us/anti-abortion-center-s-ads-ruled-misleading.html.

"Today when women seek help" Alistair Barr and Alicia Ritcey, "Tech Company Shareholder Meetings Turn Testy," *Bloomberg*, June 6, 2018, www.bloomberg.com/news/articles/2018-06-06/tech-company-shareholder-meetings-turn-testy-as-backlash-grows; Tiffany Hsu, "Google Changes Abortion Ad Policy," *New York Times*, May 21, 2019, www.nytimes.com/2019/05/21/business/media/google-abortion-ads.html.

"For now, it appears" National Institute of Family and Life Advocates v. Becerra, 138 S. Ct. 2361 (2018).

"Of course, abortion patients" National Rural Health Association, "About Rural Health Care," n.d., accessed July 28, 2019, www.ruralhealthweb.org/about-nrha/about-rural-health-care.

"What is known about traveling" Jonathan Bearak, Kristen Burke, and Rachel Jones, "Disparities and Change over Time in Distance Women Would Need to Travel to Have an Abortion in the USA: A Spatial Analysis," *Lancet Public Health* 2, no. 11 (2017): e492–e500; Cartwright et al., "Identifying National Availability";

Daniel Grossman, Kari White, Kristine Hopkins, and Joseph E. Potter, "Change in Distance to Nearest Facility and Abortion in Texas, 2012 to 2014," *JAMA* 317 (2017): 437–39.

"Sometimes women will get a ride" Ushma Upadhyay, Tracy Ann Weitz, Robert K. Jones, Rana E. Barar, and Diana Foster, "Denial of Abortion Because of Provider Gestational Age Limits in the United States," *American Journal of Public Health* 104 (2014): 1687–94.

"Another group that faces unique barriers" Brief of National Latina Institute for Reproductive Health et al. as Amici Curiae Supporting Petitioners, Whole Woman's Health v. Hellerstedt, 136 S. Ct. 2292 (2016) (No. 15–274), 9, 31.

4. COMING UP WITH THE MONEY

"What these providers' patients face" Ellen Frankfort and Frances Kissling, *Rosie: The Investigation of a Wrongful Death* (New York: Dial Press, 1979); Alexa Garcia-Ditta, "Reckoning with Rosie," *Texas Observer*, November 3, 2015, www.texasobserver.org/rosie-jimenez-abortion-medicaid/.

"Compared to many other medical procedures" Rachel K. Jones, Meghan Ingerick, and Jenna Jerman, "Differences in Abortion Service Delivery in Hostile, Middle-Ground and Supportive States in 2014," *Women's Health Issues* 28, no. 3 (2018): 215–16; Rachel K. Jones, Ushma D. Upadhyay, and Tracy A. Weitz, "At What Cost? Payment for Abortion Care by U.S. Women," *Women's Health Issues* 23 (2013): 173.

"While the nonhospital and non-third-trimester averages" Guttmacher Institute, "Abortion Patients More Likely to Be Poor in 2014 than in 2008," May 10, 2016, www.guttmacher.org/news-release/2016/abortion-patients-more-likely-be-poor-2014–2008.

"This is even more challenging" Stan L. Bowie and Donna M. Dopwell, "Megastressors as Barriers to Self-Sufficiency among TANF-Reliant African American and Latina Women," *Affilia* 28 (2013): 117–93.

"For various reasons, this level" Khaing Zaw, Jhumpa Bhattacharya, Anne Price, Darrick Hamilton, and Willam Darrity, Jr., "Women, Race and Wealth," *Research Brief Series*, January 2017, www.insightcced.org/wp-content/uploads/2017/01/January2017_ResearchBriefSeries_WomenRaceWealth-Volume1-Pages-1.pdf.

"This disparity affects" Pew Research Center, "Demographic Trends and Economic Well-Being," June 27, 2016, www.pewsocialtrends.org/2016/06/27/1-demographic-trends-and-economic-well-being/.

"Perhaps most relevant" Federal Reserve, "Report on the Economic Well-Being of U.S. Households in 2017," May 2018, 2, www.federalreserve.gov/publications/files/2017-report-economic-well-being-us-households-201805.pdf; Dedrick Asante-Muhammad, Chuck Collins, Josh Hoxie, and Emanuel Nieves, "The Road

to Zero Wealth," *Prosperity Now,* September 2017, prosperitynow.org
/files/PDFs/road_to_zero_wealth.pdf.

"Generations of discrimination" Institute for Women's Policy Research, "The
Gender Wage Gap: 2017," March 2018, iwpr.org/wp-content/uploads
/2018/03/C464_Gender-Wage-Gap-2.pdf; Zaw et al., "Women, Race and
Wealth," 3.

"In particular, Medicaid provides" Office of the Assistant Secretary for Planning and Evaluation, US Department of Health and Human Services, *2019 Poverty Guidelines,* 2019, aspe.hhs.gov/2019-poverty-guidelines; Rachel Garfield,
Anthony Damico, and Kendal Orgera, "The Coverage Gap: Uninsured Poor
Adults in States That Do Not Expand Medicaid," Kaiser Family Foundation,
March 21, 2019, www.kff.org/medicaid/issue-brief/the-coverage-gap-
uninsured-poor-adults-in-states-that-do-not-expand-medicaid/.

"But pregnancy is different" "Medicaid and CHIP Income Eligibility Limits
for Pregnant Women as a Percent of the Federal Poverty Level," Kaiser Family
Foundation, last updated January 1, 2018, www.kff.org/health-reform/state-
indicator/medicaid-and-chip-income-eligibility-limits-for-pregnant-women-as-a-
percent-of-the-federal-poverty-level/?currentTimeframe=0&sortModel=%7B%
22colId%22:%22Medicaid%22,%22sort%22:%22desc%22%7D; Kathy Gifford,
Jenna Walls, Usha Ranji, and Alina Salganicoff, "Medicaid Coverage of Pregnancy and Perinatal Benefits: Results from a State Survey," Kaiser Family Foundation, April 27, 2017, www.kff.org/womens-health-policy/report/medicaid-
coverage-of-pregnancy-and-perinatal-benefits-results-from-a-state-survey/.

"Constitutional amendments which prohibit" Representative Hyde, speaking
on H. 6083, *Congressional Record* 123 (1977), quoted in Zbaraz v. Quern, 596
F.2d 196 (7th Cir. 1979), 201 n.14. It is impossible not to be skeptical of Representative Hyde's professed concern for poor minority children given his record of
voting for cuts in welfare benefits and his dismal record on the funding of public
health programs. On the Issues, "Henry Hyde," www.ontheissues.org/IL/Henry_
Hyde.htm.

"Furthermore, Congress included" Alina Salganicoff, Laurie Sobel, and
Amrutha Ramaswamy, "Coverage for Abortion Services in Medicaid, Marketplace Plans and Private Plans," Kaiser Family Foundation, January 20, 2016,
www.kff.org/womens-health-policy/issue-brief/coverage-for-abortion-services-
in-medicaid-marketplace-plans-and-private-plans/. The Guttmacher Institute
reports that the number is now twenty-six states. Guttmacher Institute,
"Restricting Insurance Coverage of Abortion," March 1, 2019, www.guttmacher
.org/state-policy/explore/restricting-insurance-coverage-abortion.

"In two cases" Harris v. McRae, 448 U.S. 297 (1980); Maher v. Roe, 432 U.S.
464 (1977).

"Justice Marshall also connected the dots" Beal v. Doe, 432 U.S. 438 (1977),
456.

"The Hyde Amendment" Congressional Research Service, "Abortion: Judicial History and Legislative Response," December 7, 2018, 12–14, fas.org/sgp /crs/misc/RL33467.pdf; Deborah Kacanek, Amanda Dennis, Kate Miller, and Kelly Blanchard, "Medicaid Funding for Abortion: Providers' Experiences with Cases Involving Rape, Incest and Life Endangerment," *Perspectives on Sexual and Reproductive Health* 42 (June 1, 2010): 79–86; Amanda Dennis and Kelly Blanchard, "Abortion Providers' Experiences with Medicaid Abortion Coverage Policies: A Qualitative Multistate Study," *Health Services Research* 48 (February 2013): 236–52; Amanda Dennis, Kelly Blanchard, and Denisse Córdova, "Strategies for Securing Funding for Abortion under the Hyde Amendment: A Multistate Study of Abortion Providers' Experiences Managing Medicaid," *American Journal of Public Health* 101 (November 2011): 2124–29; US Government Accountability Office, *Medicaid: CMS Action Needed to Ensure Compliance with Abortion Coverage Requirements,* January 2019, www.gao.gov/assets/700/696338.pdf.

"There is one other way" Hawaii, Illinois, Maine, Maryland, New York, Washington, and Oregon have passed laws covering abortion. Alaska, Arizona, California, Connecticut, Massachusetts, Minnesota, Montana, New Jersey, New Mexico, and Vermont have court decisions requiring coverage. "State Funding of Abortions under Medicaid," Kaiser Family Foundation, last updated November 16, 2018, www.kff.org/medicaid/state-indicator/abortion-under-medicaid/? currentTimeframe=0&sortModel=%7B%22colId%22:%22Location%22,%22sort% 22:%22asc%22%7D; Zack Huffman, "New Maine Law Forces Insurers Public and Private to Cover Abortions," *Courthouse News Service,* June 13, 2019, www .courthousenews.com/new-maine-law-forces-insurers-public-private-to-cover-abortions/.

"Even though seventeen states" Katrina Kimport and Brenly Rowland, "Taking Insurance in Abortion Care: Policy, Practices, and the Role of Poverty," in *Health and Health Care Concerns among Women and Racial and Ethnic Minorities,* ed. Jennie Jacobs Kronenfeld (Bingley, UK: Emerald, 2017), 35.

"Finally, to round out the picture" Guttmacher Institute, "Restricting Insurance Coverage."

"But what's different about abortion" Kimport and Rowland, "Taking Insurance."

"In essence" Gretchen E. Ely, Travis Hales, D. Lynn Jackson, Eugene Maguin, and Greer Hamilton, "The Undue Burden of Paying for Abortion: An Exploration of Abortion Fund Cases," *Social Work in Health Care* 56 (2017).

"Although it may seem counterintuitive" Guttmacher Institute, "How do Women Pay for Abortions?," 2013, www.guttmacher.org/image/2016/how-do-women-pay-abortions.

"The amount of money" Nikita Stewart, "New York City Allocates $250,000 for Abortions, Challenging Conservative States," *New York Times,* June 14, 2019, www.nytimes.com/2019/06/14/nyregion/abortion-funding-ny.html.

"In contrast to the complexities" Amanda Dennis, Ruth Manski, and Kelly Blanchard, "Does Medicaid Coverage Matter? A Qualitative Multi-state Study of Abortion Affordability for Low-Income Women," *Journal of Health Care for the Poor and Underserved* 25 (November 2014): 1579.

"Patients also sometimes" Military women frequently have trouble accessing abortion for reasons related to these. Kate Grindlay Kelly, Jane W. Seymour, Laura Fix, Sarah Reiger, Brianna Keefe-Oates, and Daniel Grossman, "Abortion Knowledge and Experiences among U.S. Servicewomen: A Qualitative Study," *Perspectives on Sexual and Reproductive Health* 49 (November 2017): 242.

"What everyone working to help patients fears" Stanley K. Henshaw, Theodore J. Joyce, Amanda Dennis, Lawrence B. Finer, and Kelly Blanchard, "Restrictions on Medicaid Funding for Abortions: A Literature Review," Guttmacher Institute, June 2009, 1, www.guttmacher.org/sites/default/files/report_pdf/medicaidlitreview.pdf; Sarah C.M. Roberts, Nicole E. Johns, Valerie Williams, Erin Wingo, and Ushma D. Upadhyay, "Estimating the Proportion of Medicaid-Eligible Pregnant Women in Louisiana Who Do Not Get Abortions When Medicaid Does Not Cover Abortion," *BMC Women's Health* 19, art. no. 78 (2019).

"Brittany is one such woman" Katie McDonough, "Neither of These Women Wanted to Be Pregnant. Only One Could Get an Abortion," *Splinter*, May 1, 2017, splinternews.com/neither-of-these-women-wanted-to-be-pregnant-only-one-1794668225. This is a different Brittany from the person whose story is included to start the Introduction of the book.

5. GETTING IN

"Not every patient" Feminist Majority Foundation, *2018 National Clinic Violence Survey*, 2018, 7, www.feminist.org/anti-abortion-violence/images/2018-national-clinic-violence-survey.pdf.

"The Turnaway Study" Diana Greene Foster, Katrina Kimport, Heather Gould, Sarah C.M. Roberts, and Tracy A. Weitz, "Effect of Abortion Protesters on Women's Emotional Response to Abortion," *Contraception* 87 (January 2013): 83.

"Emily's, Jada's, and Elizabeth's observations" Foster et al., "Effect of Abortion Protesters," 85.

"Older and smaller studies" Katrina Kimport, Kate Cockrill, and Tracy A. Weitz, "Analyzing the Impacts of Abortion Clinic Structures and Processes: A Qualitative Analysis of Women's Negative Experience of Abortion Clinics," *Contraception* 85 (February 2012): 207; Catherine Cozzarelli and Brenda Major, "The Effects of Anti-abortion Demonstrators and Pro-choice Escorts on Women's Psychological Responses to Abortion," *Journal of Social and Clinical Psychology* 13 (December 1994): 414; Catherine Cozzarelli, Brenda Major, Angela Karrasch, and Kathleen Fuegen, "Women's Experiences of and Reactions to

Antiabortion Picketing," *Basic and Applied Social Psychology* 22 (2000): 274–75; Davida Becker, Claudia Díaz-Olavarrieta, C. Rodas de Juárez, Sandra Gallach García, Patricio Sanhueza, and Cynthia C. Harper, "Clients' Perceptions of the Quality of Care in Mexico City's Public-Sector Legal Abortion Program," *International Perspectives on Sexual and Reproductive Health* 37 (December 2011): 197; Graeme Hayes and Pam Lowe, "'A Hard Enough Decision to Make': Anti-abortion Activism outside Clinics in the Eyes of Clinic Users," Aston University, Birmingham, UK, report collating survey data from the British Pregnancy Advisory Service, September 2015, 11.

"These intense emotional reactions" Guy H. Montgomery, Julie B. Schnur, Joel Erblich, Michael A. Diefenbach, and Dana H. Bovbjerg, "Presurgery Psychological Factors Predict Pain, Nausea and Fatigue One Week following Breast Cancer Surgery," *Journal of Pain and Symptom Management* 39 (June 2010): 1044; Paula M. Trief, William A. Grant, and Bruce A. Fredrickson, "A Prospective Study of Psychological Predictors of Lumbar Surgery Outcome," *Spine* 25 (October 2000): 2616; Aleksander Perski, Elehu Feleke, Gillian Hopkins Anderson, Bassem Abdel Samad, Hugo Westerlund, Christina Ericsson, and Nina Rehnqvist, "Emotional Distress before Coronary Bypass Grafting Limits the Benefits of Surgery," *American Heart Journal* 136 (September 1998): 510.

"The Turnaway Study" Foster et al., "Effect of Abortion Protesters," 85.

"In an odd twist" Kimport, Cockrill, and Weitz, "Analyzing the Impacts," 207.

"For a particular group of patients" Brief of Amici Curiae The Victim Rights Law Center, Renee Devesty, et al., In Support of Respondents, McCullen v. Coakley, 573 U.S. 464 (2014) (No. 12–1168), 3.

"These kinds of zones" "Buffer Zones," National Abortion Federation, n.d., accessed March 10, 2019, prochoice.org/education-and-advocacy/violence/buffer-zones/; Feminist Majority Foundation, "1999 National Clinic Violence Survey Report," January 2000, www.feminist.org/research/cvsurveys/1999/1999ClinicSurvey.htm.

"Unfortunately, the Supreme Court's most recent case" Brief of Amici Curiae Planned Parenthood League of Massachusetts and Planned Parenthood Federation of America in Support of Respondents, McCullen v. Coakley, 573 U.S. 464 (2014) (No. 12–1168), 6–16.

"Despite this evidence" McCullen v. Coakley, 573 U.S. 464 (2014); Hill v. Colorado, 530 U.S. 703 (2000). In early 2019, the judges of the Seventh Circuit ruled that Chicago's buffer zone was constitutional, relying on the Colorado precedent rather than the Massachusetts precedent. Price v. City of Chicago 915 F.3d 1107 (7th Cir. 2019). In 2016, the Third Circuit indicated otherwise in an as-yet-not-final challenge to Pittsburgh's buffer zone. Bruni v. City of Pittsburgh, 824 F.3d 353 (3d Cir. 2016).

"This has been a difficult task" Paige Winfield Cunningham, "Abortion Clinics: Drawing the Line," *Politico*, July 30, 2014, www.politico.com/story/2014/07

/testing-boundaries-abortion-clinic-buffer-zones-109570; Jeannie O'Sullivan, "Clinic Buffer Zone Hurts Abortion Foes' Speech, 3rd Circ. Told," *Law360*, February 6, 2019, www.law360.com/articles/1126074/clinic-buffer-zone-hurts-abortion-foes-speech-3rd-circ-told.

"Like the law" Madsen v. Women's Health Center, Inc., 512 U.S. 753 (1994), 772–73; March v. Mills, 867 F.3d 46 (1st Cir. 2017); Pine v. City of West Palm Beach, 762 F.3d 1262 (11th Cir. 2014); Gaughan v. City of Cleveland, 212 F. App'x 405 (6th Cir. 2007).

"When there's no buffer zone" Freedom of Access to Clinic Entrances Act, 18 U.S.C. § 248.

"The part of the law" David S. Cohen and Krysten Connon, *Living in the Crosshairs: The Untold Stories of Anti-abortion Terrorism* (New York: Oxford University Press, 2015), 207–11.

"There has been little research" Cozzarelli and Major, "Effects of Anti-abortion Demonstrators," 423–24.

"One of Frances Easton's clinics" Lori A. Brown, *Contested Spaces: Abortion Clinics, Women's Shelters and Hospitals: Politicizing the Female Body* (New York: Routledge, 2016).

6. COUNSELING AT THE CLINIC

"Curtis Boyd" Carole Joffe, *Dispatches from the Abortion Wars: The Costs of Fanaticism to Doctors, Patients, and the Rest of Us* (Boston: Beacon Press, 2009), 119.

"Once a woman overcomes" Anne Baker and Terry Beresford, "Informed Consent, Patient Education, and Counseling," in *Management of Unintended and Abnormal Pregnancy: Comprehensive Abortion Care,* ed. Maureen Paul, E. Steve Lichtenberg, Lynn Borgatta, David A. Grimes, Phillip G. Stubblefield, and Mitchell D. Creinin (Oxford: Blackwell, 2009), 49.

"The decision whether or not to have an abortion" National Abortion Federation, "Ethical Principles for Abortion Care," 2011, 1–2, prochoice.org/wp-content/uploads/NAF_Ethical-_Principles.pdf.

"One issue frequently comes up" Baker and Beresford, "Informed Consent," 48–62.

"It is with the Presidential Commission's third aspect" National Partnership for Women and Families, *Bad Medicine: How a Political Agenda Is Undermining Abortion Care and Access* (Washington, DC: National Partnership for Women and Families, 2018), 7, www.nationalpartnership.org/our-work/resources/repro/bad-medicine-third-edition.pdf.

"Not only are these brochures" Cynthia Daniels, Janna Ferguson, Grace Howard, and Amanda Roberti, "Informed or Misinformed Consent: Abortion

Policy in the United States," *Journal of Health, Politics, Policy and Law* 41, no. 2 (April 2016): 181.

"The misinformation" Mayo Clinic, "Pregnancy Week by Week," www .mayoclinic.org/healthy-lifestyle/pregnancy-week-by-week/in-depth/prenatal-care/art-20045302.

"Beyond the fetal development inaccuracies" Louisiana Department of Health, "Women's Right to Know," accessed March 3, 2019, ldh.la.gov /index.cfm/page/1035; La. Stat. Ann. § 40:1061.17 (2018).

"Back to the Louisiana form" Susan J. Lee, Henry J. Peter Ralston, Eleanor A. Drey, John Colin Partridge, and Mark A. Rosen, "Fetal Pain: A Systematic Multi-disciplinary Review of the Evidence," *JAMA* 294, no. 8 (2005): 952; Later Abortion Initiative, "Fetal Pain, Analgesia, and Anesthesia in the Context of Abortion," Ibis Reproductive Health, April 2018, ibisreproductivehealth.org/sites /default/files/files/publications/LAI_factsheet_fetal_pain_Apr18.pdf.

"Mandates that providers tell patients" National Academies of Sciences, Engineering and Medicine, *The Safety and Quality of Abortion Care in the United States* (Washington, DC: National Academies Press, 2018), 9–10.

"Informing patients" American Congress of Obstetricians and Gynecologists, "Facts Are Important: Medication Abortion 'Reversal' Is Not Supported by Science," August 2017, www.acog.org/-/media/Departments/Government-Relations-and-Outreach/FactsAreImportantMedicationAbortionReversal.pdf ?dmc=1&ts=20180206T1955451745; see also www.nejm.org/doi/full/10.1056 /NEJMp1805927.

"Yet several states now require" Kimberlee Kruesi, "Idaho Joins Other Red States with 'Abortion Reversal' Law," *AP News*, March 20, 2018, apnews .com/ac0f6029b4724c43adaf0fe8358ee68d; Associated Press, "North Dakota Gov. Burgum Signs 'Abortion Reversal' Bill," *Valley News Live*, March 22, 2019, www.valleynewslive.com/content/news/North-Dakota-Gov-Burgum-signs-abortion-reversal-bill-507546521.html; Scott Richters, "Bad Medicine: States Force Doctors to Refer Abortion Patients to Google: The Truth about Medication Abortion Reversal Laws," ACLU of Nebraska, June 2019, www.aclunebraska.org/sites /default/files/field_documents/abortion_reversal_report.pdf.

"Given this predicament" Mara Buchbinder, Anne Lyerly, Rebecca Mercier, Dragana Lassiter, and Amy Bryant, "'Prefacing the Script' as an Ethical Response to State-Mandated Abortion Counseling," *AJOB Empirical Bioethics* 7, no. 1 (2016): 48–55.

"Erica went even further" Brenda Major, Mark Appelbaum, Linda Beckman, Mary Ann Dutton, Nancy Felipe Russo, and Carolyn West, *Report of the APA Task Force on Mental Health and Abortion* (Washington, DC: American Psychological Association, 2008), 92, www.apa.org/pi/women/programs/abortion /mental-health.pdf; Brenda Major, Pallas Mueller, and Katherine Hildebrandt,

"Attributions, Expectations, and Coping with Abortion," *Journal of Personality and Social Psychology* 48, no. 3 (March 1985): 585–99.

"However, this tactic" Dana Ferguson, "Planned Parenthood Bill Called a 'Medical Travesty' Heads for Daugaard's Desk," *Argus Leader*, February 26, 2018, www.argusleader.com/story/news/politics/2018/02/26/bill-condemning-how-planned-parenthood-talks-patients-heads-daugaards-desk-abortion-south-dakota/372283002/.

"However, abortion patients" Heather Gould, Diana Foster, Alissa C. Perrucci, Rana E. Barar, and Sarah Carolyn Roberts, "Predictors of Abortion Counseling Receipt and Helpfulness in the United States," *Women's Health Issues* 23, no. 4 (2013): e253–54.

"Nearly all abortion facilities" Guttmacher Institute, "Requirements for Ultrasound," April 1, 2019, www.guttmacher.org/state-policy/explore/requirements-ultrasound.

"Researchers who have studied the impact" Ushma Upadhyay, Katrina Kimport, Elise K. O. Belusa, Nicole E. Johns, Douglas W. Laube, and Sarah C. M. Roberts, "Evaluating the Impact of a Mandatory Pre-abortion Ultrasound Viewing Law: A Mixed Methods Study," *PLoS ONE* 12, no. 7 (2017): 18, journals.plos.org/plosone/article?id=10.1371/journal.pone.0178871.

"Finally, with respect to ultrasound viewing" Mary Gatter, Katrina Kimport, Diana Greene Foster, Tracy A. Weitz, and Ushma D. Upadhyay, "Relationship between Ultrasound Viewing and Proceeding to Abortion," *Obstetrics & Gynecology* 123 (January 2014): 81–82.

"The main issue in the litigation" Planned Parenthood v. Casey, 505 U.S. 833 (1992), 882.

"Under this standard" Planned Parenthood Minnesota v. Rounds, 530 F.3d 724 (8th Cir. 2008), 735–38; Planned Parenthood Minnesota v. Rounds, 686 F.3d 889 (8th Cir. 2012), 894–95.

"Other courts have found" Planned Parenthood of Heartland v. Heineman, 724 F. Supp. 2d 1025 (D. Neb. 2010), 1048.

"In a separate strand of cases" Wooley v. Maynard, 430 U.S. 705 (1977); West Virginia State Board of Education v. Barnette, 319 U.S. 624 (1943); Texas Medical Providers Performing Abortion Services v. Lakey, 667 F.3d 570 (5th Cir. 2012); Stuart v. Camnitz, 774 F.3d 238 (4th Cir. 2014).

"The Supreme Court hinted at a resolution" National Institute of Family and Life Advocates v. Becerra, 138 S. Ct. 2361 (2018). In early 2019, a federal appeals court in Ohio relied on this Supreme Court ruling to uphold the state's ultrasound mandate. EMW Women's Surgical Center v. Beshear, 920 F.3d 421 (6th Cir. 2019).

"As abortion became a more and more politicized issue" Carole Joffe, "The Politicization of Abortion and the Evolution of Abortion Counseling," *American*

Journal of Public Health 103 (November 2012): 57; Alissa C. Perrucci, *Decision Assessment and Counseling in Abortion Care* (Louisville, CO: Rowman and Littlefield, 2012), xxi.

"Floyd Moore" Jenna Jerman, Rachel K. Jones, and Tsuyoshi Onda, "Characteristics of U.S. Abortion Patients in 2014 and Changes since 2008," Guttmacher Institute, May 2016, www.guttmacher.org/report/characteristics-us-abortion-patients-2014.

"The challenge for clinics" Lauren Ralph, Diana Greene Foster, Katrina Kimport, David Turok, and Sarah C. M. Roberts, "Measuring Decisional Certainty among Women Seeking Abortion," *Contraception* 95, no. 3 (October 2016): 269.

"To tackle this problem" Baker and Beresford, "Informed Consent," 52–53.

"There is no an adequate body of research" Baker and Beresford, "Informed Consent," 50.

"But state mandates" Whole Woman's Health v. Hellerstedt, 136 S. Ct. 2292, 2318 (2016). Though those interviewed for this book would include "clinic staff" as well as the "doctors" in the Court's statement, they were otherwise very buoyed by this recognition of the importance of this kind of engagement with patients.

7. WAITING PERIODS

"Twenty-six years old" Dana Liebelson, "The Waiting Game," *Marie Claire*, June 24, 2016, www.marieclaire.com/politics/a21141/abortion-waiting-periods/; Angie Leventis Lourgos, "'My Last Resort'—Thousands Come to Illinois to Have Abortions," *Chicago Tribune*, July 14, 2017, www.chicagotribune.com/news/ct-abortion-out-of-state-met-20170714-story.html.

"These problems are endemic" Institute of Medicine, *Crossing the Quality Chasm: A New Health System for the 21st Century* (Washington, DC: National Academy Press, 2001), 5–6.

"The Institute of Medicine" Gary Kaplan, Marianne Hamilton Lopez, and J. Michael McGinnis, eds., *Transforming Health Care Scheduling and Access: Getting to Now* (Washington, DC: National Academies Press, 2015), 9–10.

"For the most part" Rachel K. Jones and Jenna Jerman, *Time to Appointment and Delays in Accessing Care among U.S. Abortion Patients* (New York: Guttmacher Institute, August 2016), 8; Lawrence B. Finer, "Timing of Steps and Reasons for Delay in Obtaining Abortions in the United States," *Contraception* 74 (October 2006): 335; Kaplan, Lopez, and McGinnis, *Getting to Now*, 9–10.

"That abortion clinics have figured out" Monica R. McLemore, Sheila Desai, Lori R. Freedman, Evelyn Angel James, and Diana L. Taylor, "Women Know Best—Findings from a Thematic Analysis of 5,214 Surveys of Abortion Care Experience," *Women's Health Issues* 24 (2014): 597–98; Diana Taylor, Debbie A. Postlethwaite, Sheila Desai, Evelyn Angel James, Amanda W. Calhoun,

Katharine Sheehan, and Tracy Ann Weitz, "Multiple Determinants of the Abortion Care Experience: From the Patient's Perspective," *American Journal of Medical Quality* 23 (November/December 2013): 514–16.

"What Andrea and Mary can do" Guttmacher Institute, "Counseling and Waiting Periods for Abortion," April 1, 2019, www.guttmacher.org/state-policy /explore/counseling-and-waiting-periods-abortion.

"The empirical research" Jones and Jerman, *Time to Appointment*, 4.

"Mississippi was the first state" Ted Joyce and Robert Kaestner, "The Impact of Mississippi's Mandatory Delay Law on the Timing of Abortion," *Family Planning Perspectives* 32 (January/February 2000): 12; Frances A. Althaus and Stanley K. Henshaw, "The Effects of Mandatory Delay Laws on Abortion Patients and Providers," *Family Planning Perspectives* 26 (September/October 1994): 231–33; Theodore Joyce, Stanley K. Henshaw, and Julia DeClerque Skatrud, "The Impact of Mississippi's Mandatory Delay Law on Abortions and Births," *JAMA* 278 (August 1997): 4–13.

"The other state" Sarah C. M. Roberts, Elise Belusa, David K. Turok, Sarah Combellick, and Lauren Ralph, "Do 72-Hour Waiting Periods and Two-Visit Requirements for Abortion Affect Women's Certainty? A Prospective Cohort Study," *Women's Health Issues* 27 (July/August 2017): 403; Sarah C. M. Roberts, David K. Turok, Elise Belusa, Sarah Combellick, and Ushma D. Upadhyay, "Utah's 72-Hour Waiting Period for Abortion: Experiences among a Clinic-Based Sample of Women," *Perspectives on Sexual and Reproductive Health* 48 (December 2016): 185; Jessica N. Sanders, Hilary Conway, Janet C. Jacobson, Leah N. Torres, and David K. Turok, "The Longest Wait: Examining the Impact of Utah's 72-Hour Waiting Period for Abortion," *Women's Health Issues* 26 (September /October 2016): 485.

"Despite these burdens" Akron v. Akron Center for Reproductive Health, 462 U.S. 416 (1983), 450–51; Planned Parenthood v. Casey, 505 U.S. 833 (1992), 885.

"That the US Supreme Court upheld" Planned Parenthood of Indiana and Kentucky v. Indiana Health Commissioner, 896 F.3d 809 (7th Cir. 2018), 833.

"Plus, as is always the case" Gainesville Woman Care v. Florida, 210 So. 3d 1243 (2017), 1261; Planned Parenthood of the Heartland v. Reynolds, 915 N.W.2d 206 (Iowa 2018), 242.

"The absurdity" Diana Greene Foster, Heather Gould, Jessica Taylor, and Tracy A. Weitz, "Attitudes and Decision Making among Women Seeking Abortions at One U.S. Clinic," *Perspectives on Sexual and Reproductive Health* 44 (June 2012): 118; Heather Gould, Alissa C. Perrucci, Rana E. Barar, Danielle Sinkford, and Diana Foster, "Patient Education and Emotional Support Practices in Abortion Care Facilities in the United States," *Women's Health Issues* 22 (July/August 2012): 361–62.

"Other medical care providers" Patients on Medicaid are also subject to waiting periods when they request sterilization, a policy that was instituted because of this country's history of forced sterilization, particularly of women of color. Maya Manian, "The Story of *Madrigal v. Quilligan:* Coerced Sterilization of Mexican-American Women," in *Reproductive Rights and Justice Stories,* ed. Melissa Murray, Kate Shaw, and Reva Siegel (St. Paul, MN: Foundation Press, 2019). However, many, including clinicians, have come to see this waiting period as unduly burdensome. Sonya Borrero, Nikki Zite, Joseph E. Potter, and James Trussell, "Medicaid Policy on Sterilization—Anachronistic or Still Relevant?," *New England Journal of Medicine* 370 (2014): 102–4.

"With these laws having no benefit" National Academies of Sciences, Engineering, and Medicine, *The Safety and Quality of Abortion Care in the United States* (Washington, DC: National Academies Press, 2018), 164.

"These requirements also deliver" Planned Parenthood of Indiana and Kentucky v. Indiana Health Commissioner, 833.

8. THE PROCEDURE

"In 2017, a young woman" Nara Schoenberg, "On the Anniversary of *Roe v. Wade,* a Look at the Future of Pill-Induced Abortion," *Chicago Tribune,* January 19, 2018, www.chicagotribune.com/lifestyles/health/ct-life-abortion-pill-future-0119-story.html.

"Kate's story is emblematic" Kate Carson, "Outlawing Late Abortion Seemed Like Such a Reasonable Idea until I Needed One Myself," *Elle,* January 29, 2018, www.elle.com/culture/a15911671/late-abortion-senate-vote-2018/.

"Medication abortion" Mitchell D. Creinin and Kristina Gemzell Danielsson, "Medical Abortion in Early Pregnancy," in *Management of Unintended and Abnormal Pregnancy,* ed. Maureen Paul, E. Steve Lichtenberg, Lynn Borgatta, David A. Grimes, Phillip G. Stubblefield, and Mitchell D. Creinin (Oxford: Wiley-Blackwell, 2009), 111–34; Margaret Talbot, "The Little White Bombshell," *New York Times Magazine,* July 11, 1999, archive.nytimes.com/www.nytimes .com/library/magazine/home/19990711mag-abortion-pill.html.

"But although it is common" Ushma D. Upadhyay, Nicole E. Johns, Sarah L. Combellick, Julia E. Kohn, Lisa M. Keder, and Sarah C. M. Roberts, "Comparison of Outcomes before and after Ohio's Law Mandating Use of the FDA-Approved Protocol for Medication Abortion: A Retrospective Cohort Study," *PLOS Medicine* 13, no. 8 (August 30, 2016): 1–2, doi.org/10.1371/journal.pmed .1002110; Rachel K. Jones and Heather D. Boonstra, "The Public Health Implications of the FDA Update to the Medication Abortion Label," Guttmacher Institute, June 30, 2016, www.guttmacher.org/article/2016/06/public-health-implications-fda-update-medication-abortion-label.

"Nonetheless, there continue to be ways" Thomas Beaton, "71% of Healthcare Providers Use Telehealth, Telemedicine Tools," mHealth Intelligence, April 28,

2017, mhealthintelligence.com/news/71-of-healthcare-providers-use-telehealth-telemedicine-tools.

"The safety of medication abortion" Daniel Grossman and Kate Grindlay, "Safety of Medical Abortion Provided through Telemedicine Compared with In Person," *Obstetrics & Gynecology* 130, no. 4 (October 2017): 778–82; Planned Parenthood of the Heartland v. Iowa Board of Medicine, 865 N.W.2d 252 (Iowa 2015), 266.

"Telemedicine abortions" Guttmacher Institute, "Medication Abortion," March 1, 2019, www.guttmacher.org/state-policy/explore/medication-abortion; Eric Wicklund, "Texas Medical Board Adopts New Telehealth, Telemedicine Rules," mHealth Intelligence, December 5, 2017, mhealthintelligence.com /news/texas-medical-board-adopts-new-telehealth-telemedicine-rules.

"However, the reality on the ground" Jackson Women's Health Organization v. Currier, 320 F. Supp. 3d 828 (S.D. Miss. 2018), 836–41.

"Peculiarities of state laws" Mary Anne Freedman and Lloyd F. Novick, "Comparison of Complication Rates in First Trimester Abortions Performed by Physician Assistants and Physicians," *American Journal of Public Health* 76, no. 5 (May 1986): 550–54; National Abortion Federation, *Who Will Provide Abortions? Ensuring the Availability of Qualified Practitioners* (Washington, DC: National Abortion Federation, 1991), 7; National Abortion Federation, "The Role of Physician Assistants, Nurse Practitioners and Nurse-Midwives in Providing Abortion," Atlanta, GA, December 13–14, 1996, 5aa1b2xfmfh2e2mk03kk8rsx-wpengine .netdna-ssl.com/wp-content/uploads/1996_symposium_report.pdf.

"Currently, seventeen states" Guttmacher Institute, "Medication Abortion."

"In five states currently" Tracy Weitz, Diana Taylor, Ushma D. Upadhyay, Sheila Desai, and Molly Battistelli, "Research Informs Abortion Care Policy Change in California," *American Journal of Public Health* 104, no. 10 (October 2014): e3–4.

"Laws that prohibit APCs" Jacob Gershman, "Lawsuits Challenge Rules Limiting Who Can Perform Abortions," *Wall Street Journal*, January 15, 2019, www .wsj.com/articles/new-challenges-to-state-abortion-laws-11547571601; National Academies of Sciences, Engineering and Medicine, *The Safety and Quality of Abortion Care in the United States* (Washington, DC: National Academies Press, 2018), 112–19.

"By the early 2000s" Stenberg v. Carhart, 530 U.S. 914 (2000), 936.

"Though abortions in the second trimester" Johanna Schoen, *Abortion after Roe* (Chapel Hill: University of North Carolina Press, 2015), 219–37. The rhetoric—and distortions—of the partial birth abortion campaign persists to this day among anti-abortion forces, with Donald Trump famously claiming, at one of the presidential debates in 2016, that abortion providers "rip the baby out of the womb of the mother just prior to the birth of the baby." Kim Painter, "Ripped from the Womb? Late-Term Abortion Explained," *USA Today*, October 21, 2016, www.usatoday.com/story/news/2016/10/21/doctors-trump-wrong-late-abortions /92515324/. Trump used essentially the same language at his State of the Union address in 2019. Anna North, "Why Trump Spent So Much Time Criticizing Abortion during the State of the Union," *Vox*, February 6, 2019, www.vox .com/policy-and-politics/2019/2/5/18212521/state-of-the-union-trump-abortion-northam.

"The Supreme Court twice considered bans" Stenberg v. Carhart, 930; Gonzales v. Carhart, 550 U.S. 124, 133 (2007).

"In justifying the Court's willingness" Cassing Hammond and Stephen Chasen, "Dilation and Evacuation," in Paul et al., *Management*, 157–77.

"Ten states have passed bans" Guttmacher Institute, "Bans on Specific Abortion Methods Used after the First Trimester," May 1, 2019, www.guttmacher.org/state-policy/explore/bans-specific-abortion-methods-used-after-first-trimester; West Alabama Women's Center v. Miller, 299 F. Supp. 3d 1244, 1281 (M.D. Ala. 2017).

"These lower federal court decisions" Hammond and Chasen, "Dilation and Evacuation," 157. The very small number of women who have abortions in the third trimester—largely because of fetal anomalies or their own health issues—typically undergo the induction procedure because D&E is not medically possible.

"The ramifications of the vilification" Gabrielle Goodrick, "When *Roe* Ends, Be Prepared for the Rippling Life or Death Consequences," August 27, 2018, drgabriellegoodrick.com/2018/08/27/when-roe-ends-be-prepared-for-the-rippling-life-or-death-consequences/.

"Among the saddest and most frustrating stories" Diana Greene Foster, M. Antonia Biggs, Sarah Raifman, Jessica Gipson, Katrina Kimport, and Corinne H. Rocca, "Comparison of Health, Development, Maternal Bonding, and Poverty among Children Born after Denial of Abortion vs after Pregnancies Subsequent to an Abortion," *JAMA Pediatrics* 172, no. 11 (November 2018): 1054, jamanetwork.com/journals/jamapediatrics/fullarticle/2698454; Sarah C. M. Roberts, M. Antonia Biggs, Karuna S. Chibber, Heather Gould, Corinne H. Rocca, and Diana Greene Foster, "Risk of Violence from the Man Involved in the Pregnancy after Receiving or Being Denied an Abortion," *BMC Medicine* 12, no. 144 (2014): 6. For a full listing of the Turnaway Study results, see ANSIRH, "Introduction to the Turnaway Study," January 2019, www.ansirh.org/sites /default/files/publications/files/turnaway-intro_1-14-2019.pdf.

"One question" Later Abortion Initiative, "Who Needs Abortion Later in Pregnancy in the United States, and Why?," Ibis Reproductive Health, December 2018, www.laterabortion.org/sites/default/files/lai_who_needs.pdf.

"However, consistent with what we described" Ushma Upadhyay, Tracy Ann Weitz, Robert K. Jones, Rana E. Barar, and Diana Foster, "Denial of Abortion Because of Provider Gestational Age Limits in the United States," *American Journal of Public Health* 104, no. 9 (September 2014); 1687–94.

"The situation facing women" Guttmacher Institute, "State Bans on Abortion throughout Pregnancy," March 1, 2019, www.guttmacher.org/state-policy /explore/state-policies-later-abortions; Anne R. Davis, Sarah K. Horvath, and Paula M. Castaño, "Trends in Gestational Age at Time of Surgical Abortion for Fetal Aneuploidy and Structural Abnormalities," *American Journal of Obstetrics & Gynecology* 216, no. 3 (March 2017): 216:278.e.1–278.e5.

"Yet another complicating factor" Carole Joffe, *Dispatches from the Abortion Wars: The Costs of Fanaticism to Doctors, Patients, and the Rest of Us* (Boston: Beacon Press, 2011), 81.

"Although some state courts" McCormack v. Herzog, 788 F.3d 1017, 1029 (9th Cir. 2015); Isaacson v. Horne, 716 F.3d 1213, 1225–27 (9th Cir. 2013).

"Nonetheless, as we have seen" Jackson Women's Health Organization v. Currier, 2018 WL 6072127 (S.D. Miss. 2018) (Mississippi fifteen-week ban); MKB Mgmt. Corp. v. Stenehjem, 795 F.3d 768, 770 (8th Cir. 2015) (North Dakota six-week ban); Edwards v. Beck, 786 F.3d 1113, 1117 (8th Cir. 2015) (Arkansas twelve-week ban); Elizabeth Nash, "A Surge in Bans on Abortion as Early as Six Weeks, before Most People Know They Are Pregnant," Guttmacher Institute, March 22, 2019, www.guttmacher.org/article/2019/03/surge-bans-abortion-early-six-weeks-most-people-know-they-are-pregnant.

"But it is no simple matter" Amy Littlefield, "'Not Dead Enough': Public Hospitals Deny Life-Saving Abortion Care to People in Need," *Rewire*, March 7, 2019, rewire.news/article/2019/03/07/not-dead-enough-public-hospitals-deny-life-saving-abortion-care-to-people-in-need/.

"Moreover, despite the emotional pull" Lori Freedman, Callie Langton, Uta Landy, Elizabeth Ly, and Corinne Rocca, "Abortion Care Policies and Enforcement in US Obstetrics-Gynecology Teaching Hospitals: A National Survey," *Contraception* 96 (2017): 265.

"The challenges of in-hospital abortions" Lori R. Freedman, *Willing and Unable: Doctors' Constraints in Abortion Care* (Nashville, TN: Vanderbilt University Press, 2010), 128.

"In other cases, Freedman tells" Freedman, *Willing and Unable*, 132–33.

"This willingness of politicians" Roe v. Wade, 410 U.S. 113, 165–66 (1973), emphasis added; Gonzales v. Carhart, 1636.

9. AN ALTERNATE VISION

"In fact, the cumulative effect" Diana Greene Foster, "Dramatic Decreases in US Abortion Rates: Public Health Achievement or Failure?" *American Journal of Public Health* 107 (December 2017): 1860–62.

"In states where this happens" Storyteller, "No Regrets," *We Testify*, n.d., accessed July 31, 2019, wetestify.org/stories/no-regrets/.

"There is a better way" For instance, experts, including one representing ACOG, recently suggested that the best and safest way to regulate abortion facilities is to treat them like any other medical facility. "Our consensus determined that requiring facilities performing office-based procedures, including abortion, to meet standards beyond those currently in effect for all general medical offices and clinics is unjustified based on an analysis of available evidence." Barbara S. Levy, Debra L. Ness, and Steven E. Weinberger, "Consensus Guidelines for Facilities Performing Outpatient Procedures: Evidence over Ideology," *Obstetrics & Gynecology* 133 (2019): 255.

"Another huge difference maker" National Academies of Sciences, Engineering, and Medicine, *The Safety and Quality of Abortion Care in the United States* (Washington, DC: National Academies Press, 2018), 77–80.

"The stories in this book" Daniel Grossman and Kate Grindlay, "Safety of Medical Abortion Provided through Telemedicine Compared with In Person," *Obstetrics & Gynecology* 130 (October 2017): 778; M. Endler, A. Lavelanet, A. Cleeve, B. Ganatra, R. Gomperts, and K. Gemzell-Danielsson, "Telemedicine for Medical Abortion: A Systematic Review," *British Journal of Obstetrics and Gynaecology* 126, no. 9 (August 2019): 1094–1102, doi.org/10.1111/1471-0528.15684.

"As described at the start" Gynuity Health Projects, "Medical Abortion," n.d., accessed March 11, 2019, gynuity.org/programs/medical-abortion.

"For women who live" Elizabeth Raymond, Erica Chong, Beverly Winikoff, Ingrida Platais, Meighan Mary, Tatyana Lotarevich, Philicia W. Castillo, et al., "TelAbortion: Evaluation of a Direct to Patient Telemedicine Abortion Service in the United States," *Contraception* 100 (September 2019): 173–177.

"As it stands now" "Risk Evaluation and Mitigation Strategies (REMS)," US Food and Drug Administration, updated February 2, 2018, www.fda.gov/Drugs /DrugSafety/REMS/default.htm.

"The pro-choice medical community" Sarah Raifman, Megan Orlando, Sally Rafie, and Daniel Grossman, "Medication Abortion: Potential for Improved Patient Access through Pharmacies," *Journal of the American Pharmacists Association* 58 (July/August 2018): 377–81.

"Preliminary evidence" Daniel Grossman, Kate Grindlay, Anna L. Altshuler, and Jay Schulkin, "Induced Abortion Provision among a National Sample of Obstetricians-Gynecologists," *Obstetrics & Gynecology* 133 (2019): 477; Complaint, Chelius v. Azar, No. 1:17-cv-00493 (D. Haw. October 3, 2017).

"Two other ideas" Nathalie Kapp, Daniel Grossman, Emily Jackson, Laura Castleman, and Dalia Brahmi, "A Research Agenda for Moving Early Medical Pregnancy Termination over the Counter," *British Journal of Obstetrics and Gynaecology* 124 (2017): 1646.

"For example, as part of a 2017 national study" M. Antonia Biggs, Lauren Ralph, Sarah Raifman, Diana Greene Foster, and Daniel Grossman, "Support for and Interest in Alternative Models of Medication Abortion Provision among a National Probability Sample of U.S. Women," *Contraception* 99 (February 2019): 118.

"It is of course impossible" Jenna Jerman, Rachel K. Jones, and Tsuyoshi Onda, *Characteristics of U.S. Abortion Patients in 2014 and Changes since 2008* (New York: Guttmacher Institute, May 2016), 8, www.guttmacher.org/sites /default/files/report_pdf/characteristics-us-abortion-patients-2014.pdf; Daniel Grossman, Kari White, Kristine Hopkins, and Joseph E. Potter, "The Public Health Threat of Anti-abortion Legislation," *Contraception* 89 (February 2014): 73–74; Daniel Grossman, E. Hendrick, Liza Fuentes, K. White, Kristine Hopkins, Amanda Jean Stevenson, Celia Hubert Lopez, Sara Yeatman, and Joseph E. Potter, Texas Policy Evaluation Project, "Knowledge, Opinion and Experience Related to Abortion Self-Induction in Texas," Research Brief, November 2015, liberalarts.utexas.edu/txpep/_files/pdf/TxPEP-Research-Brief-Knowledge OpinionExperience.pdf; Seth Stephens-Davidowitz, "The Return of the D.I.Y. Abortion," *New York Times*, March 5, 2016, www.nytimes.com/2016/03/06 /opinion/sunday/the-return-of-the-diy-abortion.html.

"For some time" Olga Khazan, "Women in the U.S. Can Now Get Safe Abortions by Mail," *Atlantic*, October 18, 2018, www.theatlantic.com/health /archive/2018/10/women-on-web-safe-abortion-mail/573322/.

"In the past, Women on Web" Hannah Devlin, "Revealed: 21,000 US Women Order Abortion Pills Online in Past Six Months," *Guardian*, May 22, 2019, www .theguardian.com/world/2019/may/22/revealed-21000-us-women-order-abortion-pills-in-six-months.

"However, the level of legal scrutiny" Clarence Y. H. Lo, "Countermovements and Conservative Movements in the Contemporary U.S.," *Annual Review of Sociology* 8 (1982): 107; David S. Meyer and Suzanne Staggenborg, "Movements, Countermovements, and the Structure of Political Opportunity," *American Journal of Sociology* 101 (May 1996): 1631–33.

"What this means" American College of Obstetricians and Gynecologists, "Position Statement: Decriminalization of Self-Induced Abortion," December 2017, www.acog.org/Clinical-Guidance-and-Publications/Position-Statements /Decriminalization-of-Self-Induced-Abortion; Michelle Oberman, *Her Body, Our Laws: On the Front Lines of the Abortion War, from El Salvador to Oklahoma* (Boston: Beacon Press, 2018); Michelle Oberman, "What Happens When Abortion Is Banned?," *New York Times*, May 31, 2018, www.nytimes.com /2018/05/31/opinion/sunday/abortion-banned-latin-america.html.

"It is not far-fetched" Chelsea Conaboy, "She Started Selling Abortion Pills Online. Then the Feds Showed Up," *Mother Jones*, March/April 2019, www .motherjones.com/politics/2019/02/she-started-selling-abortion-pills-online-then-the-feds-showed-up/; Julia Belluz, "Abortions by Mail: The FDA Is Going after Online Pill Providers," *Vox*, March 12, 2019, www.vox.com/2019/3/12/18260699

/misoprostol-mifepristone-medical-abortion; SIA Legal Team, *Roe's Unfinished Business: Decriminalizing Abortion Once and for All* (Berkeley: University of California, Berkeley School of Law, 2018), 6, docs.wixstatic.com/ugd/8f83e4_dd27a51ce72e42db8b09eb6aab381358.pdf.

"These seemingly disparate events" In an eight-part series, starting in late 2018, the *New York Times* editorial board gave a sobering account of the progress abortion opponents have made toward establishing a case for the legal recognition of fetal personhood. "The Future of Personhood Nation," *New York Times*, December 28, 2018, www.nytimes.com/interactive/2018/12/28/opinion/abortion-law-pro-life.html. The National Advocates for Pregnant Women has been warning us about the risks associated with the personhood movement for decades. Lynn Paltrow and Jeanne Flavin, "Arrests of and Forced Interventions on Pregnant Women in the United States, 1973–2005: Implications for Women's Legal Status and Public Health," *Journal of Health Politics, Policy and Law* 38 (2013): 299–343.

"To offer an analogy" Theresa Morris, *Cut It Out: The C-Section Epidemic in America* (New York: New York University Press, 2013); Boston Women's Health Collective, *Our Bodies, Ourselves* (New York: Atria Books, 2011); Joanna Moorhead, "Freebirthing: Is Giving Birth without Medical Support Safe?," *Guardian*, September 14, 2013, www.theguardian.com/lifeandstyle/2013/sep/14/freebirthing-birth-without-medical-support-safe; "Unassisted Childbirth," Unassisted Childbirth, accessed March 11, 2019, www.unassistedchildbirth.com/.

"Second, it seems that the more people learn" Maria Caspani, "Support for Abortion Rights Grows as Some U.S. States Curb Access: Reuters/Ipsos Poll," Reuters, May 26, 2019, www.reuters.com/article/us-usa-abortion-poll/support-for-abortion-rights-grows-as-some-us-states-curb-access-reuters-ipsos-poll-idUSKCN1SW0CD; PRRI Staff, "The State of Abortion and Contraception Attitudes in All 50 States," August 13, 2019, www.prri.org/research/legal-in-most-cases-the-impact-of-the-abortion-debate-in-2019-america/.

"A 2018 poll" PerryUndem, "45 Years after Roe v. Wade: What We Don't Know about Public Opinion on Abortion . . . Because We've Never Asked," January 2018, view.publitas.com/perryundem-research-communication/perryundem-report-on-public-opinion-toward-abortion.

"This poll also revealed" Helen Branswell, "Most Americans Favor Late-Term Abortion if Zika Harms Fetus, STAT-Harvard Poll Finds," *Stat*, August 6, 2016, www.statnews.com/2016/08/05/stat-harvard-poll-zika-abortion/; "Storytelling," Abortion Conversation Projects, n.d., accessed March 11, 2019, www.abortionconversationproject.org/storytelling; "Shout Your Abortion," Shout Your Abortion, accessed March 11, 2019, shoutyourabortion.com/; Amelia Bonow and Emily Nokes, eds., *Shout Your Abortion* (Oakland, CA: PM Press, 2018).

"Third, in another encouraging development" Elizabeth Nash, Rachel Benson Gold, Zohra Ansari-Thomas, Olivia Cappello, Sophia Naide, and Lizamarie

Mohammed, "State Policy Trends 2018: With *Roe v. Wade* in Jeopardy, States Continued to Add New Abortion Restrictions," Guttmacher Institute, December 11, 2018, www.guttmacher.org/article/2018/12/state-policy-trends-2018-roe-v-wade-jeopardy-states-continued-add-new-abortion; National Institute for Reproductive Health, "Gaining Ground: Year in Review 2018," January 2019, www.nirhealth.org/wp-content/uploads/2018/12/NIRH-EOY-Report-2018.pdf; National Institute for Reproductive Health, "Local Reproductive Freedom Index," 2017, localrepro.org.

"In contrast, in 2018" Elizabeth Nash, Olivia Cappello, Sophia Naide, Lizamarie Mohammed, and Zohra Ansari-Thomas, "Radical Attempts to Ban Abortion Dominate State Policy Trends in the First Quarter of 2019," Guttmacher Institute, April 3, 2019, www.guttmacher.org/article/2019/04/radical-attempts-ban-abortion-dominate-state-policy-trends-first-quarter-2019; Caitlin O'Kane, "New York Passes Law Allowing Abortions at Any Time If Mother's Health Is at Risk," *CBS News*, January 24, 2019, www.cbsnews.com/news/new-york-passes-abortion-bill-late-term-if-mothers-health-is-at-risk-today-2019-01-23/; Amelia Thomson-Deveaux, "Abortion Rights Haven't Been a Priority in Blue States—Until Now," *FiveThirtyEight*, June 10, 2019, fivethirtyeight.com/features/abortion-rights-havent-been-a-priority-in-blue-states-until-now/.

"One of the most important political developments" SisterSong, "Our Mission," accessed March 11, 2019, www.sistersong.net/; Loretta Ross and Rickie Solinger, *Reproductive Justice: An Introduction* (Berkeley: University of California Press, 2017); Loretta Ross, Lynn Roberts, Erika Derkas, Whitney Peoples, and Pamela Bridgewater, eds., *Radical Reproductive Justice: Foundation, Theory, Practice, Critique* (New York: Feminist Press, 2017).

"As its founder, Parker Dockray, has described" Carole Joffe, "'Abortion and Parenting Needs Can Coexist': A Q&A with Parker Dockray," *Rewire*, August 19, 2016, rewire.news/article/2016/08/19/qa-parker-dockray/.

Acknowledgments

First and foremost, our greatest debt, of course, is to those providers, advocates, and volunteers who took time from their busy lives to reflect with us on the challenges and gratifications of their work. We also are indebted to the other people in this field, though not interviewed for this book, from whom we have learned for decades, including the many people at the Abortion Care Network, National Abortion Federation, and Planned Parenthood Federation of America who assisted us in countless ways. As we hope this book conveys, without their extraordinary efforts, abortion care would be out of reach for many who need it.

We are very grateful to the following colleagues who read all or parts of the manuscript and gave us useful feedback: Lori Freedman, Dan Grossman, Kristin Luker, Maya Manian, Jennifer Reich, Sarah Roberts, Rickie Solinger, and Mary Ziegler. We are also grateful to all of the researchers, scholars, storytellers, advocates, and others whose work we cite throughout this book.

Early in this book's development, we were fortunate enough to work with Cecelia Cancellaro of Word Creative Literary Services, and we thank her for her very knowledgeable guidance. At the University of California Press, Naomi Schneider has been a source of superb editorial advice, and we greatly appreciate her strong support of this work. Others at UC Press we wish to thank include Alex Dahne, Summer Farah, Katryce Lassle, Elisabeth Magnus, Elena McAnespie, Benjy Malings, Dawn Raffel, Francisco Reinking, and Kate Warne. Louise Seiler provided excellent work on the index.

From Carole: I wish to thank my colleagues at the Bixby Center for Global Reproductive Health and especially the ANSIRH (Advancing New Standards in Reproductive Health) program, both located within the Department of Obstetrics, Gynecology and Reproductive Sciences at the University of California, San Francisco. I am particularly grateful to Dan Grossman, the director of ANSIRH, and ANSIRH administrative staff for their support of my work in ways too numerous to mention. I am daily inspired by the work done by Bixby and ANSIRH researchers, and my debt to their cutting-edge scholarship is reflected throughout this book.

I also want to thank Sara Daniel, Heather Gould, Tanvi Gurazada, Jason Harless, Shelly Kaller, Natalie Morris, Erin Wingo, and especially Clare Cook for their technical assistance. Peggy James did an excellent job of transcribing our interviews, for which David and I are both grateful.

I additionally want to thank a group of friends with whom I have enjoyed spirited discussions of various aspects of abortion politics and provision, and who have helped me better understand the complexities involved in these realms: Talcott Camp, Diana Greene Foster, Marji Gold, Rivka Gordon, Maureen Paul, and Susan Yanow.

From David: I am immensely grateful to my colleagues who have supported this project from the beginning. In particular, my deans at Drexel Kline School of Law, first Roger Dennis and then Dan Filler, jumped at the opportunity to support this work and have never wavered. Drexel students Justin Hollinger, Kait O'Donnell, and Alice Thornewill provided excellent research assistance.

I stopped working with the Women's Law Project in 2006, but my heart has never left it. Two of my colleagues there, Carol Tracy and Susan Frietsche, read the proposal for this book and have been enthusiastic about helping and offering advice from start to finish. They and everyone else at the Law Project continue to show me every day how to be a powerful feminist lawyer and advocate.

I also want to thank the Philadelphia and Pennsylvania reproductive health, rights, and justice community—from the abortion providers whom I have been lucky enough to have as clients (and friends), to the Women's Medical Fund and their amazing staff and volunteers, to the practical support activists doing critical work every day. I learn from everything they do.

Finally, we both thank our families for their love, support, and valuable feedback throughout this project. Carole thanks Fred, Miriam, Jude, and Andrew. David thanks Cassie, Josh, Leo, Marcia, Arnold, John, Kathleen, Rachel, and Seth. Without all of them, none of this would be possible.

Index

Founded in 1893,
UNIVERSITY OF CALIFORNIA PRESS
publishes bold, progressive books and journals
on topics in the arts, humanities, social sciences,
and natural sciences—with a focus on social
justice issues—that inspire thought and action
among readers worldwide.

The UC PRESS FOUNDATION
raises funds to uphold the press's vital role
as an independent, nonprofit publisher, and
receives philanthropic support from a wide
range of individuals and institutions—and from
committed readers like you. To learn more, visit
ucpress.edu/supportus.